Wilderness Politics and Indian Gifts

The Northern Colonial Frontier

1748-1763

By

WILBUR R. JACOBS

D1431632

UNIVERSITY OF NEBRASKA PRESS · LINCOLN

First Bison Book printing October, 1966

Bison Book edition published by arrangement with the author, and reproduced from the original edition published by the Stanford University Press.

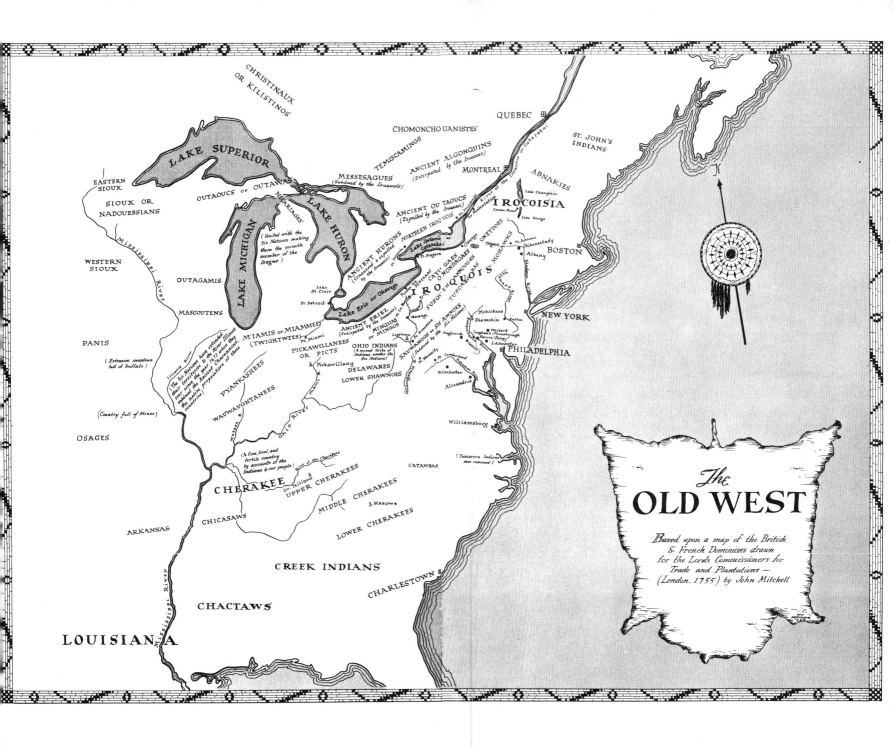

The
OLD WEST

Based upon a map of the British
& French Dominions drawn
for the Lords Commissioners for
Trade and Plantations —
(London, 1755) by John Mitchell

To Louis Knott Koontz

PREFACE

This study of gifts to the Indians is an attempt to illuminate a hitherto almost obscure factor in the Colonial westward movement. These "presents," comprising such eighteenth-century items as fabrics, hardware, munitions, food, toys, jewelry, clothing, wampum, and liquors, were a potent factor in the complex diplomatic history of Indian politics along the old Northwest frontier. Thousands of pounds sterling were expended both by the French and by the English in observing this old Indian custom that was so necessary to Indian diplomacy. Indeed, the civilizing influence of this concomitant of Western culture reached ahead of the fur trade far into the wilderness to the Mississippi Valley. These so-called presents also served as a measure of compensation for the vast areas of virgin forest that were bought by the English. The French competed with the British in securing the friendship of the powerful Indian confederacies, which, even as late as 1750, held the balance of power in North America. During the years 1748–1763, it became the policy of the colonies bordering the Ohio and Northwest frontiers to "brighten the chain of friendship" by giving presents to such influential "nations" as the members of the Iroquoian confederacy. Moreover, in some cases the Indians became so accustomed to these frequent outlays of free merchandise that they came to be almost completely dependent upon European goods. After the conquest of Canada by the British, these extensive presents were sliced to a bare minimum. It was then that the powerful Algonquian tribes, who were formerly allied with the French, felt the pain of the lack of ammunition and clothing—items so necessary to their very existence. To a surprising degree, therefore, the Indian rebellion under Pontiac was caused by the lack of presents.

W. R. J.

CONTENTS

CONTENTS

LIST OF ILLUSTRATIONS

I. AN OLD INDIAN CUSTOM: GIVING AND RECEIVING PRESENTS

Today, those Indians living along the Eastern coast of North America are but a shadow in the history of the westward movement. Manuscripts and printed sources, however, have kept fresh the story of diplomacy, wars, and conflicts with the Europeans. Once again the sachems deliberate while the business of politics and presents unfolds. (Contemporary records refer to these gifts as presents.)

Prestige was all-important in native diplomacy as denoted by the use of wampum and other gifts. Hospitality and loyalty traveled hand in hand with cunning and strategem. Edmond Atkin, superintendent of Indian Affairs for the Southern Department, once said that no people understood and pursued their national interest better than the Indians.[1] This factor is well exemplified in the numerous lists of expensive gifts that the Indians received.

The old Indian custom of giving and receiving presents proved to be a decisive factor in the story of Indian diplomacy along the Ohio and Northwest frontiers during the years 1748–1763. The French and the English found that in order to carry on diplomatic relations with the aborigines all conferences had to follow adherence to custom with painstaking regularity, especially with regard to the delivering of presents.

The competition between France and England in the giving of presents to the Indians in order to secure native friendship and alliance was a part of the struggle for empire in America—a struggle that culminated in 1763. England won the contest abroad for maritime and Colonial empire, while her continental allies occupied France in Europe. In America the power lay with England when she chose to exert herself. The large white Colonial population of the British colonies and the commercial, industrial, and maritime strength of England enabled her to undersell the French. Moreover, England was able to hinder France from sending soldiers, arms, supplies, and presents to the New World. The very mass strength of Britain and her colonies eventually brought the Indians over to the stronger side. Rum and

---

[1] Edmond Atkin to the Board of Trade, May 30, 1755, Huntington Collection of Loudoun Papers, 578. Hereafter cited as LO. This remarkable document, of fifty-five finely written pages, reveals Atkin as an authority on Indian Affairs. Contemporaries apparently did not appreciate his farsighted policies and criticized him in terms of their immediate needs.

strouds were used to purchase Indian lands, and the hunting grounds gradually disappeared. Thus the Indian, who was used as a warrior by both sides during the Anglo-French conflict, was bound to lose unless he lived in the Hudson's Bay Territory where British policy for many years protected him as a hunter.

The period of the so-called peace, 1748–1754, between the third and the last of the Intercolonial Wars marked the beginning of accelerated competition for native allegiance between the English and the French. The French, thanks to a centralized government, could boast of a unified system of giving presents. The British, on the other hand, were hampered by conflicting colonial and imperial authority in the handing out of large subsidies to the Indians.

Thousands of pounds sterling were expended by both the British and the French for these presents, which were a spearhead in the civilizing influence of Western culture. Castor hats trimmed with lace, gaudy waistcoats, and brightly colored strouds pleased the vanity of the warrior. A sinister note was sounded by such presents as scalping knives, bullet molds, and vermilion war paint. The tone was relieved, however, by gifts like wampum, duck shot, tin pots, needles, thread, and scissors—items that were needed by native women as well as by the men.

During the years from 1748 to 1763, the French were constantly hampered by a lack of goods for presents. Those gifts which were available in the form of ratteen, blankets, powder, and lead were readily handed out to the Indians. It was far cheaper to hold the friendship of the Western confederacies by "kindly" presents than to keep an expensive army stationed throughout the vast hinterland of New France. When the supply of French presents dwindled, military leaders such as Montcalm had no alternative other than to promise plunder to native auxiliaries.

In contrast, the British were able to recruit thousands of warriors by tremendous outlays of gifts made by such outstanding representatives as Sir William Johnson, Conrad Weiser, George Croghan, and Andrew Montour. With British victories and British presents came the loss of French prestige. The conquest of Canada in 1760 brought a parsimonious policy with regard to presents. The Indians, with no supplies, no munitions, and, worst of all, no French finery for their women, sought a solution in rebellion. The conspiracy of Pontiac was, therefore, to a surprising degree, a direct result of the lack of presents after 1763.

The pattern of Indian politics on the old Northwest frontier during the period of the French and Indian War is focused mainly on three parties: the French, the English, and the Indians. It was a game for empire, and the stakes were high. In consequence, thousands of pounds—

yes, tens of thousands—were expended by the British on gifts for the natives. In an effort to equal, if possible to better, their rival's success, the French countered with expensive presents, often for the same Indians. Both parties sought to outbid the other, while the Indian enjoyed the position of maintaining the traditional balance of power.[2]

Since the archives and Colonial records dealing with the frontier are punctuated with lists of presents, the historian is faced with the problem of fitting into place the pieces of a difficult puzzle. Moreover, the issue is somewhat clouded by the already existing custom among the Indians of exchanging presents. Actually, therefore, both contestants in the war for empire utilized what was an established custom among the aborigines of bestowing gifts. For this reason, it is fitting that a preliminary chapter be devoted to this interesting phase of Indian life. Such an introduction will serve as a setting for the discussions of presents in the forest diplomacy of the Northwest Colonial frontier.

Among the Iroquois, Algonquian, Muskhogean, and other linguistic families living along the Eastern seaboard, presents connoted "words." In the metaphorical language of the forest, each gift might signify a wish or a greeting. Several gifts might denote special emphasis of one kind or another.[3] For example, one gift might offer a prayer that the price of trading goods be reduced.[4] Another might figuratively "light" a warm council fire; still a third might signify that all could speak freely.[5] The Jesuit fathers observed that presents spoke more clearly than the lips.[6] From these illustrations, it is evident that the ambassador of the forest had to be well-stocked with suitable presents before he could make his wishes known in a public meeting.

The freedom derived from what was essentially a democratic government, plus the fact that each warrior had to provide for himself, promoted

---

[2] For many years there was an agreement among the Iroquois to allow the French and English to fight each other without interfering on either side. See E. B. O'Callaghan *et al.* (eds.), *Documents Relative to the Colonial History of New York Procured in England, Holland and France*, X, 94. Hereafter cited as the *New York Colonial Documents*. The French bitterly complained that the Six Nations followed the above policy. Their sachems talked a great deal but "said nothing clear," and went home loaded with presents. See *ibid.*, X, 888.

[3] Reuben Gold Thwaites (ed.), *The Jesuit Relations and Allied Documents, Travels and Explorations of the Jesuit Missionaries in New France, 1610–1791, The Original French, Latin, and Italian Texts, With English Translations and Notes; Illustrated By Portraits, Maps, and Facsimiles*, XXXII, 187. Hereafter cited as the *Jesuit Relations*.

[4] *Ibid.*

[5] *Ibid.*, XXVII, 281–83; *ibid.*, XXI, 47.

[6] *Ibid.*

individualism. A spirit of independence prevailed. The father's authority over his son was limited, while the sachem had difficulty in restraining his warriors.[7] If the sachems had authority over their fighting men, it was for the most part due to the liberal presents that the native leaders bestowed.[8] To be a sachem presupposed the individual to be a wealthy man. Gifts induced the warriors to pay respect to their leaders. One early account states that the tribesmen always inclined to those who gave them the most and those who flattered them the most.[9] Rank, authority, and prestige were important. The exchange of suitable gifts among headmen during council meetings followed precedence of rank with painstaking adherence to custom. Privately bestowed gifts and those made in public meetings often stripped influential leaders of almost all their earthly possessions.[10] As a matter of fact, generosity was much admired among the Indians. The successful hunter usually made a point of advertising his skill and his virtues of generosity by giving away part of his meat.[11]

In some tribes, the close observer could trace the bestowal of gratuities through the entire life of the aborigine, from childhood to death. It was common to deliver gifts to the parents of a child five or six months old during the naming ceremony. These ceremonial favors, usually of bark and ointment, were presented when the child had its ears pierced.[12]

When a young warrior reached the age for selecting a mate, a ceremony centering around an exchange of presents was customary. According to some accounts, the young man who sought a mate asked his prospective bride for her hand in marriage.[13] Upon her acceptance, his parents sent favors to the mother and father of the betrothed. Pending acknowledgment of these offerings, and of the generous presents that were given in return to the parents of the suitor, marriage plans were consummated.[14] Sometimes the nearest relative proposed for the suitor. Then, upon the agreement of both families, relatives met to decide what gifts would be bestowed upon the

---

[7] Emma Helen Blair (ed.), *The Indian Tribes of the Upper Mississippi Valley and the Region of the Great Lakes as Described by Nicolas Perrot, French Commandant in the Northwest; Bacqueville de la Potherie, French Royal Commissioner to Canada; Morrell Marston, American Army Officer; and Thomas Forsyth, United States Agent at Fort Armstrong,* I, 145. Hereafter cited as Blair, *Indian Tribes.*

[8] *Ibid.*

[9] *Ibid.*

[10] *Ibid.*, I, 303.

[11] *Ibid.*, I, 129–30. It is interesting to note that young hunters were flattered and given presents of vermilion, silver, and wampum.

[12] *Ibid.*, I, 76–77.

[13] *Ibid.*, II, 214.

[14] *Ibid.*

young people.[15] Among the Delawares, a mother could take meat to the girl's parents and receive a compensation denoting approval of marriage.[16] Another variation of the custom allowed the young man to take the bride on a short hunting trip. Upon their return, the couple would bestow presents upon the relatives with whom they wished to live.[17]

Occasionally, wealthy Indians had more than one wife. In cases of this kind, wives tried to keep harmony in the household through the exchange of offerings. They would reward each other with gifts of grain and make presents to the husband as well.[18]

If a warrior's wife died, he (at least, in one situation of record) gave presents to her surviving relatives. Another case obligated the parents of the deceased wife, or squaw as she was called, to give to the "widower" compensating presents.[19] Among the Ottawas, two years of mourning was necessary before a second marriage could take place; then it could take place only with the permission of the mother-in-law.[20]

These presents given at time of death, already mentioned in connection with marriage, were of the utmost importance to individuals and to the tribe as a whole. The ceremony of sadness at time of death, with its connotation of gifts, was important in the diplomatic story of Indian politics along the Colonial frontier. When a warrior was about to die, he was garbed in the most expensive clothes, his hair was greased, his body and face were painted with vermilion, and great exhibitions of sorrow took place. Hired women moaned aloud with relatives while presents were made to the widow.[21] When death at last came to the Indian, a mat was laid out for the body to rest upon. At this point, a great feast began. Gifts were exchanged among relatives and other mourners while all were congratulated upon their charitable disposition.[22]

Sir William Johnson frequently gave strouds and blankets to cover the dead. The natives required that this custom be observed before any business could be transacted because the Indians could not proceed with "blood on their garments."[23] In addition, goods actually had to be spread upon the ground and accepted as a condolence. They could not be promised belts,

---

[15] *Ibid.*, I, 68.   [16] *Ibid.*, I, 65.   [17] *Ibid.*, II, 214.

[18] *Ibid.*, I, 73.   [19] *Ibid.*, I, 74–75.

[20] *Ibid.*, I, 73. William Johnson asked his subordinates to make presents acceptable to wives and mistresses of the warriors of the Six Nations. See "Some Hints for a Commanding Officer," May 24, 1755, in James Sullivan *et al.* (eds.), *The Papers of Sir William Johnson*, I, 539–40. Hereafter cited as the *Sir William Johnson Papers.*

[21] Blair, *Indian Tribes*, I, 78–79.   [22] *Ibid.*, I, 83.

[23] *Minutes of the Provincial Council of Pennsylvania From the Organization to the Termination of the Proprietary Government*, V, 665–70. Hereafter cited as the *Pennsylvania Colonial Records.*

strings, and lists of goods. Consequently, in 1753, the Pennsylvania Indian Commissioners, Benjamin Franklin, Isaac Norris, and Richard Peters, were embarrassed because they were able to offer only lists of goods representing the Carlisle condolence present.[24]

Sir William Johnson wrote that the Indians expected the custom of giving condolence gifts to be observed; moreover, he stated there was an absolute necessity for doing so.[25] Indiscretion on the part of friends in over-looking the grief of a tribe might cause even a change in alliance. Illustrating this point, the Chickasaws and Miamis at one time changed their alliance to the French because French Indians were the only tribes who had made condolence offerings.[26]

Accounts of the Northern Department of Indian Affairs record many donations to surviving widows and to families of the Six Nations, particularly among the Mohawks.[27] An interesting account tells of Sir William Johnson's having clothed a lad who had taken the name of his dead father in order to take the place of the latter in the tribe.

Condolence offerings had a particular function in the religious ceremony of the dead. One nation of the Iroquois refused to allow the name of the deceased to be mentioned during the presentation of gifts, according to Conrad Weiser, Indian interpreter for Pennsylvania.[28] Presents were used to "raise" the body of a certain chief so that he could cross a particular river.[29] These donations gave him a free passage over the river and "dried" the tears of his friends.[30]

More recent writers on Indian anthropology, such as Henry Schoolcraft, Clark Wissler, and George Bird Grinnel, have pointed out that Indian customs varied. This inconsistency was marked for the most part by language barriers. Nevertheless, differences in observing traditions followed each group down from the large confederacies to individual tribes. Different settlements of the same tribe had deviations in ceremonies. This is true of the natives living along the Northwest frontier during 1748–1763.

In previous illustrations it has been noticed that when Indians communicated with each other presents often served as "words." With this

[24] *Pennsylvania Colonial Records*, V, 665–70.

[25] William Johnson to Sir Charles Hardy, December 7, 1755, *Sir William Johnson Papers*, II, 387–89.

[26] Blair, *Indian Tribes*, II, 127–28.

[27] Volumes I, II, and III of the *Sir William Johnson Papers* record hundreds of presents to the Mohawks.

[28] "A Journal of the Proceedings of Conrad Weiser in His Journey to Onandago . . . . ," August 15 to October 10, 1750, *Pennsylvania Colonial Records*, V, 470–80.

[29] *Jesuit Relations*, XXII, 291–93.

[30] *Ibid.*

assumption, it is not difficult to imagine the many functions that a gift might have. Presents were used in government, in law—as "law" was understood among the aborigines—and in almost every kind of personal relationship. Generally speaking, these gifts served as a measure of compensation. If a murder was committed, lawful revenge could be taken on the murderer unless compensation was made. If this was not done, relatives could kill the guilty party without trial.[31] In the same light, a knife and some tobacco would "heal" a warrior who had been physically injured.[32] These atonement offerings were quite expensive in the case of murder. By way of example, the Sauks and Foxes gave horses and silverwork.[33] If a murder was committed outside the tribe, there was a possibility of war unless compensation was made. Indeed, if the eye-for-eye justice was not administered, the whole tribe had to contribute to the atonement presentation in order to keep the peace.[34]

Relations between tribes and confederacies were often governed by presents. They were used for peace,[35] for reward,[36] for requests,[37] for declaring war,[38] as a tribute,[39] as a mark of distinction,[40] as a bribe,[41] for thanks,[42] and as a token of friendship.[43]

With periodic inconsistencies in the legend of the chain of friendship as it

---

[31] Blair, *Indian Tribes*, I, 137–40.

[32] *Ibid.*, I, 321. Presents were also an atonement for an insult. In the case of an accident, gifts were not always necessary. A quiet smoke with no spoken words was sufficient evidence of sympathy. See *ibid.*, I, 137,

[33] *Ibid.*, II, 186–87.

[34] *Ibid.*, I, 137–40. The Indians would sometimes merely take valuable presents. In case a horse was taken, the Indian would merely reply that he needed a horse and he did not take all the horses he saw. See *ibid.*, II, 187. James Adair, Indian trader, reported that the Indians expected a present for returning horses and other articles that had been taken. See Samuel Cole Williams (ed.), *Adair's History of the American Indians*, p. 318. Hereafter cited as *Adair's History of the American Indians*.

[35] *Jesuit Relations*, XXII, 291–93.

[36] *Adair's History of the American Indians*, p. 318.

[37] *Jesuit Relations*, XXII, 291–93.

[38] *Ibid.*

[39] Reuben Gold Thwaites (ed.), *Early Western Travels 1748–1849, a Series of Annotated Reprints of Some of the Best and Rarest Contemporary Volumes of Travel, Descriptive of the Aborigines, Social and Economic Conditions of the Far West, During the Period of Early American Settlement*, XXVIII, 169. Hereafter cited as *Early Western Travels*.

[40] *Sir William Johnson Papers*, I, 662–65. As a mark of distinction, William Johnson frequently gave presents to sachems and head warriors.

[41] Blair, *Indian Tribes*, I, 188.

[42] *Ibid.*, I, 152.

[43] *Jesuit Relations*, XXII, 291–93.

concerned the Six Nations and the British, the story is repeated at many treaties. From numerous accounts, the gist of the story follows.

Many moons ago, when the English first came to Albany, the Indians and their white brethren became friends. The Six Nations came to love their brethren, the English, so much that they tied their ship to a bush so that it would not float away. Perceiving that the bush would not hold the ship, the Indians then tied the ship to a great tree with a strong rope. As many moons passed, the sachems felt that the rope might rot. As they wished to make their friends more secure, the Indians chained the ship to the distant mountains. The chain was of silver to represent what was to be everlasting friendship.[44]

The significance of this remarkable chain was that it needed to be brightened or polished periodically with gifts. Thus, thousands of pounds were spent annually during the eighteenth century by the colonies. Especially did the Quaker colony drain the provincial treasury to "brighten the chain of friendship."[45] The implication was that each so-called "brightening" strengthened an alliance. Likewise, previous treaties were confirmed by investments in goods.[46] Articles were commonly exchanged by both parties in a gesture of friendship.[47] This usage was most evident at peace treaties. One officer in the British army tells of an incident which gives the individual side of this picture. The son of a friendly Indian chief called upon the officer to deliver a volume of Shakespeare's plays. In return, the Indian begged for a gift of powder, which was more precious to him than Shakespearean drama![48]

The Indians cleverly made small gifts as a token of friendship and demanded larger ones in return. Northern Indian Department accounts record a treaty where the Indians came to "shake hands" and renew friendship. Declaring that they were a poor people, the tribesmen gave three small deerskins, eight muskrats, and two minks to the English. The native spokesman then declared that since the tribesmen could not make a better present, perhaps the English and the Indians ought to assist each other.[49] This is an

---

[44] *Pennsylvania Colonial Records*, V, 348–58. Conrad Weiser's journal of his trip to the Ohio country contains perhaps the best example of the chain of friendship legend as told by Thanayieson, speaker for the Senecas.

[45] Mention is made in almost all Indian treaties involving the Iroquois and the English. See *Pennsylvania Colonial Records,* Vols. V, VI, and VII, and Samuel Hazard (ed.), *Pennsylvania Archives* (1st Series), Vols. I, II. Hereafter cited as *Pennsylvania Archives.*

[46] For example, the conference at Winchester in 1753 was held to confirm the Treaty of Lancaster in 1748.

[47] *Sir William Johnson Papers*, I, 16.

[48] *Early Western Travels*, I, 308.

[49] *Ibid.*

excellent example depicting the origin of the practice known as "Indian giving." This is the process of making a gift and expecting either an equivalent or the return of the original gift.

Friendly Indians sometimes made gifts of prisoners to their allies.[50] Live prisoners were valuable for ransom; dead ones, for scalp bounties.[51]

The type of present that circulated among the aborigines was necessarily what they had to offer. Before the coming of the white man, the articles were essentially primitive. After securing European goods, the natives used them as gifts; however, wampum continued to be the principal article used in the exchange of presents.

In diplomatic circles, wampum was important for two reasons. It was a common medium of exchange, and it had certain mystic qualities never fully understood by Europeans. Beads, often called grains, had a definite value in terms of beaver pelts, deerskins, or even English coin.[52] White wampum was worked out of the inside of the conch shell, a large spiral univalve marine shell.[53] The dark wampum, usually purple or blue inclining to black, was taken from the quahog, or quahaug, a thick-shelled American clam.[54] Since no record has been found for the source of black wampum, it was probably erroneously called black because of its resemblance to dark purple.

The size of the grains varied. Grains of the "Penn Wampum Belts" were approximately one-fourth of an inch wide and three-eighths to one-half inch in depth. According to X-ray reproductions, the perforations

---

[50] Edmond Atkin to the Board of Trade, May 30, 1755, LO 578.

[51] The prices offered for scalps and prisoners during the French and Indian War varied. For instance, on one occasion £10 were offered for a scalp, while £20 were given for each prisoner taken alive. See Charles H. McIlwain (ed.), *An Abridgement of the Indian Affairs Contained in Four Folio Volumes Transacted in the Colony of New York, from the Year 1678 to the Year 1751 by Peter Wraxall*, p. 244. Hereafter cited as *Wraxall's Abridgement*. In 1756, at the time of the Delaware and Shawnee raids on the Pennsylvania frontier, that colony offered £30 for scalps and £50 for prisoners brought in alive. See Daniel Claus to William Johnson, April 5, 1756, *Sir William Johnson Papers*, II, 440.

[52] *Collections* of the Rhode Island Historical Society, I, *Containing Roger Williams' Key to the Indian Language*, pp. 128–30. Hereafter cited as *Roger Williams' Key*.

[53] Public Record Office, Colonial Office, 5/1328, L.C. 41–42, C.O. 46. Hereafter cited as P.R.O.,C.O.

[54] See *Roger Williams' Key*, pp. 128–30, for the color of wampum beads. Williams notes that the blue beads were inclined to be black in color. Frederick W. Hodge, *Handbook of the American Indians*, I, 446–47, states that white purplish beads were taken from the quahog. Conrad Weiser's memorandum of wampum contains records of only black and white wampum. See *Pennsylvania Archives* (1st series), II, 17. Contemporaries have established the fact that white and dark wampum were taken from different types of shell. See P.R.O., C.O., 5/1328, L.C. 41–42, C.O. 46.

were between one-eighth and one-sixteenth of an inch in diameter.[55] The grains were laced together with deerskin, cut into narrow strips. When laced, the grains were made into necklaces, bracelets, strings, belts, girdles, and collars.[56] Each grain had its known value, the black or purple being worth twice to three times as much as the white.[57]

Since the grains had to be fashioned near the seashore, inland tribes traveled as many as six hundred miles to trade skins and pelts for this precious commodity.[58] Wampum was popular enough to be carried as far west as the Dakota Indians.[59] It would appear that the Atlantic seaboard Indians' possession of these raw materials for making primitive currency should have been a boon to them. Powerful inland confederacies, however, sometimes exacted backbreaking tribute from them in the form of wampum.

In diplomatic circles, wampum was used in various ways. Collars and girdles were often employed, but strings and belts were more common.[60] A string consisted of a group of leather strips (called strands) which were about three feet in length and tied together at one end. These were strung with grains of various colors. These colors were superimposed upon the white and purple grains to signify war, peace, friendship, or whatever the occasion demanded.[61] Red was most popular, being painted over grains in both strings and belts. The strings were used for minor occasions; the belts, for major. The greater the size of the belt or string the more valuable it was and the more emphatic it made any speech that accompanied the wampum. In each case, the string and the belt served as a "word" or even a complete statement.

In the construction of belts, the design was based on the pattern of leather strips which ran horizontally and vertically. Particular events war-

---

[55] *Leaflets of the Museum of the American Indian*, No. 4, *Penn Wampum Belts*, Plate IV. Hereafter cited as *Penn Wampum Belts*.

[56] Apparently the collars and girdles of wampum were worn to serve as credentials. A belt would serve the same purpose. Collars were frequently passed among the Indians. See Reuben Gold Thwaites (ed.), *Collections* of the State Historical Society of Wisconsin, XVIII, 465. Hereafter cited as *Wisconsin Historical Collections*.

[57] P.R.O., C.O., 5/1328, L.C. 41–42, C.O. 46 states that every bead had its known value. It might be added that there was some difference of opinion among contemporaries of the eighteenth century as to the value of dark grains over the white.

[58] *Roger Williams' Key*, pp. 128–30.

[59] Hodge, *op. cit.*, I, 446–47.

[60] The Iroquois and the Ohio Indians used strings and belts almost exclusively. However, the inland tribes often used collars and girdles.

[61] Lewis H. Morgan, *League of the HO-DÉ-NO-SAU-NEE or Iroquois* (edited by Herbert M. Lloyd), II, 52. This plate shows green, red, and blue beads. In William Trent's journal of 1752, P.R.O., C.O., 5/1327, L.C. 431–47, C.O. 549–69, a green belt is used by the Twightwees.

ranted the construction of large belts, some six feet in length.[62] Sir William Johnson's accounts of Indian expenses show that he bought wampum in large allotments of 3,000 grains and over.[63] The grains were ordered with leather and thread, the latter being easier to use as lacing for the grains. Conrad Weiser's accounts list 2,000 grains in one belt; but the average belts used by the interpreter contained about 900 grains.[64] Weiser's large belts were entirely of black grains, while his smaller belts were either all white or contained a few black grains. His strings ranged from 185 to 600 grains, and were either all white or contained some black grains.[65]

Roger Williams, an early authority, noted that the making of wampum beads was difficult. For one thing, before the natives received awls[66] from Europe, they had to bore the shell currency with sharp stones.[67] The English, observing the value placed on beads, made imitation porcelain beads which were sold to the Indians at what was probably a handsome profit.

Designs on belts carried a special meaning. Conrad Weiser, in a meeting in 1748 with the Wyandots,[68] described a very interesting pattern. Here the Indians showed Pennsylvania's interpreter a belt 25 grains wide and 265 grains long, in all containing almost 7,000 grains.[69] In the design were seven Indians holding each other by the hand. Beneath the Indian figures were two rows of black wampum beads. Since the Governor of New York had bestowed the belt on the Wyandots, it had a specific connotation. The first figure represented the governor of New York or his superior, the king of Great Britain. The next five figures represented the Five Nations; and the seventh, the Wyandots.[70] The two rows of black wampum signified a road running from Albany through the territory of the Five Nations to the Wyandots. The belt here described by the Ohio tribesmen is similar to Sir William Johnson's description of wampum. The superintendent's famous letter to Arthur Lee on Indian culture, dated February 21, 1771, reads:

Their belts are mostly black Wampum, painted Red when they denote War they describe Castles [tribes] sometimes upon them as figures of White Wampum, & in Alliances Human figures holding a Chain of Friendship, each figure represntg [sic] a nation, an ax is also sometimes described . . . .[71]

---

[62] *Sir William Johnson Papers*, III, 159.   [63] *Ibid.*, III, 172.

[64] *Pennsylvania Archives* (1st series), II, 17.   [65] *Ibid.*

[66] Awls were usually referred to in contemporary records as "awl blades."

[67] *Roger Williams' Key*, pp. 128–30.

[68] The spelling varies: Wondats, Owandaets, and Owandats.

[69] The Journal of Conrad Weiser, Indian Interpreter to the Ohio, *Pennsylvania Colonial Records*, V, 348–58. See chapter vi, *passim*.

[70] See note 69.

[71] William Johnson to Arthur Lee, February 28, 1771, E. B. O'Callaghan (ed.), *Documentary History of the State of New York*, IV, 273. Hereafter cited as *Documentary History of the State of New York*.

Returning to the particular belt described by the Wyandots, in 1748, these tribesmen told Conrad Weiser that they had received their belt from the Governor of New York over fifty years before. Furthermore, the Indians asserted that their alliance with the English had been renewed. This was accomplished by sending the belt to Albany, accompanied by deputies, six years before that time. One is naturally puzzled as to the safekeeping of these belts over such a long period of time. As a matter of interest, their preservation and safeguarding was a sacred duty that devolved upon a special officer of the tribe, usually a sachem.[72]

Rows of black or white wampum on belts generally represented paths to a specific place. These paths connoted friendship since they could not be used freely during time of war.[73] Several of the "Penn Wampum Belts" are still preserved in the Museum of the American Indian, Heye Foundation, New York. Authorities of the Museum, in 1925, called upon surviving members of the Onondaga and Seneca tribes to interpret the meaning of these belts. An illustration of their mystic reading was the interpretation of the "Freedom Belt." This belt, with a white background and purple beads running in a rectangular pattern across the length of the belt, denoted the idea of freedom. The concept of the Indian was that he reserved the right perpetually to traverse, whenever necessary, lands previously sold to the whites.[74]

The method of presenting belts and strings is equally interesting. It was usually done in council meetings; and the main participants, who were elected by their tribes, were called "speakers." Holding a belt or string in his hand, the speaker would rise and begin his talk. At its conclusion, he would give the wampum to the group of persons just addressed.[75]

Records of Indian treaties occasionally contain these words: "Shew'd the String & Retook it."[76] When a belt or string was returned, it denoted that the party addressed did not comply with the request.[77] Illustrations of this practice were frequent when the war hatchet was presented, but not accepted; in that case, the speaker took back the hatchet.[78]

Conventional practice was for wampum to be displayed as a record and

---

[72] *Documentary History of the State of New York*, IV, 271.

[73] P.R.O., C.O., 5/15, L.C. 285, C.O. 397.

[74] *Penn Wampum Belts*, pp. 10–11.

[75] P.R.O., C.O., 5/1328, C.O. 47–52, L.C. 43–72 contains the journal of William Fairfax, Indian Commissioner. Here, the Twightwees are described as taking the belt in their hand as they begin to speak and holding it throughout their talk.

[76] *Sir William Johnson Papers*, II, 126–27.   [77] *Ibid.*

[78] Theodore Calvin Pease (ed.), *Collections* of the Illinois State Historical Library, XXIX, French Series, III, *Illinois on the Eve of the Seven Years' War, 1747–1755*, p. 129. Hereafter cited as *Illinois on the Eve of the Seven Years' War.*

evidence of previous treaties, as in the case of Conrad Weiser and the Wyandots. Since the Indians preserved no written record of public meetings, their archives, in the form of wampum, were kept, as has been observed, by a sachem.[79]

One use of Indian wampum strings was in connection with formal talks at Indian treaties. George Croghan, deputy superintendent of the Northern Department of Indian Affairs, greeted the Shawnees and other visiting Indians in this fashion:

> Brethren,
>> with this String I wipe the Sweat & dust off Your Bodies Pick the bryars out of Your feet & clean Your eyes that You may see Your Brethren's faces and look cheerfull—
>>
>> Gave a String
>
> Brethren,
>> With this String I clear Your hearts & Minds that You may Speak perfectly free and open to us—
>>
>> Gave a String
>
> Brethren,
>> With this String I wipe the Blood from off the Council Seats, that Your Cloaths [sic] may be not Stained nor Your minds disturbed—
>>
>> Gave a String[80]

When a belt was presented, the Indians usually gave a shout to indicate their approval.[81] Belts, being more valuable than strings, were used for emphasis. The war belt, employed for the same purposes as the tomahawk or hatchet, was important in connection with the declaration of war. To illustrate: at a conference at Mount Johnson[82] in 1755, William Johnson threw down the war belt in General Braddock's name. The belt was picked up by an Oneida sachem; and Arent Stevens, interpreter, began the war dance while the sachems sang the conventional song.[83]

Belts were generally used for alliances,[84] to prevent disputes,[85] to identify a messenger,[86] for friendship,[87] and to assure future fidelity.[88] As William

---

[79] *Documentary History of the State of New York*, IV, 271.

[80] *Sir William Johnson Papers*, III, 209.

[81] *New York Colonial Documents*, VI, 966–67.

[82] Sir William Johnson's home on the Mohawk River.

[83] *New York Colonial Documents*, VI, 974–75.

[84] *Wraxall's Abridgement*, p. 245; *Sir William Johnson Papers*, II, 500.

[85] *Sir William Johnson Papers*, I, 524.

[86] A belt was used by the Mohawks that requested a fort to be built for the Oneidas. In this case, the belt holder was identified as the official messenger. See *ibid.*, II, 293, 297, 298.

[87] *New York Colonial Documents*, X, 206. In this case, the Cayugas gave the French their promise of neutrality and friendship.

[88] *Ibid.*, X, 141.

Johnson has said, the belt was a "Sacred Engagement" among the Indians.[89]

Like wampum, the mystic connotations of the calumet pipe probably will never be fully comprehended by the white man. As a gift it had profound meaning and implications. French sources tell the story of early European contacts with the calumet. English records note the use of the pipe with the Miamis (or Twightwees). The Iroquois smoked, but the pipe as a religious and sacred object does not appear to have been generally used. For this reason, it would be safe to assume that the calumet pipe was more limited to the Algonquian and Sioux families, rather than to the Muskhogean and Iroquois. In appearance, the calumet was characterized by a long stem sometimes curiously wrought and wrapped with wampum.[90] Delawares and Miamis used a feathered calumet, and tobacco appears to have been the only plant smoked.[91] Possibly other plants were smoked when tobacco was not available.

French emissaries stated that the calumet had authority to confirm everything and to render agreements solemn and binding.[92] It could arrest lawful vengeance on a tribe accused of murder or even compel the suspension of hostilities.[93] When the calumet was given to a visitor, it was a sign that all in the village should honor and respect him. To speak with the calumet was to make a serious request.[94] In relations between the Six Nations and the Twightwees, for instance, the calumet served as wampum. In this case, an ancient pipe was preserved as the record of an old alliance between the two peoples. According to custom among the Twightwees, they —and not the Six Nations—kept the calumet. The latter declared that they were glad that the pipe had been kept safe, signifying the careful observance of friendship.[95]

Frequently the calumet was presented with a blanket or with wampum.[96] Rather than an emblem of war, the calumet was, in such cases, regarded as a token of peace by the people to whom it was sent.[97] At conferences it was solemnly smoked by the deputies of the various nations. Then, as it was pre-

---

[89] *Sir William Johnson Papers*, II, 500.

[90] "A Treaty at the Court House in Lancaster," July 19, 1748, *Pennsylvania Colonial Records*, V, 307–19.

[91] P.R.O., C.O., 5/1327, L.C. 431–47, C.O. 549–69.

[92] Blair, *Indian Tribes*, I, 186.

[93] *Ibid.*, I, 185.

[94] *Illinois on the Eve of the Seven Years' War*, p. 513.

[95] P.R.O., C.O., 5/1327, L.C. 431–47, C.O. 549–69.

[96] *Ibid.*

[97] P.R.O., C.O., 5/1327, L.C. 415–24, C.O. 531–36. Occasionally the pipe was used as a war pipe. See *Wisconsin Historical Collections*, XII, 104.

sented, it carried with it the meaning of a link in the chain of friendship.[98] Again, a popular conception of the "peace pipe" had its origin in this unusual custom of the first Americans.

The human scalp was another gift exchanged between tribes! According to a contemporary of the French and Indian War period, "Scalping is the cuting [sic] the Skin round the Head, & by drawing quite to the eyes . . . ."[99] These barbarous trophies were highly prized among warriors and were exchanged as tokens of alliance.[100] Bounties in most of the colonies were offered for scalps, thus increasing their value.[101] Apparently the English colonists were prepared to pay for scalps of marauding warriors, but they accepted those of the Frenchmen as well.

Of all the gifts with a symbolic background, the tomahawk has survived with a familiar meaning in modern speech. To "bury the hatchet" universally meant to make peace; while, accordingly, to "take it up" meant to declare war. To bury the hatchet in the "bottomless hole" appeared to be one method of declaring everlasting friendship.[102] Sir William Johnson, in one of his letters in which he has described its use, emphasized that the ax served at times as a symbol of war and at other times as a symbol of peace.[103]

Wars which involved the Iroquois and their allies were always preceded by conferences. At such conferences, when the Iroquois desired that their allies "take up the hatchet," the procedure was to lay the tax upon a blanket Then the speaker would inform his listeners that he wished them to "take it up." Thereupon, the hatchet either would be "taken up" or be refused, depending upon the circumstances.[104] Should a war dance already be in progress, the acceptance of one more ax merely added fuel to the fire.[105] Other gifts usually followed.

The tomahawk and its construction are familiar to all students of Ameri-

---

[98] For the manner of smoking the pipe, see the "Journal of the Commissioners at Logstown, May 28, to June 13, 1752," *Virginia Magazine of History and Biography,* XIII (October 1905), pp. 154–74. For the pipe as a link in the chain of friendship, see *Pennsylvania Colonial Records,* V, 307–18.

[99] P.R.O., C.O., 5/1327, L.C. 415–24, C.O. 531–36.

[100] *Ibid.*

[101] *Vide,* note 51.

[102] *Pennsylvania Colonial Records,* V, 663–70. Herein is the report of the commissioners from Carlisle in 1753. A conversation between Half King of the Senecas and a French officer is recorded. The Indian pleads, ". . . . Let us exchange Hatchets—Let us bury our Hatchets in this bottomless Hole . . . ." In return the French commander stated that he meant no harm, ". . . . You seem to think I carry my Hatchet under my Coat; I alway [sic] carry it openly, not to strike you but those who shall oppose me."

[103] *Documentary History of the State of New York,* IV, 273.

[104] *Illinois on the Eve of the Seven Years' War,* p. 129.

[105] Blair, *Indian Tribes,* I, 232–34.

can history. Nevertheless, it is interesting to recall to mind that the Indians kept a war record on its handle. Hereon human figures represented prisoners, while bodies without heads counted as scalps.[106]

Sticks tied in bundles were another kind of gift and served as a token of brotherhood.[107] One account states that these fasceslike sticks were the size of matches. Sir William Johnson, however, has described the sticks as generally about six inches in length, very thin, and painted bright red if they were presented in time of war. He calls them "Bloody Sticks,"[108] though actually they were probably not painted with blood. Bundles of sticks connoted an alliance, each stick representing an individual. This was the Iroquois' simple arithmetic. Conrad Weiser has stated that the Mingoes and their allies on the Ohio held up a number of sticks to tell him how many people they had in their respective tribes.[109]

Other types of gifts that circulated among the Indians were beaver pelts,[110] deerskins, blankets, and tobacco. Tobacco was valued not only for its use by smokers, but also as a remedy for rheumatism and toothaches.

Items of clothing were likewise common offerings. Actually, the Indian in his native environment wore few items of apparel. He envied, however, the clothes worn by the whites and, in exchange for native wares, was overjoyed to receive, as presents, elaborate shirts, coats, and hats trimmed with lace and ribbon.[111] These presents were, in turn, often circulated among the Indians themselves.

Indian diplomacy, as it concerned presents, is closely related to the organization of government among the Ohio and Iroquois tribes. Generally speaking, the tribal system of most Indian families of the old West resembled that of the Iroquois, though on a smaller scale. Sir William Johnson has described the chief sachem (the head sachem or king) as being in authority.[112] In the South, the Cherokee counterpart was called emperor by the English. This leader held his authority by virtue of presents, given and received, and also by his superior wisdom, influence, and military ability. Among the Iroquois, the sachems formed a grand council; but the local sachem of each tribe deliberated over the affairs of their particular unit.[113] It is worthy of emphasis that, among the aborigines, deliberations proceeded with "regularity and decorum." The speaker at the Onondaga Coun-

---

[106] *Documentary History of the State of New York*, IV, 273.

[107] *New York Colonial Documents*, VI, 964–66.

[108] *Vide*, note 106.

[109] *Pennsylvania Colonial Records*, V, 348–58.

[110] A medium of exchange among the Indians.

[111] Presents of this kind are discussed under "types" of gifts. *Vide.*, chapter iii.

[112] *Documentary History of the State of New York*, IV, 271.

[113] *Ibid.*

cil[114] of the Iroquois was never interrupted; and harsh language was never used, no matter what thoughts may have been in mind.[115] The representatives of the six united tribes (or "nations" as they were called), the Mohawks, Oneidas, Onondagas, Cayugas, Senecas, and Tuscaroras, customarily met at the council house in Onondaga to decide matters for the whole confederacy. All of these nations were located in the present limits of the state of New York. The Mohawks, situated north of the Mohawk River and east to the present border of Vermont, were generally the recipients of English goods; consequently, they were in alliance with the English. On the other hand, the Senecas, located in western New York, south of Lake Ontario, their territory bordering on Lake Erie, were more likely to be under French influence. As a result, they were frequent recipients of French presents. Other members of the Iroquois vacillated in their disposition—depending upon the flow of goods, whether as gifts or as trade, through their territory. It was a general policy of the sachems who met at Onondaga, notwithstanding the pressure on the east and west, to observe a strict neutrality. This policy was carried through the Colonial wars, culminating in the French and Indian War of 1754–1763.[116] Iroquois-English relationships were based upon the chain of friendship legend.[117] In contrast, therewith, a long record of bad feeling between the French and the Iroquois dated back to the seventeenth century, when Champlain is reported to have taken the side of the Algonquians against the Iroquois. Thus, at a disadvantage, the French gifts were always directed toward maintaining the neutrality of the Six Nations. British policy, however, was more aggressive. It sought, by gifts and even by subterfuge, to induce the whole confederacy to take up arms against the French.[118] Sir William Johnson, for instance, was quite successful in securing military aid from the Mohawks by means of presents. In turn, the Onondaga Council admonished their erring brethren for deviating from the established policy.[119]

The Southern Indians, principally the Cherokees and the Catawbas, had a long-standing feud with the Six Nations.[120] British gifts were directed toward breaking up this quarrel so that peace could be maintained among those Indians friendly to Britain. In all of these affairs, the influence of the Six Nations was paramount. Gifts to the sachems at Onondaga

---

[114] Located in present-day Onondaga County, New York State.

[115] *Vide*, note 112.

[116] LO 578; *Sir William Johnson Papers*, I, 514; *Pennsylvania Colonial Records*, V, 635–37.

[117] *Vide*, note 44.

[118] *Sir William Johnson Papers*, I, 514, 628–31.

[119] *New York Colonial Documents*, X, 97.

[120] *Pennsylvania Colonial Records*, V, 470–80.

could compel even the Delawares and Shawnees to bury the hatchet with the Quaker colony.[121] The vast influence of the Six Nations reached the Mississippi River, culminating in an alliance with the powerful Miami confederacy.

A brief survey of general Indian politics serves to show that the Onondaga Council held the balance of power. As early as 1720, the British came to realize this fact and accordingly channeled their presents in the direction of the Iroquois.[122] Appreciating the situation, the Iroquois were able to demand presents.[123] Overconfident young warriors went so far as to take gifts by force.[124] Even Sir William Johnson, who rarely spoke against the Indians to his close friends, referred to them as a ". . . . begging & insatiable set of People & expect to be denied nothing they ask for . . . ."[125]

Gifts for whole tribes, as well as individual presents, were showered upon that confederacy. The situation came to such a pass that the sachems regularly expected private gifts and refused to share in public donations.[126] Moreover, the young sachems would often carry presents to the older sachems. In turn, presents were redistributed by the older men in order to maintain prestige. Thus, the never ending cycle of presents became an inseparable part of Indian politics.

Following the above preliminary view of the custom of giving and receiving presents, it is now pertinent to inquire into the comparative methods used by the British and the French in distributing presents. The expedient of presents—a type of bribery—to obtain an end was by no means a foreign element either to English or to French diplomacy. As Talleyrand shrewdly remarked at a later date, "Every man has his price."

---

[121] *Sir William Johnson Papers*, II, 452–54.

[122] *New York Colonial Documents*, V, 571.

[123] Thomas Pownall, "Notes on Indian Affairs, 1753–1754," LO 460.

[124] *Sir William Johnson Papers*, II, 326.

[125] *Ibid.*, I, 514.

[126] LO 460.

II. PRESENTS: THE BRITISH AND FRENCH
SYSTEMS COMPARED

Comparison of the British and the French systems of giving presents on the old Northwest frontier, 1748–1763, involves a discussion of government regulation as it concerned the distribution of such presents. The French government lends itself more readily to study because of its centralization.

In New France, the government formed a counterpart to the hierarchical system of the mother country. Indian policy, and the corresponding distribution of presents, could be consistent and unified throughout the vast hinterland that formed a vital part of New France. Running from north to south, a long chain of inland lakes and rivers linked Canada to the Illinois country, while the Mississippi formed a final connection with Louisiana in the south. Interwoven in this network of communication so necessary to the French was a series of powerful Indian confederacies. These confederacies could be either a threat to French security or a source of protection against the English and their native allies. Consequently, the governor-general of New France (Father Ontontio[1] as he was called by the Indians) desired a tight control over the natives in order to keep them closely bound to the French. Presents were one of the best methods of accomplishing this purpose.

Governors-general, governors, commanders, priests, and all representatives were a part of the closely knit chain of government control in the disbursement of goods. The governor, in accordance with custom, gave present for present and speech for speech whenever he wanted to win the Indians to his point of view.[2] However, instructions for Vaudreuil,[3] governor-general of New France, stated that he was not to allow the Indians to accept British collars and flags. Such a procedure would prove costly because the Indians brought the British goods to the French, asking presents in return for them.[4] Vaudreuil's appointment as governor-general was

---

[1] According to an English account, the name Ontontio, or Onondio, signified the name of the governor of Canada or of a chief commander among the French. See P.R.O., C.O., 5/1328, L.C. 41–42, C.O. 46. See Blair, *Indian Tribes,* I, 268, for the use of the name.   [2] *Jesuit Relations,* XL, 167.

[3] Pierre de Vaudreuil de Cavagnal served as governor of Louisiana until 1753. At this time, he went to France, returning in 1755. He is not to be confused with his brother, Francois Pierre or Pierre Francois Rigaud de Vaudreuil, who was made governor of Montreal in 1757. See *Illinois on the Eve of the Seven Years' War,* pp. xix–xx.

[4] Instructions for Vaudreuil, March 22, 1755, *Wisconsin Historical Collections,* XVIII, 151–53.

chiefly based upon the fact that he had influence with the vast numbers of tribesmen surrounding the Canadian settlements. This influence enabled the governor-general to recruit warriors by the use of presents for the Marquis de Montcalm during the French and Indian War.[5]

The problem of transportation made necessary annual shipments of goods to be used for presents.[6] These presents were sent inland from New Orleans or Canada to each of the colonies and to the far-flung outposts, where representatives doled out clothes, food, and arms to the natives. Yet, despite the handicap of distance, all of these presents seemed to fit the general pattern of French Indian policy. This consistency was in sharp contrast to British decentralization. In New France, commanders, governors, and governors-general received reports on Indian affairs and gifts from the outposts. Such reports were forwarded across the Atlantic to the French home government.[7] Alert English governors, such as James Glen of South Carolina, complained about this unified French command.[8]

In the long series of Colonial wars between the French and the English, the French had proved themselves worthy adversaries. La Galissonière,[9] governor-general, in a memoir of 1750, points out that the Indians, knowing how dependent the French were upon them, often took presents from

---

[5] Vaudreuil was not always successful in securing warriors. A major controversy between Montcalm and Vaudreuil resulted after only sixteen Indians made an appearance to aid the French at Ticonderoga in 1758. See *New York Colonial Documents*, X, 732.

[6] Such shipments are mentioned, for example, in *Illinois on the Eve of the Seven Years' War*, pp. 234–35. See also Dunbar Rowland (ed.), *Mississippi Provincial Archives English Dominion, 1763–1766, Letters and Enclosures to the Secretary of State for Major Robert Farmer and Governor George Johnston*, I, 28–29.

[7] See the reports in the *New York Colonial Documents*, X. These reports are in the form of letters, memoires, or general surveys of the "Occurrences in Canada" covering a whole year. Occasionally reports were enclosed in the governor-general's letters. For example, in *ibid.*, X, 876, Montcalm wrote on "General Reflections on the Measures to be Adopted for the Defence of this Colony." This account, where Montcalm states that the Indians should be given what they require instead of having it sold to them, is enclosed in Vaudreuil's letter to M. de Massiac, Minister of Marine and Colonies, dated November 1, 1758.

[8] A summary of Glen's views is related in Lee to Hamilton, October 22, 1750, *Pennsylvania Archives* (1st series), II, 58. Cadwallader Colden, in writing to Governor Clinton of New York, August 8, 1751, noted that the French advantage was that with one council no expense was too great to accomplish a purpose. For this reason, he said that the French could perform the same service at half of the expense that it would cost the British. See *New York Colonial Documents*, VI, 744.

[9] Roland Michel, Comte, and later Marquis, de la Galissonière, was governor-general of New France during the years 1747–1749. The distinguished historian, Theodore Calvin Pease, states that he was the most able man to rule New France in the eighteenth century. See *Illinois on the Eve of the Seven Years' War*, pp. xx-xxi.

both contestants.[10] Continuing, La Galissonière shows that the French Canadians who lived among the Indian tribes were vital factors in French-Indian politics because they either could lead the tribesmen to war or wage war against the same Indians, if need be.[11] Many of these sons of the forest entered the service of the Church,[12] whose priests were among the most important agents for the distribution of presents for New France.

Religion was a powerful force in the eighteenth century, particularly with the Indians; and representatives of the Church believed in learning the Indians' customs, especially the custom of giving presents.[13] In order to Christianize the natives the Jesuits and other orders combined catechism, pictures, baptism, and presents in a successful manner. Presents, for instance, were used in a resurrection ceremony which was enacted when an adopted native was welcomed into a family to take the place of a dead warrior. The most important part of this ritual occurred when the adopted son received a gift from the family. At this point in the procedure there was great rejoicing over the symbolic resurrection of a departed loved one.[14] To introduce warriors to Christianity the Jesuits held up a picture of the French king and told the Indians that he desired that they love Jesus. To consummate this ceremony robes were given to the Indian chiefs as an expression of royal affection.[15] Presents were also associated with baptism. To the Indians baptism meant that they were subjects of the governor of Canada,[16] and it was at this time that they received presents of fine clothes and liquor.[17] Conrad Weiser reported, however, that the newly converted Indians frequently returned home to their original tribes and sold their clothes for more liquor. As a matter of fact, the Indians sometimes joked about erring brethren who incurred the anger of the priests when the gifts and holy water had no effect on them.[18] Notwithstanding this factor, Weiser observed, in 1748, that most of the Onondaga Indians

---

[10] "Memoir on the French Colonies in North America by M. de La Galissonière," December 1750, *New York Colonial Documents*, X, 223.

[11] *Ibid.*

[12] For an example, see note 26.

[13] *Jesuit Relations*, XL, 167.

[14] *Ibid.*, XXXII, 209–11.

[15] *Ibid.*, XXVIII, 235.

[16] William Johnson had prevailed upon the Cagnawaga Indians to be neutral. Their reply was that baptism made them the French allies. In their own words ". . . . for the French & we are one Blood, & where they are to dye [sic] we must dye [sic] also." See *Sir William Johnson Papers*, II, 379.

[17] "A Journal of the Proceedings of Conrad Weiser in his Journey to Onandago . . . .," August 15, 1750, to October 10, 1750, *Pennsylvania Colonial Records*, V, 470–80.

[18] *Ibid.*

were sympathetic to the French. So it was that Church and State worked together as agents in the distribution of gifts to the Indians.

That the Indians seriously accepted the teachings of their robed leaders is shown in accounts of how the tribesmen had great drops of sweat on their foreheads from efforts in remembering prayers.[19] These so-called "praying Indians," the receivers of many French gifts, were a source of anxiety among the English, who feared that the former would leave their peaceful mode of life.

The Jesuit records show that the priests successfully used presents to pacify savage tribes who practiced cannibalism. Blankets and kettles, used figuratively as "words," were employed to make the hatchet fall from the hands of the Iroquois, to "break" the kettle which was used to boil enemies, to "wash off" red war paint, and to "hide" bows, arrows, and war canoes.[20] Some priests, showing heroic bravery, boldly went forth to present collars to soften the hearts of hostile Indians who had tortured captives.[21] Further-more, General Amherst records a letter wherein a priest was the agent in suing for peace on behalf of French Indians in 1759.[22]

Priests did not always give presents for such pacific purposes, however. French records tell a long story of giving arms to the Indians through the intermediary of the Church. These warlike gifts were a source of great con-cern to the English, who had not lost their fear of popery. The black robes were seen from the Six Nations in the North[23] to the Ohio Indians, from the Chickasaws to the Catawbas and Creeks in the South.[24] Robert Din-widdie, lieutenant-governor of Virginia, complained that the priests were able to make the Creeks declare war on South Carolina.[25] New York Colonial documents cite the activities of Father Germain, resident missionary in Acadia, who distributed arms to the Indians during King George's War.[26]

It is James Adair, however, who paints the most alarming picture of the activities of these priests. Adair relates that the first step in the process of Christianization was to give the Indian ward a string of colored beads with a silver cross. This symbolized that they were engaged in the battle for

---

[19] *Jesuit Relations*, XL, 193–94.

[20] *Ibid.*, XL, 167–69.

[21] *Ibid.*, XLIII, 213–15.

[22] J. Clarence Webster (ed.), *The Journal of Jeffery Amherst Recording the Mili-tary Career of General Amherst in America from 1758 to 1763*, p. 241.

[23] P.R.O., C.O., 5/1327, L.C. 197, C.O. 257. See the journal of Conrad Weiser in the *Pennsylvania Colonial Records*, V. 470–80.

[24] Robert Dinwiddie to Sir Thomas Robinson, November 24, 1755, P.R.O., C.O., 5/17, L.C. 1, C.O. 461.

[25] *Ibid.*

[26] For Father Germain's activities in distributing presents, see the *New York Colonial Documents*, X, 13, 14, 43, 67, 71, 73, 74, 126.

Christianity. Next, using the catechism method, the priests taught the Indians that the English were not true Christians.[27] After the Indians were thus indoctrinated, the priests gave the tribesmen hundreds of scalping knives to be used to kill English subjects without regard to age, sex, or station in life.[28]

No documentary evidence has been found to substantiate this report, however; and Adair's viewpoint, no doubt distorted, illustrates the British fear of "praying Indians." Although French sources mention that the priests were used to mold the Indians to serve the ends of the government, raids by Christianized Indians, as such, were not often reported.[29] On the other hand, English sources frequently mention that the "praying Indians" had attacked various portions of the frontier, killing settlers.[30] The English reported that priests spared no expense in presents for this purpose.[31] Governor George Clinton of New York felt that a church near the Oneidas should be crushed by force for the preservation of the colonies.[32] Even so able a diplomat as William Johnson found that the French priests were among his most competent rivals in dealing with the Iroquois.

Probably the most skilled of all the priests who doled out presents and sermons was Abbé Piquet, member of the Sulpitian order. His mission-fort, La Présentation, was located on the upper St. Lawrence, just north of Fort Frontenac and thirty-five leagues south of Montreal.[33] This mission-fort, which was probably built in 1747, was the scene of much activity. Here the land was cleared off, guns were mounted for a fort, and pigs, cows, and poultry were raised. It was here, also, that Indian spies were sent out, and goods, clothes, and supplies of arms were delivered in large quantities. Duquesne,[34] writing to France in 1753, declared that Piquet's talent for mold-

[27] *Adair's History of the American Indians*, pp. 160–61.

[28] *Ibid.*

[29] The Indians who accompanied Baron Dieskau were the Cagnawaga or "praying Indians." However, they betrayed him. For accounts of this battle, see Vaudreuil to Machault, September 25, 1755, *New York Colonial Documents*, X, 318–27; Arch. Nat. Col. F. 3, 14, 144–46 (photostat); *New York Colonial Documents*, VI, 1003–4. See *ibid.*, Vol. X, for numerous accounts of Indian raiding parties sent out by the French.

[30] *Pennsylvania Archives* (1st series), II, 11.

[31] See *Adair's History of the American Indians*, pp. 160–61; Cadwallader Colden to George Clinton, August 8, 1751, *New York Colonial Documents*, VI, 741–43. John Sergeant, missionary to the Mohawks, complained of British lack of interest in using ". . . . our Religion, & fasten[ing] them [the Mohawks] to our Interest." See *Sir William Johnson Papers*, I, 233–34.

[32] *Sir William Johnson Papers*, I, 199.

[33] *New York Colonial Documents*, X, 203–5.

[34] Duquesne served as governor-general after the death of Jonquière in 1752. When Vaudreuil arrived in 1755, he took over the office from Duquesne.

ing the Indians to his ends had succeeded admirably.[35] There are plentiful records which testify to Piquet's activities in giving presents to induce the Indians to go to war on behalf of the French during the year 1760.[36] In this year, Amherst reported that Abbé Piquet actually led one hundred and fifty Indians into war, urging them to plunder and to give quarter to none.[37] Thus, it would seem that the representatives of the Church were formidable Indian agents on behalf of the government, distributing presents wherever the need was greatest.

The French also employed interpreters and gunsmiths[38] to work among the Indians and to apportion gifts. Second only to the priests as influential representatives, however, were the French officers. The Joncaire brothers, Philip Thomas and Daniel, Sieur de Chabert et de Clausonne, were two of these officer-interpreters who played a vital part in the drama of forest diplomacy and gifts.[39] Since both brothers were known as Sieur Joncaire, or simply as Joncaire, it is difficult to trace their movements.[40] About the year 1744, Philip Thomas, ensign, had been sent to reside among the Senecas, then living in what is now western New York; and by 1745, his reports covering the affairs of all of the Iroquois tribes were being transmitted to France. It appears that Philip Thomas Joncaire's chief duty at this time was to keep the Iroquois neutral.[41] In 1748, ill health caused him to relinquish his post to his younger brother, Chabert Joncaire[42] (sometimes known by his Indian name, Ontachsina). Available records indicate that Philip Thomas next worked among the Ohio Indians, whom he furnished with presents, much to the annoyance of the English.

The younger brother, Chabert, continued to reside in the Seneca country, where he was still active as late as 1758, bringing goods, arms, armorers, and smiths to the Iroquois and to the Delawares.[43] Like his brother, he was a disturbing element to the British; but when they complained of his numerous gifts among the Senecas in 1755, the Indians said that Chabert could not be molested because he had children amongst them.[44] It was in

---

[35] Duquesne to Rouillé, October 31, 1753, *Illinois on the Eve of the Seven Years' War*, p. 850.

[36] *New York Colonial Documents*, X, 154, 237–38.

[37] Webster, *op. cit.*, p. 139.

[38] *New York Colonial Documents*, X, 698.

[39] See the note in *Illinois on the Eve of the Seven Years' War*, p. xxxiv.

[40] *New York Colonial Documents*, X, 163.

[41] For an early account of the Joncaire brothers, see "Military and Other Operations in Canada During the Years 1745–1746," *New York Colonial Documents*, X, 38–75.

[42] *Ibid.*, X, 163. Both of these brothers were supposedly captured by William Johnson at Niagara in 1759.

[43] *Ibid.*, X, 698.

[44] *Wraxall's Abridgement*, p. 243.

1755, also, that William Johnson became so irritated by Chabert's competition in distributing presents that he offered a reward to any Frenchman in New York who would make Joncaire a prisoner.[45] The situation was not improved by the fact that Chabert Joncaire even secured from Albany traders English goods which he used for his presents.[46] There are records which tell of the younger Joncaire's being on the Ohio also,[47] and it appears that he was at the French post at Venango in 1753. It was in October 1753, when young George Washington went on his memorable journey to warn the French, that Chabert Joncaire used every artifice at his command to entice Washington's guide, Half King, to desert the English.[48] Hence, these Joncaire brothers, Philip Thomas and Chabert, had a long and varied career in Indian diplomacy on the frontier. The fact that their orders emanated from, and their reports were forwarded to, the governor-general of New France is significant,[49] for this is another indication of the French centralization of Indian policy.

The Joncaire brothers are only two examples of the host of capable leaders employed by the French to distribute gifts among the Indians. Céloron de Blainville,[50] who led the memorable Ohio expedition in 1748, and deposited leaden plates, was another competent donor of gifts,[51] as well as Major MaCarty Mactigue of the Illinois country[52] and Captain Charles de Raymond, commandant of the Miami post.[53] These and other alert young officers followed Indian affairs closely and fully realized the value of gifts to influence the Indians.

While centralization characterized the French administration of Indian affairs and gifts, decentralization, especially before 1755, fittingly describes the British system of disbursing gifts to the Indians. With the English, everyone seems to have been an "authority" on how to treat the Indians. Consequently, conflicting gifts, meetings, and plans appear to have been the

---

[45] *Sir William Johnson Papers*, II, 388.   [46] *Ibid.*

[47] *New York Colonial Documents*, X, 233–35.

[48] John C. Fitzpatrick (ed.), *The Diaries of George Washington, 1748–1799*, I, 56–57. Hereafter cited as *George Washington's Diaries*.

[49] Jonquière was well informed of their activities. See *New York Colonial Documents*, X, 207. For Montcalm's interest in Chabert Joncaire's presents see *ibid.*, X, 678.

[50] Louis Jean Baptiste Céloron de Blainville (or Bienville) should not be confused with his older brother, Pierre Joseph Céloron de Blainville. See note, *Illinois on the Eve of the Seven Years' War*, p. xxviii.

[51] See Céloron's journal of the Ohio expedition in the *Wisconsin Historical Collections*, XVIII, 36–37.

[52] *Illinois on the Eve of the Seven Years' War*, p. 510. In Illinois, the farmers furnished the Commandant with goods for gifts and were paid thirty percent of the original cost. See *ibid.*, pp. 27–29.

[53] *Illinois on the Eve of the Seven Years' War*, p. 177.

rule rather than the exception. Governors and various groups within a colony, such as the Quakers, traders, army officers, and special agents of the Crown, all doled out goods to the natives with no particular policy in mind. As a consequence of this practice, the Indians called the English colonies by different names instead of having one name for the king of England as they had for the king of France. Virginia's Governor was dubbed with the name Brother Assaraquoa, the Indian appellation for a cutlass which the Governor had given to an Indian chief.[54] Brother Onas was the name for Pennsylvania; and the proprietor of Maryland was known as Brother Tocarry-Hogan, a name which denoted his geographical position between Brother Assaraquoa and Brother Onas.[55]

Men like James Adair, William Johnson, Edmond Atkin, Thomas Pownall, and George Washington deplored such haphazard methods of dealing with the Indians. They felt that one responsible person should represent the Crown in the giving of presents.[56] They lamented the disorganization that occurred when each colony took care of its own presents. Under such a system many confusing practices arose. The Pennsylvania Assembly showered the Ohio tribes with large donations. Virginia dispensed presents so freely that a tax was proposed in order to lift the burden of expense from the assembly.[57] South Carolina's aggressive James Glen practically regarded the Southern Indians as wards of his colony; and when Robert Dinwiddie took an active interest in their affairs and gave them presents, Glen strenuously objected.[58] Farseeing men felt that all of this conflict of interest undoubtedly had a bewildering effect upon the Indians.

---

[54] P.R.O., C.O., 5/1325, L.C. 41–42, C.O. 46.

[55] Indian names such as father and brother were important in native diplomacy. For example, Count Zinzendorf, German missionary among the Iroquois, relates, "These Nations are divided into Fathers, or Children, or Brethren, or Members of the Covenant, and such as do not belong to one of the three Classes they call *Cousins*, which signifies as much as Subjects; and these former are again by them called *Uncles*." See William C. Reichel (ed.), *Memorials of the Moravian Church*, I, 120–21.

[56] See *Adair's History of the American Indians*, pp. 399–400; William Johnson to James Delancy, July 30, 1755, *Sir William Johnson Papers*, I, 794–97; LO 578; *Sir William Johnson Papers*, I, 853–56; John C. Fitzpatrick (ed.), *The Writings of Washington from the Original Manuscript Sources, 1745–1799*, II, 39–42. Hereafter cited as the *Writings of Washington*.

[57] James Munro and Sir Almeric W. Fitzroy (eds.), *Acts of the Privy Council of England, Colonial Series*, IV, 200–203. The tax was upon tobacco.

[58] For the Dinwiddie-Glen dispute, see, for instance, the following letters: Robert Dinwiddie to James Abercromby, October 23, 1754, R[obert] A[lonzo] Brock (ed.), *The Official Records of Robert Dinwiddie, Lieutenant Governor of Virginia, 1751–1758*, I, 375 (Hereafter cited as the *Dinwiddie Papers*); Robert Dinwiddie to James Glen, October 25, 1754, *ibid.*, I, 379; Robert Dinwiddie to Thomas Robinson, November 24, 1755, *ibid.*, II, 283.

Even the establishment of the Indian superintendencies in the North and in the South did not solve the problem of decentralization of Indian policy. In New York, William Johnson, Indian authority par excellence, found his powers hampered by the assembly, which was apparently intent on counting pennies.[59] Even after Johnson had received his commission as sole superintendent of the Northern Indians, William Shirley, commander-in-chief of His Majesty's forces in America, intrigued against him. Shirley was abetted in this action by John Lydius, who handed gifts to the very Indians whom Johnson regarded as his wards.[60] Lydius apparently regarded himself as a personal enemy of the superintendent.

So it was that many different agencies and officials continued to confuse the issue by dispensing presents. The Quakers, for instance, now and then took it upon themselves to distribute presents separately, despite the protests of their Governor.[61] Georgia insisted upon presenting gifts on her own initiative, even after Edmond Atkin's appointment as Southern superintendent. Theoretically, all the Southern colonies could contribute to the gifts, but they were to be handed out by the superintendent.[62] If he was not available, as was frequently the case, special representatives, such as Christopher Gist in Virginia, were to give out presents in his name. In 1763, John Stuart, who succeeded Atkin, complained that the Southern governors nullified his work by giving "separate presents." Some colonies left the whole business of Indian presents to traders, who were often "unfit persons."[63] Further difficulties were created by the fact that each governor seemed to occupy himself with Indian problems, especially with the ordering of gifts, immediately upon his arrival in America—sometimes even before![64] The ideas of the preceding governor relating to Indian policy seemed to have had little weight since the very fact of his having to leave the colony served to discredit him.

Lord Loudoun, as a military commander, had definite ideas about presents. He stated that large gifts should be presented only to those Indians who were principals, and presents should be given sparingly to those who had no influence. He also warned that the giving of arms to potential

---

[59] George Clinton to William Johnson, September 24, 1750, *Sir William Johnson Papers*, I, 301.

[60] *Ibid.*, I, 794–97.

[61] Henry F. Depuy, *Bibliography of the English Colonial Treaties with the American Indians, Including a Synopsis of each Treaty*, p. 37. Depuy has published a facsimile of the title page of a treaty between the Quakers and the Indians in April 1756.

[62] Edmond Atkin to the Board of Trade, May 30, 1755, LO 578.

[63] LO 578.

[64] George Clinton, before leaving London, made arrangements for gifts to be sent to the Indians near New York. See Huntington Manuscript, 9846. Hereafter cited as HM.

enemies was dangerous.[65] Although Sir William Johnson seemed to have showered presents on all Indians, he, too, concentrated on the influential tribesmen. Women, children, and the very old men were also important as recipients of presents. British authorities declared that their Colonial representatives did not recognize sufficiently the aged tribesmen who still exercised great influence, though they could not hunt and fight.[66] On the other hand, the French took especial care to present gifts to the old men even though those gifts might be mere trifles.[67] Such conflict in administration and practice in some degree explains the lack of co-operation between the Indians and the English.

The role played by the English Church in respect to the giving of gifts is in direct contrast to the aggressive work of the Catholic emissaries such as Abbé Piquet, who was a direct arm of the French government. By and large, the missionaries in the British colonies were genuinely interested in Christianizing the Indians; but the several expressions of this interest were as different, one from another, as were the sects themselves. The Anglican Church, through the Colonial governors and through the Society for the Propagation of the Gospel in Foreign Parts, attempted to establish schools to teach the Indians the elements of Christianity.[68] Moravian missionaries brought the gospel directly to the Indians in the forest, but the Quakers appear to have been the only religious group which used presents extensively to influence the Indians.[69] German sects in Pennsylvania, along with the Quakers, pacified the Indians with gifts which were "necessaries" rather than ammunition.

Gifts from the English to the Indians were supplied by the Crown, by private individuals such as traders, or through funds voted by the provincial assemblies. The *Journals of the Board of Trade* furnish an opportunity to observe the manner in which the home government provided for official gifts. Some of the recorded dealings concerning the colony of Georgia follow.

On June 19, 1754, Benjamin Martyn, agent for Georgia, had a memorial read, requesting presents to be sent over for the Indians in his colony.[70]

---

[65] Lord Loudoun to William Johnson [June 1757], *Sir William Johnson Papers,* II, 719–25.

[66] LO 567.

[67] *Ibid.* See *Adair's History of the American Indians*, pp. 307 ff. for a discussion of French skill in making trifles go a long way as regards control of the Indians. William Johnson noted that the French donors were always officers and not incompetent traders. See *Sir William Johnson Papers*, I, 430.

[68] For example, the College of William and Mary had an Indian school.

[69] See the *Pennsylvania Colonial Records*, Vols. IV, V, and VI, and the *Pennsylvania Archives* (1st series), Vol. II.

[70] *Journal of the Commissioners for Trade and Plantations*, X, 49. Hereafter cited as the *Journals of the Board of Trade.*

Eight days later, a draft of the agent's memorial was sent to the king. On January 21, 1755, the secretary laid before the Board of Trade a warrant directing the payment of £1500 to Martyn for the purpose of purchasing the desired presents. Of this fund, only £1000 were to be used for merchandise; the remainder was to cover the cost of packaging, freight, insurance, and delivery.[71] Almost three months elapsed before an order appeared directing the secretary of the Board of Trade to write to the secretary of the Lords Commissioners of the Admiralty. This was to request the usual protection for the master and the crew of the sloop *Juno*, bound for Georgia, carrying presents for the Indians bordering on that province.[72] Then on February 4, 1757, the secretary of the Admiralty informed the Board of Trade that the stores of presents and other articles were aboard the *Juno*, which would sail in two or three days, convoyed by two ships of war.[73] More time was consumed while the Board of Trade asked that the convoy see the *Juno* safely into the Savannah River. Finally, almost three years after the original memorial had been presented, Lieutenant-Governor Henry Ellis of Georgia wrote, on May 25, 1757, to inform the Board that the presents and ammunition had arrived safely.[74]

Under ordinary circumstances, shipments of presents arrived within a few months. Colonial agents on duty in London were responsible for ordering such presents by memorials. For example, one Wright, acting as agent for South Carolina, had such a memorial read in 1758.[75] In this case, the Board of Trade made a draft of his memorial and sent it to the Lords of the Treasury. Sir Danvers Osborn, governor of New York for a brief term, apparently employed one Milliquet for the sole purpose of having presents sent over for the Indians.[76] During the years 1755–1756 the time in transit must have been especially long. Robert Dinwiddie and William Johnson both noted the tardy arrival of ships with Indian goods through this period.[77]

The foregoing description of the English system does not, by any means, exhaust the difficulties which arose in connection with obtaining gifts and presents for the Indians. There were many occasions, for instance, when merchandise for the natives was almost impossible to secure.[78] For example, gifts from the Crown sometimes came in the form of warrants for cash. In

---

[71] *Ibid.*, X, 53–54, 103, 107.

[72] *Ibid.*, X, 119.

[73] *Ibid.*, X, 295–96.

[74] *Ibid.*, X, 343.

[75] *Ibid.*, X, 410–11.

[76] *Ibid.*, X, 3.

[77] See *Documentary History of the State of New York*, II, 422; *Sir William Johnson Papers*, II, 466–77; and *Dinwiddie Papers*, II, 487–88.

[78] *Documentary History of the State of New York*, II, 422.

this case, the goods had to be procured by the agents and local merchants, who sometimes found it necessary to search extensively in all the large centers, such as New York, Philadelphia, and Boston, before they could find the needed products. This condition was further aggravated by the fact that the British army often bought up ammunition stores and other articles of a military nature. In this manner, the army itself competed directly with the agents, who wished to secure such items for gifts.[79]

Once the gifts had arrived in a particular colony, commissioners[80] were appointed, interpreters[81] were selected, and the goods were sent inland. Batteaux,[82] wagons,[83] and pack horses[84] were used to transport the precious merchandise to the Indians, who eagerly awaited its arrival. On the inland journey, oilcloths were used to cover the goods in transit; and tents were set up to serve as temporary storehouses.[85] Altogether, freighting the gifts to the interior was an expensive procedure.

The actual distribution of the gifts might be accomplished in several ways. The French often allowed the Indians to come for presents to such designated points as Montreal. Sometimes the Canadians sent their gifts into the interior to forts and missions for distribution.[86] Like the French, the British sometimes permitted the Indians to come to Charleston and Philadelphia, or other designated cities, to claim presents. For special occasions, they often selected a frontier rendezvous such as Logstown, located near the modern town of Economy, Pennsylvania. Many problems were attendant upon this kind of procedure, however. One such difficulty was the fact that the Indians were exposed to diseases and to the temptation of liquor when they came to the cities. Indeed, the "sickly season" in Philadelphia and Charleston frequently prevented the natives from coming to accept their gifts.[87] Aside from this danger, the journey to the cities was

---

[79] *Sir William Johnson Papers*, II, 466–67.

[80] For the work of the commissioners, see the journal of William Fairfax, at the Winchester conference in 1753, P.R.O., C.O., 5/1328, L.C. 43–72, C.O. 47–72. For the Georgia presents, see *Journals of the Board of Trade*, X, 110.

[81] For the recommendation of an interpreter, see Cresap to Dinwiddie, December 27, 1751, William Palmer *et al.* (eds.), *Calendar of Virginia State Papers and Other Manuscripts, 1752–1781*, I, 245–47.

[82] *Sir William Johnson Papers*, III, 219.

[83] *Ibid.*, III, 226.

[84] George Croghan often provided horses for moving the goods inland. See the *Pennsylvania Colonial Records* for his activities.

[85] *Sir William Johnson Papers*, III, 255–56.

[86] *New York Colonial Documents*, VI, 898.

[87] Diseases, such as smallpox, spread from village to village, wiping out whole populations. At Colonial cities, native delegates frequently were exposed to this disease and "fevers" during the sickly season.

often long and arduous.[88] And, finally, transporting the goods home constituted a real task. After their trip to Philadelphia, the Indians were usually loaded down with as much goods as they could carry.[89]

At the time a gift was to be presented to the Indians, commissioners, interpreters, and influential colonists were usually in attendance at the place designated. In view of the importance of this work, the commissioners were always leaders in their colony. For instance, Benjamin Franklin, William Fairfax, and Richard Peters served in this capacity.[90] The interpreters were selected from among those traders and half-breeds who had a good reputation. Andrew Montour, considered a member of the Six Nations by the Indians themselves, was employed as interpreter both by Pennsylvania and by Virginia.[91] Conrad Weiser, religious leader, farmer, and head of a large family, was one of the few interpreters who was not a trader. George Croghan, holder of a military commission, and an outstanding trader, was entrusted with holding conferences without commissioners being in attendance.[92]

When the commissioners could not be in attendance, the interpreters usually read off a speech which had been prepared by the governor. Such a speech was important because it was the "word" that accompanied the goods. If there was a language handicap, the Iroquois sachems sometimes made the speech on behalf of the English.[93] In these instances, cautious Pennsylvania leaders directed the verbose sachems to stick to the subject of the speech lest the intended purpose of the gift be lost.[94]

These interpreters carried on a lucrative business, being employed first by one official, then by another. Occasionally they served two masters simultaneously. Interpreters were scarce in the British colonies, for few trustworthy men could be found to perform this service. On the other hand, the French were fortunate in having an abundance of interpreters, chosen from among the many of their countrymen living among the Indians. As one

---

[88] The emperor of the Cherokees suffered abuses from traders in making a journey to Virginia. See Draper MSS 1 QQ 71 (film).

[89] See the numerous accounts throughout the *Pennsylvania Colonial Records*.

[90] Benjamin Franklin's interest in publishing Indian treaties probably stems from his work as a commissioner. See Carl Van Doren and Julian P. Boyd (eds.), *Indian Treaties Printed by Benjamin Franklin.* Hereafter cited as *Indian Treaties Printed by Benjamin Franklin.*

[91] *Early Western Travels*, I, 58–69; William Trent to Robert Dinwiddie, August 11, 1753, Historical Society of Pennsylvania, Etting Collection of Ohio Company Papers (film).

[92] *Early Western Travels*, I, 97.

[93] Instructions for George Croghan and Andrew Montour from James Hamilton, April 25, 1751, *Pennsylvania Colonial Records*, V, 518–22.

[94] *Ibid.*

method of relieving this shortage among the British, Conrad Weiser recommended that young men live among the Indians, possibly with the resident blacksmiths, in order to learn the Indian language.[95]

Smiths and armorers were employed by the English, as well as by the French. Resident smiths were much in demand among the Indians. Their work had become necessary once the natives started using firearms. If a part of the weapon was lost or broken, it became useless because there were no interchangeable parts.[96] It was for this reason that a good deal of gun repairing went on at most treaties. These men served also as interpreters and often distributed presents on behalf of their government.

That Indian diplomatic methods were tiresome and pedantic in their procedure is obvious from the lengthy accounts of treaties. Governor Robert Hunter Morris of Pennsylvania was among those who complained of this tedious business.[97] One cause contributing to the great length and confusion of these meetings was the conflict of authority among the British as to who was to take precedence in the distribution of the presents. Was it to be a governor, an Indian superintendent, or a military commander, such as William Shirley or Jeffery Amherst? According to orders of the Board of Trade, Edmond Atkin, Southern superintendent, was dependent for funds and orders on the commander-in-chief of the British forces in America.[98] Although Sir William Johnson was royally commissioned as the "sole" director of the Northern Indians, he, too, had to secure his orders and funds for gifts from the commander-in-chief. The situation was further complicated by the fact that some governors appear to have ignored the superintendents and to have followed their own inclinations whenever they desired to give presents.

What did the presents accomplish in terms of general policy? The French, like their English rivals, first sought the friendship of the Indians. Next, also, as in the case of the British, they sought to prevent wars among the friendly tribes in order that their numbers might not be decimated.[99] Gifts were often effective in preventing such wars. Moreover, once these

---

[95] See Conrad Weiser's journal relating to his trip to Onondaga, where he recommends this procedure for his nephew. *Pennsylvania Colonial Records*, V, 470–80.

[96] William Johnson's smith for the Senecas and the Cayugas was to repair axes, hoes, and mend all arms for the Indians. See *Sir William Johnson Papers*, I, 765. For an elaboration on the necessity of these smiths, see [Archibald Kennedy], *The Importance of Gaining and Preserving the Friendship of the Indians to the British Interest Considered*, p. 14.

[97] Robert Hunter Morris to Sir William Johnson, April 24, 1756, *Sir William Johnson Papers*, II, 442–43.

[98] *Journals of the Board of Trade*, X, 242–43.

[99] *Wisconsin Historical Collections*, XVIII, 151–53; *Wraxall's Abridgement*, p. 250.

friendly alliances were secured, both the French and the English attempted to turn their friends into actual auxiliaries.[100] The French concentrated their gifts upon winning over those Indians who would exchange furs for English goods. This "illicit trade" among the so-called French Indians occupied the limelight of native diplomacy.[101] When gifts and other overtures could not win the Indians, the French turned to force. Two examples will suffice here: the Miami massacre at Pickawillany[102] and the confiscation of English goods,[103] and the case of the Chickasaws. In the latter example, the Chickasaws' position along the Mississippi enabled them, as friends of the English, to cut communications between Louisiana and the Northern colonies. French presents were of no consequence here, and a long series of Indian wars resulted. Despite this pressure, the fierce Chickasaws withstood overwhelming onslaughts of the French, time and time again.[104]

French commanders, like some English officers, believed that the Indians' fear was a stronger power than friendship in commanding the respect of the natives.[105] When the French could not use fear, they showered the Indians with expensive gifts that occasionally dwarfed the British presents. Hence, the Iroquois in the North and the larger confederacies in the South, such as the Cherokees, received gifts to court their neutrality.[106] If the French could not get active assistance by means of their gifts, they at least hoped to keep the Iroquois neutral rather than have them allied to the English.[107] This does not mean that the Indians directly under the French control did not receive gifts. Their services as scouts and auxiliaries, in opening up trade and acting as messengers merited compensation.[108]

---

[100] See *Sir William Johnson Papers*, I, II, and III for numerous illustrations.

[101] See Raymond to La Jonquière, October 11, 1749, *Illinois on the Eve of the Seven Years' War*, pp. 120–21, reporting on the treason of La Demoiselle, Miami chief, who traded with the English.

[102] This Indian village was located near the modern town of Piqua, Ohio.

[103] For an account of presents given to La Demoiselle to induce him to come back to his old village, see instructions for Sieur de Villiers, July 10, 1750, *Illinois on the Eve of the Seven Years' War*, pp. 218–19.

[104] See LO 2272. Herein is an account of the efforts of Kerlerec, as governor of Louisiana, to induce the Cherokees to attack the Chickasaws. Also see LO 578.

[105] See Blair, *Indian Tribes*, II, 56, where an Indian gives a Frenchman presents because of fear. In LO 26, Vaudreuil actually demanded scalps and the head of Red Slipper, a chief, as a tribute gift from the Choctaws.

[106] For an example of a list of French presents, see Dunbar Rowland *et al.* (eds.), *Mississippi Provincial Archives, 1704–1743, French Dominion*, III, 327.

[107] *New York Colonial Documents*, X, 562–63.

[108] As an example of the necessity of Indian allies, Sir William Johnson wrote to William Shirley, July 29, 1755, *Sir William Johnson Papers*, I, 789–90, that he must have Indians for his command or could promise no success.

In the case of British policy, the Board of Trade felt that it was of the utmost importance to have gifts delivered to the Indians in order to insure their friendship. Moreover, this agency wanted such gifts punctually delivered.[109] Generally speaking, the British literally showered the Indians with gifts. Since friendship with the Indians was almost a byword among Colonial officials, the natives were almost overwhelmed with goods in many cases. British manufacturers studied the desires and needs of the aborigines with the express purpose that no urge for adornment or necessity would be overlooked.[110] When the gifts were apportioned, individuals had to leave the meeting satisfied. Sometimes what seemed to be a large present was not large enough. In one instance, for example, George Croghan used his own trading merchandise to complete a body of goods. He, in turn, decided to ask for reimbursement, and proceeded to charge a grumbling Pennsylvania Assembly with the amount.[111] French records bristle with complaints about these huge English presents.[112] Since French storehouses were filled with only yearly shipments, the French could not begin to compete with British textiles, which were brought over in large quantities, convoyed by a powerful navy.

At no time does there appear to have been a consistent British Indian policy. The main consideration seems to have centered around giving as many presents as possible, thus insuring British trade and westward expansion at the expense of the French.[113] Indeed, the contest developed into what might be called a "scramble" for Indian allies. To add to the confusion, the British often quarreled among themselves and resorted to giving conflicting presents, as was the case with Braddock's potential warriors. Thus, as both the British and the French attempted to win the other's allies, those Indians who remained neutral appear to have received the lion's share of gifts.

That the Indians were essential as allies is shown in the history of the campaigns of the French and Indian War. At this time, the unmapped virgin forest with its primeval trees was unfamiliar to all but a few colonials. Indians performed a valuable function in acting as guides for such compe-

---

[109] The Board of Trade admonished Governor James Glen of South Carolina for not carrying out this policy.

[110] See "Distribution of Presents to the Indians at the Congress of Augusta," November 19, 1763. In John Stuart's letter of December 5, 1763, North Carolina Historical Commission, Transcripts English Records, C.O. 5. Bdl. 65, p. 324.

[111] The *Pennsylvania Colonial Records*, Vol. V, contain much on Croghan's activities. He was accused of being dishonest on several occasions.

[112] For examples, see *New York Colonial Documents*, X, 219, 256.

[113] *Ibid.*

tent woodsmen as Conrad Weiser and Christopher Gist.[114] European generals, by contrast with the Indians, were literally lost in the forest. The failure of Braddock, with only eight Indian guides, as against a host of French and Indians in 1755, is well known. Baron Dieskau's defeat in the same year was due to the treachery of his Cagnawaga Indians.[115] The great Montcalm was dependent upon natives for the same types of services. He wrote that he could not follow up his victory at Ticonderoga because he had only sixteen Indians, while the British had five hundred to lead them through the woods.[116] So we see that Indians as allies were a necessity, and this factor explains, in some degree, the extensive amount of presents given by both the French and the English.

---

[114] Conrad Weiser became lost while on his journey to Onondaga. See *Pennsylvania Colonial Records*, V, 470–80.

[115] *Vide*, note 29.

[116] See *New York Colonial Documents*, X, 734.

III. TYPES OF PRESENTS

When considering the types of presents offered to the Indians, it is expedient to examine the motives of the donor. If gifts were used to secure the friendship of the Indians, they had to be acceptable to the recipients. This meant that the agents must know who was to be the recipient and what were the desires of that recipient. Arms and munitions were acceptable to warriors; goods intended for sachems must be of a different type; and certain items, such as food, were necessary at all times for all groups. Indeed, a wide variety of goods, ranging from tawdry ornaments to simple toys, had their place in the appetites of the Indians. The agent was familiar with these appetites as well as with the factors which stimulated them. He knew, for example, that both greed and need dictated the Indian's choice of presents, but the demands of the warriors were primarily governed by their wives and other members of their families.

Among the Iroquois, women had great influence on the young warriors. They sat in councils and deliberated in public affairs.[1] Their feminine influence prevented warriors from going on campaigns when losses were heavy. Indeed, there are even records of Indian queens, some of whom were known as "Chief Women."[2] Records bear out the fact that both the French and the British were aware of this influence and used it in their dealings with the Indians. James Adair noted that the French were shrewd in making their trifles welcome to the fair sex,[3] and William Johnson instructed his officers to make presents that would be most acceptable to wives and mistresses of the Indians.[4] Official lists abound with requests for feminine gifts. Blankets for women were a different size from those made for men. Women's scarlet hose with clocks were in demand.[5] The consistent request for "lively colors" in calicoes, ribbons, and gartering pointed to feminine tastes. Even light-colored thread was specified.[6] Color listings for textiles and laces included such hues and shades as deep red, mazarine blue, green, scarlet, and yellow. Silk handkerchiefs, silver rings, ear bobs, and barleycorn beads also found their way into feminine hands. These items portrayed the brighter side of the Indian woman's life, but she was also desirous of

---

[1] *New York Colonial Documents*, VII, 103; *Sir William Johnson Papers*, II, 80–82.

[2] *Sir William Johnson Papers*, II, 384–86. For a reference to an Indian queen see *George Washington's Diaries*, I, 66.

[3] *Adair's History of the American Indians*, p. 258.

[4] "Some Hints for a Commanding Officer," May 24, 1755, *Sir William Johnson Papers*, I, 539–40.

[5] *Ibid.*, II, 898–900.   [6] *Ibid.*

having practical objects at her command. For example, awls for boring leather and wampum beads[7] were in demand. Weeding hoes, needles, and brass kettles[8] were a boon to her in her domestic tasks.

A glance at numerous lists reveals the demand for presents designed for Indian children. Materials for children's clothing were especially desirable. At one time, ten pieces of garlix, a linen cloth imported from the Germanies, of three-fourths size, were ordered to make shirts for children of different ages.[9] Some of the garlix was ordered in seven-eighths size and ruffled with muslin to make men's shirts.[10] The shirts of the influential men were ruffled, but those for the boys and common Indians were plain. Boys' shirts were specified as being in a separate category. There seems to have been a lack of gifts for the little Indian girls, however. It appears that the Indian women utilized the numerous textiles ordered during the period of the French and Indian War to make garments for the native girls. Certainly, the orders of needles, thread, and scissors would provide the tools for this undertaking. Occasionally, clothing was ordered already made. Red Head, an Onondaga chief, for instance, accepted finished articles of clothing for his entire family.[11]

An account indicating the specialization in giving presents intended to please every station, age, and sex among the Indians has been found in the *Wisconsin Historical Collections*.[12] Although this account is undated, the editor, nevertheless, has bracketed the years 1796–1797. Despite the fact that these years fall beyond the scope of this study, the list does, notwithstanding, serve to illustrate the tendency of appealing to all groups of Indians. According to this list, a Mohawk chief was to be given a pair of arm bands, a medal with ribbon, and a chief's gun. Three and one-half yards of fine cloth were donated for a blanket, while two and one-half yards of linen were intended for a shirt. In addition, a knife, flints, a pair of shoes, a large blanket of three points[13] (points determined the size of the blanket), vermilion paint, ball and shot, ear bobs, two hundred brooches, and a tin

---

[7] "Sketch of Goods Suitable as a Present for the Indians," December, 1752, P.R.O., C.O., 5/1327, L.C. 565–66 (film). Roger Williams noted that the awl blades were used for boring wampum grains. See *Roger Williams' Key*, p. 130.

[8] Both brass and tin kettles were used as gifts. See "List of Indian Goods at Rock Creek Belonging to the Ohio Company," Stanislaus M. Hamilton (ed.), *Letters to Washington and Accompanying Papers*, I, 363–64.

[9] P.R.O., C.O., 5/1327, L.C. 565–66 (film).

[10] *Ibid.*

[11] *Sir William Johnson Papers*, III, 161.

[12] *Wisconsin Historical Collections*, XII, 102–4.

[13] Points referred to the lines woven into the blanket. These lines determined the width, as in the Mackinaw blanket; and, therefore, the value of each blanket was determined by points.

kettle are included in the list.[14] The donor also made splendid gifts for the chief's lady. She was to have five yards of fine cloth for a blanket and a petticoat, thirty-six yards of ribbon, two hundred brooches, and a smaller blanket of only two and one-half points. Two and one-half yards of linen or calico, a plain hat, and two silk handkerchiefs were added to complete her ensemble.[15] Some embossed serge for shirts and smaller blankets were provided for the chief's children, the size of the blanket to be determined by the size of the child.

In giving presents during the eighteenth century, the donors adhered to the rule of precedence in rank. The common Indian received an ordinary gun rather than a chief's rifle. In addition, he was handed a common hat, four flints, and a blanket of three points. While the chief was allowed a choice of brass or tin kettles, the common Indian could have only the brass.[16] The common Indian's wife received only a piece of stroud to be used for a blanket and petticoat. The stroud, a cheap cloth made of woolen rags, was quite different from the fine material given to the chief's wife. It is interesing to note, however, that the children received the same materials whether they belonged to a chief or to a common Indian.

The rule of precedence was applied to tribes as well as to individuals. Consequently, the lower Canadian Indians received smaller presents than the mighty Iroquois. For example, their blankets were only two and one-half points in size.[17] On the other hand, women over sixteen years of age were presented with the same articles as those received by a common Iroquois Indian wife. Boys and girls ranging from twelve to sixteen years were given a blanket of two points; children between eight and twelve years received a blanket of one and one-half points; children under eight had a blanket of only one point.[18]

The chiefs and sachems were frequently the beneficiaries of special goods. At a conference in 1756, William Johnson discreetly gave each Onondaga chief a "Handsome private Present" of clothing, money, and corn for the families of the tribal leaders.[19] Accounts of the Northern Department of Indian Affairs record one occasion wherein thirty Iroquois sachems were the recipients of one hundred thirty-nine pounds in cash as well as a share of the public present given to the whole tribe, the latter

---

[14] *Wisconsin Historical Collections*, XII, 102–4. Vermilion included in this list was a bright red pigment. Verdegris or verdegreace (original spelling), a green or greenish-blue pigment and poisonous drug, was also ordered for Indian presents. While verdegris was ordered in small quantities as "lumps," vermilion was packed in casks and appears to have been in great demand by the Indians. See "List of Goods to be Sent from London, for the Northern Indians," *Sir William Johnson Papers*, II, 898–900.

[15] *Wisconsin Historical Collections*, XII, 102–4.   [16] *Ibid.*

[17] *Ibid.*   [18] *Ibid.*   [19] *New York Colonial Documents*, VII, 186.

amounting to fifteen hundred pounds.[20] This practice of giving special presents to the sachems was widely used by British agents well acquainted with the Indians. As William Johnson aptly expressed it, arguments, promises, and the giving of presents, when conducted in private meetings with the sachems, cut a deep wound in the French interest.[21]

It has been apparent that materials for clothing were most important among the selections of suitable gifts. British textile manufacturers deliberately created a category of goods which became exclusively Indian merchandise. The stroud, a cheap woolen cloth made of rags, and used for clothing and blankets, is often linked with rum as a British monopoly. It was unusual, indeed, for a list of presents not to include the stroud as the first item of preference.[22]

Blankets were not always made of stroud material. The duffle,[23] named for a town near Antwerp, where it was originally made, was a coarse woolen cloth with a thick nap or frieze. "Duffles," when itemized in lists of presents, no doubt referred to duffle blankets.[24] A better grade of woolen cloth was found in the ratteen.[25] Like stroud cloth, this material was often used for coats; but because of its thick twill and frieze, or curled nap, it also made a fine blanket. Stockings and linings were frequently made of penistone, a coarse woolen cloth, this name being derived from the small town in Yorkshire where the cloth was made. A most welcome gift was the halfthick, found on numerous lists of Indian goods. Defined as "a kind of cloth," the halfthick is known only to be a coarse material made in Lancashire. Halfthicks were probably used as cheap blankets, since they were ordered in pieces, as were duffles and strouds.[26] Although they were listed with cotton calicoes, "calliminicoes" were actually a Flanders wool product, woven with satin twill,

---

[20] *Sir William Johnson Papers*, III, 164.

[21] William Johnson to Edward Braddock, June 27, 1755, *ibid.*, I, 662–65.

[22] Actually, strouds were the first item to be listed in almost every list of gifts. See "List of Goods to be Sent from London for the Northern Indians," *Sir William Johnson Papers*, II, 898–900; "Sketch of Goods Suitable as a Present for the Indians," December 1752, P.R.O., C.O., 5/1327, L.C. 565–66 (film); and "Distribution of the Presents to the Indians at the Congress of Augusta," November 19, 1763, North Carolina Historical Commission, Transcripts of English Records, C.O. 5. Bdl. 65, pp. 321–24.

[23] Duffle is also spelled duffel or duffil. Usually duffles were ordered in stripes. See *Pennsylvania Colonial Records*, V, 151, 393.

[24] The duffle was also used for making coats. See P.R.O., C.O., 5/175, L.C. 154 (film).

[25] For the use of ratteen as a gift, see *Sir William Johnson Papers*, II, 898–900. In this list of goods, ratteen is ordered in deep purple.

[26] P.R.O., C.O., 5/1327, L.C. 565–66 (film); *Pennsylvania Colonial Records*, IV, 446.

enabling the observer to see checks on one side only.[27] Indian agents ordered this glossy material in stripes and lively colors. Walsh cottons were equally baffling by name. Actually these "cottons" were a kind of woolen cloth with a nap.[28]

Other than woolens, cotton and linen fabrics were also used as presents. Garlix, a linen fabric, and printed cotton calico were both popular items; and the gimp, a silk worsted or cotton twist with a cord or wire running through, commonly was used for trimming purposes. These fabrics, basically cheap and drab, were dyed bright hues of red, blue, and aurora in order to make them attractive to the aborigines. Their desirability was further enhanced by the addition of alluring decorations of bed lace, tinsel, and nonsopretties, a decorative braid or tape.[29]

When we analyze the kinds of clothing used as gifts for the Indians, it becomes evident that the tribesmen prized all the items worn by colonials in the 1750's.[30] In fact, the only articles worn by contemporary Europeans that the Indians did not receive as gifts were wigs and breeches.[31] No record of either of these items has been found in any of the numerous entries of goods.

Despite the popularity of clothes as gifts, many observers noted that the Indians wore their European clothing only when they were among the English. This situation was commented upon by Roger Williams in 1643, and by Captain Arent Schuyler de Peyster in 1779.[32] Undoubtedly, the natives chose to use expensive attire for ceremonial purposes or to create a favorable impression. Otherwise, they preferred their own simple mode of dress. In 1755, a description from Fort Cumberland of the Indians who were to aid

---

[27] *Sir William Johnson Papers*, II, 898–900. Undoubtedly Johnson referred to callimanco or calamanco.   [28] *Ibid.*

[29] For a list of presents including ribbon and bed lace, see *Pennsylvania Colonial Records*, V, 393. Small bells used by the Morris dancers on their costumes during May Day celebrations were also in demand for decoration. See *ibid.* For tinsel used for lacing hats, see *Sir William Johnson Papers*, II, 504. Nonsopretties are merely called "Prettys" in the list of gifts for the Southern Indians at the Augusta Conference, North Carolina Historical Commission, Transcripts from English Records, C.O. 5. Bdl. 65, pp. 321–24.

[30] See clothing descriptions of runaway servants in the *Virginia Gazette*, April 4, 1751. Printed at Williamsburg, Virginia, reproduced in photostat by the Massachusetts Historical Society.   [31] *Ibid.*, April 11, 1751.

[32] *Roger Williams' Key*, p. 108; *Wisconsin Historical Collections*, XVIII, 387. Captain Arent Schuyler de Peyster entered the British army in 1755, and in 1774 was sent to command Mackinac, where he remained until 1779. Later he retired and went to Scotland, where he met the poet Burns. His "Miscellanies" are printed in part in Volume XVIII of the *Wisconsin Historical Collections*, pp. 377–90. Herein is a curious rhyming verse account of Indians, presents, and customs.

Braddock states that their main article of clothing was a blanket or coat, which was thrown around the shoulders. They were shod in deerskin moccasins; and their faces were painted with an odd combination of red, yellow, and black pigment. This custom had certain advantages not present in the European garb. In wet weather, for example, the Indians, not hampered by unhealthy, damp garments, could dry quickly in their minimum of clothing.[33] Furthermore, they wore no hats, having only a tuft of hair, which they dressed with feathers.[34]

On ceremonial days, the Indian attire was greatly changed. Some of the young chiefs wore as many as twelve silver gorgets, each hanging below the other. Their richly laced coats of fine scarlet cloth covered flowery chintz shirts; silk handkerchiefs, which were never used, dangled half out of the coat pockets; and hats, richly plumed around the rims, were the culminating items in this unusual ensemble. All of these costly clothes could easily be thrown off, however.[35]

To this point, waistcoats have not been mentioned in the description of gifts for the Indians. Iroquois sachems, nevertheless, prized elaborate green silk waistcoats trimmed with lace and gold.[36] As a matter of fact, William Johnson usually distinguished his favorite sachems by clothing them completely, even to the waistcoat. The French made a practice of clothing the dead Indians from head to foot.[37] In addition, they competed with the English in giving native leaders the finest suits of clothes available, although they sometimes had to give cheaper types. Edmond Atkin's list of goods included many cheap waistcoats of scarlet, blue, or green. The coats were trimmed with cheap, gaudy lace; and yellow, silver, and gold buttons adorned the ever brilliant cloth.[38] The Southern Superintendent of Indian Affairs asked that buttons be plentifully supplied. Cuffs, collars, and shirts were needed to complete the over-all effect. The shirts, some of which were ruffled, were ordered of Scotch or Irish linen.[39]

For the Indian, who seldom wore a chapeau, gaudy hats were a special treat. Apparently, however, unlaced hats were of no value as gifts; and both Edmond Atkin and William Johnson used gold and silver tinsel for decorative purposes.[40] Securing this lace, so highly prized by the Indians, was

---

[33] *Roger Williams' Key*, p. 108.

[34] Winthrop Sargent (ed.), *The History of an Expedition Against Fort Du Quesne in 1755; Under Major General Edward Braddock, Generalissimo of H.B.M. Forces in America*, p. 373.

[35] *Wisconsin Historical Collections*, XVIII, 387.

[36] *Sir William Johnson Papers*, III, 161.   [37] *Jesuit Relations*, XXXII, 245.

[38] LO 3517.

[39] *Ibid.*

[40] *Ibid.*; also see *Sir William Johnson Papers*, II, 504.

sometimes a difficult task for the Northern Superintendent.[41] Even castor hats of beaver pelts could not be used without lace decoration.

Gartering and ribbons of the most startling hues were in great demand for lacing jackets and other gaudy articles. It is interesting to note Edmond Atkin's extensive use of the term "gaudy" to describe any article of clothing to be presented to the Indians. The only rival adjective seems to be the word "cheap." Indeed, inexpensive, tawdry clothes were probably quite practical as gifts since the Indians wore these clothes only for special occasions.

The Indians often specified a desire for goods of particular colors and designs. For example, if the tribesmen wanted stripes and stars on their strouds, these strouds were made up in that fashion. It is of interest to observe that their tastes were catered to even in those cases where they demanded a special kind of stripe.[42]

Gorgets, medals which were fastened around the neck with ribbons, were used as jewelry or for identification purposes. Both the French and the British made liberal use of these medals as presents. William Johnson and other British donors generally ordered their gorgets to be made of silver. The pattern was usually the same, a likeness of the British king on one side and the British coat of arms stamped on the other.[43] The medal was one item of "dress" which usually remained on the body after the more superficial garments were discarded.

More practical as a gift than medals and clothes was food. It is well known that British settlers drove away game, thus making it difficult for those tribes who lived primarily by hunting to procure meat. Consequently, the Indians were often in need of meat, bread, corn, and flour. The prevention of famines was not the only reason why the English gave away vast amounts of food. Every time Indian warriors were called away to a conference, they had to be fed.[44] In addition, the old men, women, and children left at home in the villages had to be provided with daily rations. So it was that lists of gifts often included large amounts of beef, rice, fruit, pork, butter, sugar, loaves of bread, tea, and liquors.[45]

---

[41] *Sir William Johnson Papers*, II, 504. [42] LO 3517.

[43] William Johnson had trouble getting honest workmen to make gorgets. Sometimes supposedly silver gorgets were made of a base metal. See *Sir William Johnson Papers*, II, 523. Governor Dinwiddie ordered his medals directly from England, having the king's picture on one side and the British coat of arms on the other. Each medal had a loop to hold the ribbon. See P.R.O., C.O., 5/1327, L.C. 565-66 (film).

[44] *Sir William Johnson Papers*, III, 23.

[45] For gifts of food see *Sir William Johnson Papers*, III, 23; William Johnson's account of Indian expenses from March 1755, to October 1756, *ibid.*, II, 566-645; *Pennsylvania Colonial records*, V, 197; Draper MSS 1 QQ 161, 1 QQ 142-45 (film).

Rum was the most popular of all gifts, though wine and brandy were both in demand (the latter being supplied almost exclusively by the French). In 1753, when George Washington gave Queen Aliquippa of the Delawares a present of a matchcoat[46] and a bottle of rum, she considered the rum the more desirable of the two articles. Since the British had almost a monopoly on rum, they used it extensively in all their dealings with the Indians; and rum was widely circulated. Unfortunately, it proved to be a most effective gift for designing traders, who knew that an inebriated Indian lost almost complete control of his senses. James Logan, member of the Pennsylvania council in the 1740's, appreciating the Indian's lack of self-control, urged them to abstain from the use of alcohol. Remarking on the good sense shown by the tribesmen in many other matters, he admonished them for their lack of self-discipline when drinking, contrasting them with the whites, who seemed to be able to drink as they pleased, without actually becoming inebriated.[47]

The French declared that the persistent use of rum actually set the Indians crazy. However, brandy, the beverage dispensed by the French, resulted in as disastrous effects as did the English rum. Often, after an all-night orgy of drinking brandy, the natives found themselves in a terrible state. Noses and ears were bitten off, causing disfigurement.[48] Mothers rolled in burning coals and threw their babies into fires and boiling kettles; and husbands and sons committed "a thousand abominations."[49]

Frequently, when a conference was in progress, all business had to be held up for a day or two until the Indians became sober enough to proceed with negotiations.[50] On other occasions, interpreters deliberately used the Indian's fascination for liquor to dupe him into selling his lands in exchange for cheap presents.[51] There were a few chiefs who were able to "hold"

---

[46] *George Washington's Diaries*, I, 66.

[47] *Pennsylvania Colonial Records*, IV, 91–92.

[48] Blair, *Indian Tribes*, I, 208, 209.

[49] *Ibid.* Jeffery Amherst said the Indians were "devils" when drunk. See Webster, *op. cit.*, p. 219.

[50] See the journal of the commissioners at the Winchester conference of 1753, P.R.O., C.O., 5/1328, C.O. 47–72, L.C. 43–72.

[51] The native tribes of Virginia degenerated into drunken, miserable figures after having sold their lands. For this reason, the Nottaways and the Pamunkeys were of no significance in frontier politics. See Colonel Thomas Lee to the Board of Trade, September 29, 1750, P.R.O., C.O., 5/1327, L.C. 171–85, C.O. 231–46. James Glen of South Carolina was one of the outspoken officials who criticized the method of taking lands from the Indians by presents. See, for example, James Glen to Holdernesse, June 25, 1753, P.R.O., C.O., 5/13, L.C. 463, C.O. 595.

their liquor day after day and still transact business, much to the amazement of their tormentors.[52] Names such as "Thickup" and "The Drunkard" indicated habitual indulgence on the part of these chiefs.[53]

Although it was true that almost all of the commissioners and interpreters used rum during these conferences, moderation was the rule with the more experienced men such as William Johnson and George Croghan. They opposed the drunken traders who secretly gave large amounts of *Demon Rum* to the natives. Trouble arose after the Indians had merely tasted a dram of liquor in preliminary meetings which preceded the formal opening of a conference.[54] Once, in an attempt to solve this problem by direct action, Conrad Weiser and George Croghan deliberately smashed the kegs of one trader who had brought thirty gallons of spirits to an Indian meeting.[55]

Both the individual colonies and the departments of Indian affairs made an effort to control this undesirable situation by passing strict laws against selling and giving rum to the Indians.[56] This was done even though the beverage seemed almost necessary to open some trade negotiations. These laws were intended as a restriction upon the rascally traders, but they actually screened out only a few minor offenders. Records of subsequent trials and of contemporary correspondence to be found in the *Sir William*

---

[52] See in the *Pennsylvania Colonel Records*, Vols. VI, VII, and VIII, the accounts of Indian treaties, where Teedyuscung, Delaware sachem, consumed large amounts of liquor.

[53] Myndert Wempel to William Johnson, November 22, 1755, *Sir William Johnson Papers*, II, 325–26. See also *ibid.*, II, 517.

[54] When the Indians were welcomed to the conference at Winchester in 1753, each was given a dram of rum; then he retired. However, later in the conference, they became so drunk that the negotiations could not be continued. See the journal of the commissioners at the Winchester conference in 1753, P.R.O., C.O., 5/1328, L.C. 43–72, C.O. 47–72. Atkin thought that the Indians were so addicted to rum that the supply could be cut off to them only gradually. See Edmond Atkin to the Board of Trade, May 30, 1755, LO 578.

[55] See the journal of Conrad Weiser relating to his trip to the Ohio country in August 1748, *Pennsylvania Colonial Records*, V, 348–58. In the report of the commissioners of the Carlisle conference of 1753, the Indians are said to have been unusually drunk. A speedy remedy to change the deplorable state of the Indians was urged before it was too late because of the inconceivably large amount of rum being given the Indians. See *Pennsylvania Colonial Records*, V, 670–86. The Delawares, Six Nations, and Shawnees were described as being continually under the influence of liquor while the Twightwees or Miamis were noted for their martial spirit and sobriety. See James Hamilton to Robert Dinwiddie, November 16, 1753, *Pennsylvania Archives* (4th series), II, 208–14.

[56] *Sir William Johnson Papers*, I, 580–81, II, 562; *New York Colonial Documents*, X, 976–77; Edmond Atkin to the Board of Trade, May 30, 1755; LO 578.

Johnson Papers indicate that the magistrates and their friends were too often the real offenders themselves, not the poor women and laborers.[57]

On numerous occasions, the Indians themselves protested against this plague that decimated their population. When bodies of dead warriors were found, the stench often betrayed death by reason of intoxication.[58] Still, the Indians seemed unable to resist alcohol's fatal lure. In one breath they asked for relief; in another they requested that some of their members who had never tasted rum be given an opportunity to sip the white man's liquor. Perhaps they reasoned that all must sample these spirits in order to judge of the evil they contained!

Aside from undermining the constitution of the Indian, rum caused obfuscated natives to give away fine clothing in exchange for still more liquor.[59] William Johnson confessed that he sometimes had to clothe sachems three and four times because unscrupulous traders acquired the Indians' own clothing for themselves![60] It would seem almost as if the traders had entered into a deliberate conspiracy to drive the whole Indian population into a state of inebriety. When the store of liquors was confiscated from the traders at Fort Niagara in 1762, it amounted to 2,602 gallons.[61] Even though these traders weakened their rum with water, it had a damaging effect, nevertheless.[62] Only diseases such as smallpox, another "gift" of the white man, could rival liquor as a death knell to the warrior population of the aborigines.

War gifts of cutlasses, scalping knives, guns, powder, and bullet molds strike a grim note in the numerous lists of goods to be delivered to warriors.[63] Although this tone is somewhat relieved by the turkey and duck shot, jews'-harps, wrist plates, fishing equipment, and Dutch toys,[64] which were sent to the Indians, we cannot overlook the fact that the outfit of each Indian auxiliary contained a large assortment of equipment for the influential fighters.[65] Gimps for bending the hair, vermilion paint, light guns, flints,

---

[57] *Sir William Johnson Papers*, II, 496–98, 534.

[58] See Conrad Weiser's journal relating to his trip to the Ohio country in August 1748, *Pennsylvania Colonial Records*, V, 348–58.

[59] "Minutes of the Catawba Conference, May 18, 1757," HM 3992; *Sir William Johnson Papers*, II, 646, I, 560–61.

[60] *Ibid.*, II, 646.   [61] *Ibid.*, III, 719.   [62] *Early Western Travels*, II, 92.

[63] *Pennsylvania Colonial Records*, V, 151, 197; *Sir William Johnson Papers*, II, 898–900; P.R.O., C.O., 5/1327, C.O. 565–66 (film).

[64] See LO 2507; LO 1389; P.R.O., C.O., 5/540, L.C. 493–94 (film).

[65] See Sir William Johnson's account of Indian expenses from March 1755, to October 1756, *Sir William Johnson Papers*, II, 566–645. Jeffery Amherst was quite enthusiastic about giving medals to the Indians as a mark of distinction. See Jeffery Amherst to William Pitt, May 4, 1761, *ibid.*, III, 386. The letter is also printed in G. S. Kimball (ed.), *The Correspondence of William Pitt*, II, 427.

kettles, Walsh cottons, knives, blankets, and scissors were but a few of the items requisite for Indian service.[66] Unfortunately, unscrupulous individuals frequently purchased these valuable goods from the Indians before they had a chance to use them![67]

One perennial question always arose in connection with war goods. Against whom were these barbaric gifts to be used? To arm the Indians to the teeth was one thing, but it was quite another to have these very bullet molds and knives used against the donor. And that is precisely what occurred whenever the Indians' affections shifted! This was especially true when the natives were refused additional gifts.[68] The Pennsylvania Assembly was often embarrassed when faced with the subject of war gifts, for the Indians overcame Quaker arguments for pacifism by pointing out that they needed arms for their daily hunting. Since a diminishing supply of game made the bow and arrow almost useless, this was a most valid argument.

During wartime, the so-called "civilized" powers frequently exchanged barbaric trophies when dealing with the savages. Scalps were common, while the French demanded no less than a whole head as a tribute from obstreperous tribesmen.[69] By contrast, fierce warriors so terrified the English colonists that they were bribed by large presents. James Adair complained that loyal Indians were thus deprived of many gifts because of their friendliness.[70] Nor were these the only gifts made during the time of war. Others included prisoners, wampum, hatchets, as well as the ever desired food and clothing.

Enterprising eighteenth-century businessmen hoped these gifts would stimulate a great market for British merchandise. Basing their plans upon the principles of mercantilism, these businessmen wished that the Indians would cultivate and export tobacco, indigo, cotton, and flax in return for their gifts. Then, supposedly, after the natives had been Christianized, they would eventually be absorbed by the neighboring white population.[71] The increasingly large volume of presents sent out indicated that these

---

[66] See "Calculation of Expenses of Indian Warriors for Their Service," July 23, 1758, in *Collections* of the New York Historical Society, *The Letters and Papers of Cadwallader Colden*, V, 248. Hereafter cited as *Colden Papers*. Also see *Sir William Johnson Papers*, I, 107–10.

[67] *Ibid.*, I, 77–79.

[68] Sachems were continually asking for arms to defend themselves and families. See *New York Colonial Documents*, VI, 986.

[69] LO 26, pp. 38–39. It is interesting to note that the French controlled the chiefs by giving them medals. These leaders were known as the "Medal Chiefs." See *ibid.*, pp. 12–13.

[70] *Adair's History of the American Indians*, p. 307.

[71] *Ibid.*, p. 492.

hopes were realized in part. It took many years, however, before the proud Iroquois and Algonquian warriors became even partially adjusted to this agricultural mode of life.

It seems appropriate, at this point, to consider the "civilizing" influence of the gifts to the Indians. Despite the Indians' slow adjustment to a different economy, the increasing amounts of textiles, hardware, clothes, jewelry, and toys indicated a steady rise in the demand for merchandise. Once the Indians had become accustomed to the white man's goods, they could not live without the traders and without presents.[72] Some even became lazy with excessive gifts and refused to raise crops.[73]

This "civilizing" influence of gifts began with the settlement of Jamestown in 1607. John Smith records that he sent beads, wooden combs, fishhooks, knives, and a grindstone to Powhatan, these presents being made on behalf of Sir Thomas Dale.[74] Correspondingly, the early colonists of Plymouth and Massachusetts Bay exchanged gifts with the neighboring Indians. From this time on, the story is one of increase in the amount of gifts. With the introduction of the horse as a present, saddles and bridles became frequent gifts.[75] By 1747, the Quaker colony was giving 6,500 flints, eighteen barrels of gunpowder, and thirty brass kettles as a minor part of one present.[76] In 1756, the volume had jumped so that Sir William Johnson's casual order of 1,000 blankets and 400 shirts seemed but ordinary.[77] Hundreds of pounds of vermilion were ordered to keep pace with other items that were sent over by the dozen and by the gross.

With volume came variety. At the end of the French and Indian War, storehouses were literally eighteenth-century hardware-textile warehouses.[78] Everything from padlocks to pipes seemed to be available.[79] Tinware, haberdashery, and ironware had already created such a demand for more

---

[72] See Teedyuscung's account of the economic distress of his people, the Delawares, in 1756, in *Indian Treaties Printed by Benjamin Franklin*, p. 139.

[73] *Adair's History of the American Indians*, p. 444.

[74] Lyon Gardiner Tyler (ed.), *Narratives of Early Virginia, 1606–1625*, p. 314.

[75] Draper MSS 6 QQ 140 (film). In 1758, at Fort Loudoun, the Indians threatened to rob the English of all the horses that they encountered if they were not given a large present to take home. See Bouquet Papers, A 25, 3–6, Canada Archives. For gifts of saddles, stirrups, and bridles, see the list of gifts for the Southern Indians at the Congress of Augusta, 1763, North Carolina Historical Commission, Transcripts of English Records, C.O. 5. Bdl. 65, pp. 321–24.

[76] *Pennsylvania Colonial Records*, V, 197.

[77] *Sir William Johnson Papers*, II, 898–900.

[78] "East Florida Account of Presents Delivered to the Indians at the Congress Held at Picolata," November 15, 1765, P.R.O., C.O., 5/540, L.C. 493–94 (film).

[79] *Ibid.*

civilized items that the United States government carried right on with yearly subsidies to the Iroquois confederacy after the Revolution.[80]

It should be observed here that the civilizing influence of presents was curtailed for three years after the conquest of Canada in 1760. Up to the time of the final capitulation of the French at Montreal in this year, Jeffery Amherst approved Sir William Johnson's requests for huge warrants to be used for presents to secure warriors. After 1760, however, ". . . . the British governmental policy was parsimonious in the matter of presents," along the old Northwest frontier.[81] This policy was not always followed, however. When the Southern Department held the great Congress of Augusta in 1763, strouds, calicoes, duffles, hatchets, and barleycorn beads were doled out by the thousands to the host of Southern confederacies represented there.[82] Looking glasses, saddles, bridles, cutlery, belts, and tinware were, indeed, a measuring stick for the civilization which had been foisted upon the Indians through the medium of presents and trade.[83]

The concomitants of transportation, such as containers for liquids, brought new ideas to the Indians. The colonists' practice of using salt to preserve pork taught the tribesmen of the Ohio and Northern frontiers the use of brine. The employment of casks, kegs, bags, and the tilloting of fabrics[84] for the protection of presents revealed to the natives many methods of caring for their belongings.[85] Merchandise for Indian presents was brought overland via roads and waterways by horses, wagons, and batteaux.[86] To hold that the Indians were blind to these influences would, indeed, be naïve. The fact that Indians became superior batteau pilots

---

[80] What was probably the first treaty between the Iroquois and the United States government is preserved in manuscript form at the Henry E. Huntington Library. On April 23, 1792, the United States agreed to give the Iroquois $1,500 annually for the purchase of clothing, domestic animals, and implements of husbandry. It is noteworthy that this treaty is signed by John Knox, Thomas Jefferson, and George Washington. See "Indian Treaty, The United States and the Five Nations," April 23, 1792, HM 576. As a matter of interest, the Iroquois were receiving their yearly subsidies of calico prints as late as 1940.

[81] *Wisconsin Historical Collections*, XVIII, 228.

[82] The Choctaws, Cherokees, Upper and Lower Creeks, and Catawbas were the confederacies represented at the Congress.

[83] "Distribution of Presents to the Indians at the Congress of Augusta," November 19, 1763, in John Stuart's letter of December 5, 1763, North Carolina Historical Commission Transcripts of English Records, C.O. 5. Bdl. 65, pp. 321-24.

[84] Tillot was a kind of coarse cloth used for wrapping fabrics and garments during the eighteenth century.

[85] William Carry to William Johnson, August 6, 1756, *Sir William Johnson Papers*, II, 530.

[86] William Carry to William Johnson, August 6, 1756, *Sir William Johnson Papers*, II, 530; George Clinton to William Johnson, March 25, 1747, *ibid.*, I, 83-84.

and that stirrups, saddles, and horses became popular defeats this argument.[87] Furthermore, the storekeeper of presents, as in the case of the Northern Department of Indian Affairs, no doubt acquainted the natives with businesslike methods of accounting for merchandise, as well as teaching them how to protect such merchandise with oilcloths and tents.[88] Though not gifts, in a sense, such articles as oilcloths soon became part of the Indians' "machinery" for handling many different types of presents.

Gunsmiths and locksmiths performed services that were as valuable to the Indians as were the actual gifts themselves. No one was more welcome than these smiths, who took their equipment directly to the Indian tribes. William Shirley pointed out that the men had to be skilled and careful workmen.[89] Ordinarily, the smiths were outfitted by the Board of Ordnance. However, in those cases when the Board of Ordnance could not furnish tools, Edmond Atkins explains that these items could very properly be included in the agent's list of presents.[90] This was no small request, for one smith alone needed twenty-four different kinds of files. In addition, his equipment included:[91]

saws	pincers	drills
anvil	reamers	drill boxes
forge cart	screw plates	scouring paper
bellows	punches	drill bows
vises	cold chisels	grinding stone
wire	solder	trough for grinding stone
tongs	glue	strings for drill bows
hammers	vise bench	

Of course, the Indians quickly noticed the differences between their primitive tools and those of the skillful smiths who lived among them. Earlier their women had taken to awls and scissors.[92]

The physician was another important factor in the civilizing process. He helped the Indian learn skills useful in caring for his wounds. Numerous references in the *Sir William Johnson Papers* record the expenses of surgeons among the Indians.[93] Important as they were, medical and artisan services were overshadowed by the influence of the missionary school teachers as civilizing agencies. In these eighteenth-century records, inter-

---

[87] *Vide*, note 83.

[88] *Sir William Papers*, III, 166, 255–56.

[89] "Instructions for Major General William Johnson from William Shirley," January 13, 1756, *Sir William Johnson Papers*, II, 410.

[90] LO 3517.

[91] LO 3246.

[92] *Pennsylvania Colonial Records*, V, 151.

[93] *Sir William Johnson Papers*, I, 456; II, 596.

mingled with discussions of different types of presents, are accounts of missions and their work among the Christianized Indians.[94] Languages were among the subjects taught with religion. The Stockbridge Indians, famed companions of Robert Rogers, learned so much in school that they began to demand money wages for military service. In vain did Sir William Johnson try to bring them back to accepting occasional presents for their services after William Shirley, commander-in-chief, had set the precedent of giving them money.[95] Perhaps an education taught the Indians too much about the white man's way of living! The Mohawk sachems, for instance, soon came to appreciate the value of money over goods; and numerous accounts show how money gradually came to be used by the Indian for almost every type of compensation.[96]

Certain types of presents have not been considered in this chapter because of limitations of space. Presents for children, such as toy cannon, balance figures, and mock guns, fall into this group. Along with the jews'-harps, looking glasses, textiles, and hardware, which went to the adults, however, they played a part in that introduction of European culture to the wilderness of America which we customarily term the march of civilization westward.[97] Accompanying these aspects of "culture" were the "gifts" of rum and disease. Civilization almost came to mean extermination for the Indian.

---

[94] *Sir William Johnson Papers*, II, 410–11; I, 353.

[95] *New York Colonial Documents*, VII, 184–85. Shirley's "sin" herein was that he was merely ahead of his day.

[96] See William Johnson's accounts of Indian expenses in *Sir William Johnson Papers*, II, 566–645; III, 149–81.

[97] LO 3517.

IV. THE COST OF PRESENTS

Presents to the Indians were a source of increasing expense to the individual colonies and to the British Government from the time of colonization to the Revolution. Numerous accounts of expenditures indicate the development of several trends in the financing of presents. Most significant among these trends were the following: (1) the increased over-all expenditures for presents after the French and Indian War; (2) the Northern superintendency saw a gradual shift from the colonies to the Crown in bearing the increasing financial burden of these gifts. In the case of the Southern superintendency, however, the colonies continued to share this financial burden until the time of John Stuart's appointment in 1762;[1] (3) outwardly, there was a larger expenditure for presents in the Northern superintendency than in the Southern superintendency, although this difference was more a matter of different bookkeeping methods than actual cash expenditures; (4) the beginning of large subsidies for presents during the period, 1748–1763, because of an increased dependence on Indian auxiliaries; (5) the Industrial Revolution brought a general lowering in the cost of individual items used for gifts during 1748–1763, although prices were not lowered extensively until after 1766. Wampum was the major exception to this trend. A discussion of these trends follows.

Those colonies such as New York, Pennsylvania, and Virginia, which bordered upon large Indian populations, were constantly in need of large amounts of goods for the Indians. As early as 1687, New York paid £332:03:4 for a disbursement of presents to ransom prisoners.[2] In the long series of Colonial wars that followed, the natives were the recipients of large subsidies. Though the accounts of Indian presents were large during the French and Indian War, these costs were dwarfed by the enormous expenses for gifts of British agents after 1775. For example, the total spent for Indian presents from 1775 to 1779, excepting £500 given to the Nova Scotia tribesmen, was £87,484:18:10.[3] The diplomatic rivalry and competition between the English and the American revolutionists,

---

[1] William Knox Papers (William L. Clements Library), Vol. X (film). Hereafter cited as the William Knox Papers.

[2] Blathwayt Papers, 189, Huntington Library. See also "List of Stores Sent by the Earl of Bellomont," August 26, 1697, New England Bundle, B. No. 45, Library of Congress (film), for an invoice of goods amounting to £300. This manuscript also provides for a fort among the Onondaga Indians costing £500.

[3] William Knox Papers, Vol. X.

involving as it did large presents and promises of annuities[4] by the revolutionary agents, pressed so hard upon John Stuart, superintendent of the Southern Department of Indian Affairs, that he frequently went far beyond his quota for gifts. As a matter of fact, during the year 1787, Guy Johnson, who followed his uncle as head of Indian Affairs in the north made demands on the government for presents that fell little short of £55,000.[5] These costly grants for presents show the rising crescendo of provincial and imperial expenses. The French and Indian War can be said to mark the beginning of large subsidies to the natives.

Before the creation of the Northern and Southern Departments of Indian Affairs, the Colonial assemblies of New York, Pennsylvania, and Virginia appear to have carried most of the expense for presents along the Ohio and Northern frontiers. They were occasionally reimbursed by the imperial treasury; since the power of the purse dictated the policy to be followed, however, some colonies were willing to pay for their own goods. Pennsylvania was one of these, for the Quaker colony preferred to follow an independent policy of dealing with the various tribes.[6] These numerous gifts proved very costly to the colony. In 1751, for example, one present of £700 was given to the tribes of the Ohio.[7] Other colonies also found the cost of presents to be prohibitive. As late as 1755, the New York Assembly complained of this heavy burden which fell upon its shoulders.[8] In Virginia, during the year 1752, a tax of two shillings per hogshead of tobacco exported was used to defray the expenditures for gifts for the Six Nations and their allies.[9] When the Twightwees, a powerful western confederacy of many fighting men, were brought to the attention of the Old Dominion in 1752, it was proposed in some quarters to divert a part of the quit rent revenue to cover a £1,000 gift to them.[10] In his request to the Board of Trade for this help, Governor Dinwiddie pointed out that Virginia would bear the cost of transporting the gift to the natives. This proposal was fair,

---

[4] William Knox Papers, Vol. X.

[5] *Ibid.* For additional expenditures and gifts by John Stuart, Lieutenant-General Frederick Haldimand, governor of Quebec, and General Thomas Gage, see P.R.O., C.O., 5/149, L.C. 345–48, C.O. 671–74 and P.R.O., C.O., 5/175, L.C. 154 (film).

[6] It should be noted that the Quakers signed individual treaties with the Indians apart from those of the Pennsylvania Assembly and gave the Indians separate gifts.

[7] *Pennsylvania Colonial Records*, V, 518–22. See also *ibid.*, V, 197, for a gift in 1747 amounting to £828:8:0½. In addition, there were miscellaneous charges for transportation of separate items, the largest being £13:16:0.

[8] *Sir William Johnson Papers*, I, 614–18.

[9] P.R.O., C.O., 5/1327, L.C. 415–24, C.O. 531–36. See also Munro and Fitzroy, *op. cit.*, IV, 200–203 and P.R.O., C.O., 5/1327, L.C. 171–75, C.O. 231–46.

[10] *Vide*, note 9.

for transportation was a major expense. The charge of transporting merely one present had cost the colony a total of £1,200.[11]

It should be noted, for purposes of comparison, that expenditures for presents became so great that South Carolina and the infant colony of Georgia were not able to satisfy the voracious appetites of the Southern Indians. As a result, in 1749, the imperial government appropriated a yearly grant of £3,000 to relieve the distressed financial condition of these two colonies. Moreover, it was specified that the presents be purchased in England since the prices were cheaper there than in the colonies.[12]

The *Journals of the Board of Trade* record large grants of presents for the Indians bordering on Georgia. Since this colony was the youngest of the "thirteen," its financial resources were meager. Gifts amounting to £400 were needed in 1733 and 1739, to buy the lands adjacent to Savannah.[13] In addition, donations of £1,500 were needed in 1754 and 1758, to bolster the friendship between Georgia and the powerful Southern Indian confederacies. Georgia furnishes a good illustration of the possible complications resulting from great expenditures for gifts. The case cited here relates to the recall of John Reynolds, governor of Georgia from October 1754 to February 1757, and exemplifies the increasing concern of the Board of Trade over the possible misappropriation of valuable goods. Furthermore, this case illustrates the conflict between governor and council over the expense of presents.

The chief accusations against Reynolds were centered around the disposal of a £900 present to the Southern Indians in 1756.[14] It appears that the members of the council had a dislike for the secretary of the Governor, who, besides holding several other offices, also acted as Indian agent. While serving in the latter capacity, he was alleged to have taken a 5 percent commission of the £900 gift, over and above entertainment costs for the Indians.[15] Moreover, the councilmen maintained that they were kept in the dark in the auditing of these accounts. In addition, John

---

[11] *Ibid.*

[12] "Report of the Committee Concerning Presents Granted to the Indians in South Carolina and Georgia," May 30, 1749, LO 174.

[13] *Journals of the Board of Trade*, IX, 213.

[14] For materials relating to the recall and the appearance of Reynolds before the Board of Trade, see the following: British Add. MSS 35909 fo. 285–95, L.C. Tr. 491–93; fo. 215–16, L.C. Tr. 343–44; fo. 283–84, L.C. Tr. 481–90; P.R.O., C.O., 5/15, L.C. 3028, C.O. 421–24; P.R.O., C.O., 5/211, L.C. 161, C.O. 349–52; P.R.O., Treasury 1 Bdl. 382, fo. 2037, L.C. Tr., and *Journals of the Board of Trade*, X, 61–64, 178, 280–81, 380–85, 397.

[15] *Vide*, note 14. John Reynolds maintained that his councilmen were former highway robbers, ignorant, and obstinate, and that one had defrauded a gentleman in England out of £600.

Reynolds was accused of allowing this present to be used as a payment to the Creek Indians for lands purchased by private individuals.[16] In making his defense against these charges, and several other accusations not relating to presents, Reynolds brought out the possibility of graft on the part of some of the opposition, notably one Benjamin Martyn, Georgia agent in London. Apparently Martyn, who purchased gifts in London for shipment, was working with a corrupt group of councilmen who opposed Governor Reynolds.[17]

Though Georgia's affairs were under the supervision of the Board of Trade, this colony's presents to the natives were relatively independent of the Southern Department of Indian Affairs until the latter part of the French and Indian War. Edmond Atkin's entrance as the superintendent of this department in 1756, marked the beginning of a period of large expenditures in behalf of the Southern and Ohio tribes.

In his plan of organization for the Southern Department, Atkin provided for a provincial fund to pay for presents and other expenses of the department. He proposed that revenue for this fund be raised by a poll tax on all male inhabitants, by duties on wines, foreign sugars and molasses, and by a revenue derived from a system of Colonial post offices.[18] Actually this plan was not put into being, although a good share of his expenses was defrayed by the individual colonies. Virginia's periodic appropriations, ranging from £500 to £3,000, helped to bolster the superintendent's credit.[19] Closer examination of Atkin's accounts reveals that his disbursements were relatively great because Colonial contributions for presents were subtracted from British outlays for gifts. This factor made Atkin's expenses appear to be lower than those of William Johnson, superintendent in the North.[20] For instance, Atkin's expenses in Virginia from May 1757, to October 1757, were only £115:17:10¼.[21] Upon close scrutiny, however, it is found that the superintendent's income from Virginia was £732. This he

[16] For sources relating to the Bosomworth land controversy see the *Journals of the Board of Trade*, X, 139, 390–91, 426–27. In his defense, Reynolds claimed that the present was given to the Indians to celebrate his arrival as was customary. See British Add. MSS 35909 fo. 285–95, L.C. Tr. 491–543.

[17] British Add. MSS 35909 fo. 296–301, L.C. Tr. 545–52. For the activities of Benjamin Martyn in securing presents, see the *Journals of the Board of Trade*, X, 103, 213, 343.

[18] Edmond Atkin to the Board of Trade, May 30, 1755, LO 578.

[19] Robert Dinwiddie to Arthur Dobbs, June 20, 1757, *Dinwiddie Papers*, II, 652, Robert Dinwiddie to Horatio Sharpe, June 14, 1757, *ibid.*, II, 639.

[20] See William Johnson's expense accounts in Volumes II and III of the *Sir William Johnson Papers*.

[21] Edmond Atkin, "Accounts with the Colony of Virginia," October 14, 1757, LO 4640.

had subtracted from his total expenses amounting to £847:17:10¼, leaving the above balance of some one hundred and fifteen pounds.[22] Atkin was able to keep the cost of presents for other Southern confederacies for this same year down to £3,000, the amount allotted to South Carolina and Georgia for their Indians during time of peace.[23] In an effort to economize further, Atkin proposed that each Indian warrior give one deerskin a year to the British in exchange for more valuable gifts of powder, lead, and guns. This would pay ammunition costs. To defray the expense of transportation, he advocated having all traders carry the King's present to the natives free of charge.[24] These suggestions were never put into effect, however.

From the above illustrations it might be supposed that Edmond Atkin's financial affairs went along smoothly. Actually this was not the case. His grandiose plans for rangers, gunsmiths, deputies, surgeons, ministers, interpreters, storekeepers, commissaries, and secretaries were never realized because of lack of funds.[25] Upon his death in 1761, his widow, Lady Atkin, was required to account for his numerous debts.[26] She complained that she did not receive a shilling from the British Government for the personal fortune that her husband had expended while carrying out his duties as Southern Indian superintendent.[27] As late as 1764, Atkin's widow appealed to Lord Loudoun, former commander-in-chief, for reimbursement, although her application had been refused by General Amherst two years before because some of Atkin's debts had been contracted during the time of Lord Loudoun's command in America. These "monstrous accounts" of Atkin's (so-called by Robert Dinwiddie) were small, however, when compared with his successor's expenditures. John Stuart, who replaced Edmond Atkin as Southern superintendent in 1762, held that office until 1779, during which time he paid out enormous sums for gifts at prices that were extravagant for even the eighteenth century.[28] Pensacola storehouses held thousands of items. To supply these warehouses, Stuart's accounts in the William Knox Papers are sprinkled with expenditures ranging from five to fifteen thousand pounds.[29] These goods were sent over in storeships, filled with munitions, pork, strouds, and hardware.[30]

---

[22] Ibid.   [23] LO 3517.   [24] LO 578.

[25] LO 2502. In all fairness to Atkin, it must be noted that he intended to have all accounts of subordinates audited. Moreover, he counted on having the Society for the Propagation of the Gospel in Foreign Parts pay the salary of ministers to the Indians. See LO 578.

[26] Anne Murray to the Earl of Loudoun, May 26, 1764, LO 6350.

[27] Ibid.

[28] William Knox Papers, Vol. X.

[29] Ibid.

[30] P.R.O., C.O., 5/149, L.C. 345–48 (film.)

A view of the situation in the North reveals that William Johnson's expenses far surpassed those of Edmond Atkin, his counterpart in the South. As the agent for the New York Assembly, Johnson had gone into debt trying to please both the Six Nations and the frugal assembly.[31] However, when Edward Braddock commissioned him the sole superintendent of the Northern Indians in April 1755, Johnson's fortune changed. Now he was to have £2,000 for gifts and £800 in immediate cash;[32] and if he needed more funds, he could draw on William Shirley, who had become commander-in-chief at Braddock's death.[33] This appeared to be a congenial arrangement, but Shirley's alleged attempt to divert Indians from the Crown Point campaign to his command against Niagara nullified the effect of many expensive presents.

The provincial assemblies grudgingly contributed to Johnson's fund, Massachusetts giving £800. Eventually, Johnson did receive a full grant of £5,000 for the year 1755.[34] From this time on, William Johnson's expenses show a sharp rise. His accounts from March 1755, to October 1756, were £19,619 :9 :1½, this sum representing a period of approximately nineteen months.[35] This increase is still more evident in Johnson's accounts from November 1758, to December 1759. During this period of only thirteen months, the accounts totaled £17,072 :2 :10¼.[36] Such large expenditures did not escape official notice, for there is record of Shirley's admonishment of Johnson, cautioning him to be frugal.[37] Goldsbrow Banyar, William Johnson's loyal friend in New York, also constantly warned him against needless disbursements. On one occasion, Banyar cautioned Johnson to be sure to turn in a warrant covering an Onondaga visit amounting to £72 :9 :0; this was done in the interest of personal economy so that the superintendent would have money to live on during his old age.[38]

It is worthy of notice that General Jeffery Amherst was responsible for a cut in expenses for presents after the conquest of Canada in 1760.

[31] George Clinton to William Johnson, September 24, 1750, *Sir William Johnson Papers*, I, 301.

[32] "Minutes of the Council at Alexandria," April 14, 1755, P.R.O., C.O., 5/46, L.C. 29–34.

[33] Edward Braddock to Thomas Robinson, April 19, 1755, P.R.O., C.O., 5/46, L.C. 19–28.

[34] William Shirley gave Johnson £3,000 making a total of £5,000, considering the previous grants made by Braddock. See *Sir William Johnson Papers*, I, 769–71.

[35] *Ibid.*, II, 645.

[36] *Ibid.*, III, 181.

[37] "Instructions for Major General William Johnson from William Shirley," June 13, 1756, *ibid.*, II, 412.

[38] Goldsbrow Banyar to Sir William Johnson, April 30, 1756, *ibid.*, II, 461.

Since the war was over in Canada, a stringent policy in slicing expenses was followed through the years 1760–1763. Finally, in October 1764, Sir William Johnson concocted an interesting plan to pare the annual costs of operation for the Northern Department down to £10,850, including his personal salary.[39] That this laudable plan, based upon a £10,963 :0 :6 annual duty on fur trade, did not go into effect is deduced from the huge expenses accumulated by his nephew and successor, Guy Johnson.[40] Sir William's inventive brain, however, did help him to accumulate a large personal fortune. His pelts and skins brought the best prices; and he even attempted to market the gentian root, which was used as a tonic.[41] In 1751, Johnson's correspondence reveals that he employed many warriors of the Six Nations to gather four hogsheads of these highly prized roots, which brought a "monstrous" price.[42]

In summarizing the expenses of the Indian Departments, it should be noted that Edmond Atkin's debts were far less than those of Johnson during the same period. Helen Louise Shaw's dissertation on *British Administration of the Southern Indians 1756–1783* lists the total expenditures of Edmond Atkin's entire term of office, covering the years 1756–1761, as being only £1,472 :15 :11.[43] This figure would seem to be subject to correction since Atkin ordered £3,000 for South Carolina alone during the year 1757.[44] Furthermore, Atkin's bills for this same year in Virginia amounted to over £115.[45] By contrast, Johnson's accounts showed a marked increase over Atkin's, while those of John Stuart, Lieutenant General Frederick Haldimand,[46] and Guy Johnson climbed to even greater amounts.

Let us now turn to an overview of the trend in cost of individual items used for gifts. Wampum, the most common gift of that time, may well receive our first consideration. In 1643 (one of the earliest years for which we have statistics) one fathom[47] of wampum was worth five shillings, the

---

[39] *Ibid.*, IV, 556–63.

[40] William Knox Papers, Vol. X.

[41] *Sir William Johnson Papers*, I, 346, 371–73.

[42] *Ibid.*

[43] Helen Louise Shaw, *British Administration of the Southern Indians, 1756–1783*, p. 54.

[44] Edmond Atkin, "A List of Goods Proper to Be Sent from England to Charles Town in South Carolina, to Be Given as Presents from His Majesty to the Indians in the Southern District, for the Service of the Year 1757," March 1757, LO 3517.

[45] LO 4640.

[46] Lieutenant General Frederick Haldimand was governor and commander-in-chief of Quebec in the period following the French and Indian War.

[47] A fathom is a measure of length amounting to six feet. The original connotation referred to the space to which a man could extend his arms.

price having dropped from the ten-shilling price of a few years previous. By the year 1687, one fathom of wampum was worth only eighteen pence, another sharp decrease in value.[48] Since there were approximately 280 beads in a fathom, the above amount of ten shillings and six pence would pay for approximately 2,000 beads. Because there was a great demand for these beads during the years of the French and Indian War, however, wampum rose in price. Large belts, six feet in length, and containing almost 7,000 beads, were frequently used in Indian treaties. For this reason, the Northern Department of Indian Affairs purchased large allotments of wampum beads.[49] In 1755, 2,250 white wampum beads cost £2:11:0.[50] In the same year, black grains, which were higher priced, cost three pounds per 2,000 black beads. By comparison, 2,000 of these beads sold for only a little more than ten shillings in 1687.

The construction of wampum belts also involved some expense other than the beads themselves. For example, the cost of labor in making two large belts, over six feet in length, amounted to two pounds, eight shillings.[51] Moreover, there was an additional outlay for leather and thread. Sometimes belts were purchased from native women who procured the necessary beads and leather for the belts themselves.[52] In other cases, beads were bought separately by the pound, avoirdupois. When the beads were purchased in this manner, the belts might have been cheaper, for two and one-half pounds of beads amounted to only fifteen shillings.[53]

Fabrics were next in importance as presents after wampum. Most fabrics were ordered in "pieces." A "piece" was a unit of measurement that was approximately twelve yards in length. Since most pieces of woolen

---

[48] Blathwayt Papers, 189, Huntington Library. Roger Williams stated that the fall in the price of wampum was due to the decrease in the market value of beaver pelts. See *Roger Williams' Key*, pp. 128–30. It is of interest to note that the value of textile presents was computed in terms of pelts and skins. An illustration from the *Sir William Johnson Papers*, III, 531–32, detailing the minute regulations for trade, proves this to be true:

A stroud two yards long . . . . Two good beaver or three bucks
Men's plain shirts . . . . One beaver or a buck and a doe
Men's ruffled shirts . . . . Two beavers or three buckskins
Four bars of lead . . . . Four bucks
One fathom of calico . . . . One buck and a doe or a good beaver
One gallon tin kettle . . . . Two bucks
Wrist bands . . . . Two bucks
Women's hair plates . . . . Three beaver or four bucks

[49] *Sir William Johnson Papers*, III, 172.
[50] *Ibid.*, II, 582.
[51] *Ibid.*, III, 159.
[52] *Ibid.*, II, 579.
[53] *Pennsylvania Colonial Records*, V, 197.

fabric were approximately the same length, they can be compared in price. Strouds were the most expensive. In 1755, one piece of blue stroud was listed at nine pounds; on the other hand, one piece of white halfthick was priced at only £3 :12 :0. One piece of duffle, a better fabric, was only a little less expensive than the stroud. The duffle, costing seven pounds, was priced the same as an ordinary blanket.[54]

These textiles show some increase in prices compared to the seventeenth century, but their value dropped very low about the year 1768. In the year 1697, for example, five red strouds, five blue clothes (probably coats and waistcoats), four blue and two red duffles, and six pieces of striped blankets were sold at £161 :12 :4. These items would probably have cost about the same in 1755. By 1768, however, the Industrial Revolution had brought about a marked decrease in prices. Eighty pieces of strouds were valued at only £340, bringing the cost of one stroud down to less than one-half of the price in 1755.[55] In the same manner, by 1768, duffles had dropped to less than half of their former price. Gartering strips (fabric used for garters), which were purchased by the gross, had also declined in price by this year, one gross costing only nine shillings, eight pence, while in 1747, one gross had sold for almost twelve shillings.[56] The records of New England-British Customs illustrate the further drop in woolens and cottons by the year 1773. As an illustration, 8,994 square yards of cottons and linens were valued at only seventy-eight pounds;[57] 28,100 yards of frieze, a woolen fabric used for blankets, were estimated to be worth only £2,927 :1 :8. This meant a price of two shillings a yard for a fabric which would have cost approximately ten times as much in 1755.

During the 1750's, the Indians desired French fabrics because they were of a better quality than the British merchandise. French blankets and ratteen, which was used for stockings, were in particular demand.[58] Astute native sachems probably were not unaware of the fact that English strouds were made of woolen rags. Moreover, the French gave the Indians a complete outfit, called the *Aduapou*, which consisted of a blanket, shirt, leggings, shoes, and a breechcloth.[59] The English were able to take advantage of this desire for French goods by the use of confiscated materials. William Johnson was able to purchase French woolens, captured by British

---

[54] *Ibid.*, V, 552.

[55] P.R.O., C.O., 5/549, L.C. 69–70 (film). For a detailed list of blue and red strouds shipped to Charleston, South Carolina, in 1763, see Treasury 1 Bdl. 423, L.C. Tr. (film).

[56] P.R.O., C.O., 5/549, L.C. 69–72 (film), *Pennsylvania Colonial Records*, V, 197.

[57] Customs 3/73, P.R.O. (photographic enlargement, University of California).

[58] *Sir William Johnson Papers*, I, 376–77; III, 334–35.

[59] *Wisconsin Historical Collections*, XVIII, 193–94.

war vessels, at almost the same price as English blankets. In 1755, for instance, one stroud blanket amounted to fifteen shillings, while one French blanket cost some thirteen shillings, showing English products to be a little more expensive.[60] Undoubtedly, the French blankets were priced lower because they were confiscated goods.

Miscellaneous items of cloth called for additional appropriations for the Northern Indian Department. In one case, in 1755, a flag for a Tuscarora Sachem cost £3:10:0; in another case, an Iroquois warrior was given a fine shirt, a pair of hose, and ribbons, the total ensemble valued at only one pound, ten shillings.[61]

As hostilities between France and England became more and more imminent, a transition in the type of presents can be observed. Arms, munitions, knives, and bullet molds took the place of tandem ruffled shirts and castor hats.[62] The decline in prices continued. In 1750, one Indian gun with richly ornamented stock was valued at twelve shillings. By 1768, however, ten shillings would buy one of these so-called trading guns.[63] Furthermore, the relative drop in value is to be noticed in the costs of hatchets, butcher knives, and bullets. In New York, in 1753, Sir Danvers Osborn's list of goods states that one hatchet amounted to one shilling and one-half pence.[64] When hatchets were doled out to Florida Indians in 1768, however, they cost only one-half shilling apiece.

The manufacture of gun flints formed another excellent example of the reduction in prices of gifts because of the Industrial Revolution. As late as 1761, one thousand of these flints sold for two pounds, eight shillings.[65] But only a few years later, in 1766, one thousand of the best flints could be had for only ten shillings, almost one-fifth of the cost in 1761.[66]

It is worthy of interest to note that certain expensive items such as jewelry were given to the Indians for a specific purpose. The object in mind was to introduce a custom and thereby increase the demands on the traders.[67] When goods could not be secured from the traders, the Indians had rather unusual methods of obtaining attractive jewelry. Occasionally a warrior would approach William Johnson to request a gift to fulfill a

---

[60] *Sir William Johnson Papers*, II, 583.

[61] *Ibid.*, II, 574.

[62] This trend can be observed especially during the American revolutionary period. See P.R.O., C.O., 5/175, L.C. 154 (film). Strouds, however, were still in great demand. See Treasury 1 Bdl. 423, L.C. Tr. (film).

[63] P.R.O., C.O., 5/549, L.C. 69 (film).

[64] Treasury 1 Bdl. 353 fo. 181 L.C. Tr. (film).

[65] *Sir William Johnson Papers*, III, 503.

[66] P.R.O., C.O., 5/540, L.C. 501 (film).

[67] P.R.O., C.O., 5/549, L.C. 70 (film).

dream. These "dreams" of jewelry involved gorgets, silver arm bands, and other articles. For instance, one silver arm band handed out by Johnson cost one pound, twelve shillings.[68] Silver gorgets, cast with the king's arms, varied in price according to the honesty of the workman. A dependable silversmith could make these gorgets for a cost of twenty-five shillings apiece.[69] Although these gorgets were crescent shaped, they were much more expensive than medals. Amherst, writing to William Pitt in 1761, stated that he purchased one hundred and eighty-two medals for only £74:6:4 sterling, about eight shillings apiece.[70]

A cheap but effective gift which pleased the vanity of the warrior was the looking glass. These glasses, which probably varied in size, sold for only nineteen shillings per dozen in 1747.[71] However, by 1751, the price had gone down to only seven shillings per dozen, while in 1766, a dozen looking glasses with painted frames cost only six shillings.[72]

After 1763, better manufacturing methods also brought wire, tin quart pots, padlocks, and other hardware items to a lower price level.[73] Even though prices in the late 1760's show a decisive decrease, the mounting volume of presents forced total expenditures to a higher level.[74]

Food and drink, whether used as separate presents or for entertainment purposes, were still another source of great expense. Through the decade from 1750 to 1760, a bull, ox, or cow might bring anywhere from three to seven pounds sterling.[75] In one case, a fat cow, bought from a squaw as a present for the Mohawks, was invoiced at five pounds sterling. However, oxen seem to have been valued around four pounds, while a good bull might bring as much as seven pounds sterling.[76] Bread, peas, rice, and "biscake" are mentioned in terms of shillings, unless they were used to feed a large number of Indians attending a conference. John Stuart's superiors claimed that his order of five hundred barrels of pork to be used at a conference was purchased at the most extravagant prices.[77] Food and drink at large Indian conferences involved heavy outlays for these articles themselves as well as for their transportation. At only one small meeting

---

[68] *Sir William Johnson Papers*, II, 593.

[69] *Ibid.*, II, 523.

[70] Jeffery Amherst to William Pitt, May 4, 1761, *ibid.*, III, 386.

[71] *Pennsylvania Colonial Records*, V, 151.

[72] P.R.O., C.O., 5/540, L.C. 501 (film).

[73] *Ibid.*

[74] See William Knox Papers, Vol. X.

[75] *Sir William Johnson Papers*, II, 575. A horse used as a present sold for £8:12:0 during the year 1757. See Draper MSS 6 QQ 140 (film).

[76] *Sir William Johnson Papers*, II, 575–76.

[77] William Knox Papers, Vol. X.

in 1755, the charges involved for tea and sugar punch amounted to almost six pounds sterling.[78] After 1760, it was the British policy to cut down on food expenses. When the complete accounts of a meeting held with the Northern Indians at Niagara and Detroit in 1761 were invoiced, a total of £305 was computed for tobacco, vermilion, and other items, which did not include food.[79] Liquors were, however, the most expensive of gifts. Rum was a particularly costly item because it led the Indians to give away their valuable goods. For this reason, gifts had to be duplicated and sometimes triplicated before the Indians went home. The actual selling price of a quart of rum, however, amounted to only four shillings a quart.[80] Claret wine seems to have been only slightly higher in price, but punch made from tea and sugar was cheaper and did not intoxicate. Particularly palatable to the Indians was beer. It took about twelve barrels of beer, costing £9:12:0, to supply the Indians at one conference held by William Johnson. A hogshead of rum was also needed, the latter amounting to £19:12:0.[81] Such data might lead the student to believe that actual presents formed the greater part of Indian expenses. Contemporaries of the period of the French and Indian War, nevertheless, stated that the gifts amounted only to one-half of all accounts.[82]

Cash outlays for various chiefs and warriors were quite high. Moreover, widows of dead warriors received periodic sums that almost seemed to be as regular as a pension.[83] Sometimes these condolences in cash were small, ranging from five to ten pounds; on other occasions, after the Lake George campaign in 1755, for instance, William Johnson made one grant of £54:16:0.[84] Constant donations were made for sick Indians, old men, and starving people. In spite of the fact that such charity offerings were in the shillings, over a period of time these small donations helped to steepen the accounts of the Northern Department of Indian Affairs.

Another cause for cash outlays on the part of the British was to win over key Indians who had long been friends of the French. Only £1:18:10

---

[78] *Sir William Johnson Papers*, II, 576.

[79] *Ibid.*, III, 428–503. The Indians were very dissatisfied with the decrease in the volume of presents after hostilities had stopped. It will be noticed that this invoice of only £305 is very small compared to William Johnson's early expenses. For example, a gift in June 1755 amounted to £1,086:6:10. Undoubtedly the lack of presents contributed to the native dissatisfaction that eventually resulted in the rebellion under Pontiac.

[80] *Sir William Johnson Papers*, III, 179. The invoice lists five quarts of rum priced at one pound.

[81] *Ibid.*, II, 602.

[82] See LO 174.

[83] *Sir William Johnson Papers*, II, 607, 614.

[84] *Ibid.*, II, 607.

in cash was strong enough to turn the allegiance of one native who had lived sixteen years with the French.[85] Peter, another influential French Indian, made his "price" a little higher, costing Sir William a little over six pounds sterling before he could be prevailed upon to settle down to plowing and planting.[86]

Donations in cash were also needed to pay the wages of the Stockbridge Indians. A large number of auxiliaries, each costing four shillings per day, contributed to a mounting sum of money.[87] Moreover, these same Indians were given presents in addition to their wages. On other occasions, the natives actually sold leather, for cash, to the Northern Department; this leather was, in turn, to be given to them in the form of shoes.[88] Furthermore, warriors received money for scalps and live prisoners. Scalps were worth thirty pounds sterling; prisoners brought fifty pounds sterling. These prisoners were sometimes exchanged with the French.[89]

One of the largest allotments from the imperial treasury was necessary in order to pay the personnel of the Indian Departments. Edmond Atkin wanted the same salary as that received by Sir William Johnson for the office of superintendent, £600 per year. Deputies such as George Croghan received only £300 a year, while the salaries of interpreters ranged from seventy to eighty pounds sterling.[90] Since they were skilled craftsmen, gunsmiths were much in demand. As a result, their salaries started at the same rate as those of the interpreters; but they went up as high as £100.[91] It should also be pointed out that the bellows, tools, and materials for each smith in the Northern Department amounted to twenty pounds sterling. However, according to Edmond Atkin's enumerated list, a smith's equipment would run into the hundreds of pounds sterling.[92]

The storekeeper for goods also drew a salary. In the Northern Department, Sir William reported that twenty pounds would adequately pay such a clerk for seven months.[93] In addition, Indians had to be employed as messengers and translators. For example, it cost William Johnson twenty dollars in cash to have one speech translated for the Six Nations. However, since the families of the translators had to be provided with food and lodging, the whole charge for translating amounted to nine pounds, sixteen shillings.[94]

---

[85] *Ibid.*, II, 572.

[86] *Ibid.*, II, 572.

[87] *New York Colonial Documents*, VII, 184–85.

[88] *Sir William Johnson Papers*, II, 641.

[89] *Ibid.*, II, 440; *New York Colonial Documents*, X, 197.

[90] *Sir William Johnson Papers*, IV, 561–63.

[91] *Ibid.*   [92] LO 3517; *ibid.*, 3246.

[93] *Sir William Johnson Papers*, III, 166.   [94] *Ibid.*, II, 573.

Regardless of the above expenses, additional cash outlays for packing, shipping, insurance, and final distribution amounted to about one-third of the total allotted for goods.[95] The expense of protecting these goods with accompanying ships of war was still another charge that was borne by the imperial treasury. Before a small assortment of fabrics was ready to leave England, the charge for dyeing, pressing, folding, tilloting, and packing brought the initial estimate of £145 to £208:10:0.[96] In the Northern Department, William Johnson's accounts were punctuated with disbursements for sled, horse, wagon, batteau, and sloop transportation costs.[97]

Insurance was of particular importance. It varied in accordance with the hazards of the voyage, the cost being especially high in time of war. If a man-of-war accompanied the merchant ship, the rates were lower; but if the merchant ship went unescorted, the insurance amounted to hundreds of pounds sterling.[98] It appears, however, that no insurance charges were made if the goods were sent in a warship, the safest method of transportation.[99]

In a summary of the cost of presents, there are several factors which should be made clear. First, the price of wampum seems to have gone up from the seventeenth to the eighteenth century. This item, however, was an exception. Presents of hardware articles, textiles (both wool and cotton), munitions, and other manufactured gifts showed a decided decrease in price after 1763. In many cases there was a gradual lowering of the prices of articles through the period 1748–1763. Looking glasses illustrate this condition. Notwithstanding this example, other items, such as gun flints, maintained a high price level until 1761, but dropped after 1766.

Second, it should be pointed out that the cost of presents for the Northern Department of Indian Affairs was much greater than that of the Southern Department. The fact that the individual colonies paid for many of the gifts of the Southern Department accounts for this difference. Furthermore, Atkin's accounts record only the imperial outlays, and not those of the individual colonies.

Finally, it should be noted that the over-all picture of the inclusive costs of presents showed two trends. There was a rising crescendo of outlays for gifts from 1748 to 1760. After 1760, expenses for gifts were drastically sliced because of the parsimonious policy of General Jeffery Amherst. In the

---

[95] *Journals of the Board of Trade*, X, 103.

[96] "Bills of Parcels and Receipts for the Purchase of Goods for Presents to the Indians in South Carolina and Georgia £1,067:4:6, 1749–1751," P.R.O., C.O., 5/17, L.C. Tr. (film).

[97] *Sir William Johnson Papers*, II, 566, 573; III, 149.

[98] LO 3517.

[99] *Ibid.*

late 1760's, nevertheless, the British Government began to make heavy outlays for gifts again. By the time of the American Revolution, the accounts of the Northern Department of Indian Affairs recorded huge amounts spent on presents, sums that were far greater than any yearly outlays during the period 1748–1763.

It should also be noted that the cost of presents was higher in the colonies than in the mother country.[100] And it must be remembered that the expenses of transportation, freight, customs, and insurance were additional financial burdens for the donors of presents.[101] Generally speaking, presents to the Indians during the period 1748–1763 were, indeed, a financial problem. Fortunes were made and lost by men who sold and distributed these gifts. Provincial treasuries and the imperial war chest itself were under a constant strain from the obligation of presenting gifts to the Iroquois and their allies in order to "brighten the chain of friendship."

---

[100] There was also a difference in the buying power of provincial currencies and pounds sterling. For a comparison of New York currency and pounds sterling relating to prices of goods, see *Sir William Johnson Papers*, IV, 559.

[101] For examples of classified costs of customs, transportation, freight, commissions, and the actual price of gifts, see Treasury 1 Bdl. 353, fo. 181, L.C. Tr. (film); *Pennsylvania Colonial Records*, V, 197.

V. COLONEL WILLIAM JOHNSON AND THE DEVELOPMENT OF THE IROQUOIS ALLIANCE, 1748–1753

The story of the distribution of presents to the great Indian confederacy of the North, the Iroquois, during the last years of King George's War and the ensuing period of preparation for the final struggle centers around one of the most versatile personalities of the Colonial era.

William Johnson, man of high titles and military commissions, undoubtedly had superior qualifications as an agent for the disbursing of gifts to the Iroquois. Indeed, in this respect he was superior to any man of his period. As a cultured English gentleman of scholarly tastes and as a man versed in military affairs, he had few, if any, equals among the Colonial administrators of his day.[1] As a manager of Indian Affairs, he measured high by the standards set by that observing Indian authority, James Adair.[2] True, Johnson committed errors. In his early years, he had violated laws regarding the giving of liquor to the Indians; and in his later years, he was noted for his extravagant presents. On the other hand, his interest in aiding the Society for the Propagation of the Gospel in Foreign Parts in its work among the Indians indicated a sincere desire to help the tribesmen adapt themselves to Christian teachings.[3] Johnson, however, above all other things, realized that the successful direction of Indian politics required the extensive use of presents as well as frequent contacts with the natives.

His eminence in his field was recognized by contemporaries, who looked to him as a leader. Although capable men like Conrad Weiser criticized his squandering of money for gifts, in the same breath they asked him for advice on Iroquoian affairs.[4] Mayors, governors, and leaders of the New York Assembly sought his aid in the distribution of goods, when their own devices failed.[5] Once the provincial leaders of the New York Assembly asked Johnson to demonstrate the diplomacy involved in the presenting of goods to the Indians.[6] Anyone who hoped to compete successfully with the growing army

---

[1] William Johnson to Samuel and William Baker, February 19, 1750, *Sir William Johnson Papers*, I, 264–65.

[2] *Adair's History of the American Indians*, pp. 399–400.

[3] See William Johnson's letter in the Society for the Propagation of the Gospel in Foreign Parts (hereafter cited as S.P.G.) MSS, Series B, Volume 2, Parts 1 and 2; Frank J. Klingberg, *Anglican Humanitarianism in Colonial New York*, pp. 87–120.

[4] Conrad Weiser to Governor Hamilton, May 4, 1750, *Pennsylvania Archives* (1st series), II, 43–45. See also Conrad Weiser to William Johnson, February 8, 1751, *Sir William Johnson Papers*, I, 317–18.

[5] John Ayscough to William Johnson, May 18, 1751, *Sir William Johnson Papers*, I, 333. [6] *Ibid.*

of Catholic emissaries, who had now penetrated the strongholds of the Iroquois with their gifts and missionary zeal, was badly in need of goods for presents and trade.[7] Johnson was successful in such competition, and he did not hedge on the issue of presents.

One of Johnson's most important qualifications for the position of commissary of goods for presents was his knowledge of Indian needs, derived from his close association with the Indians themselves. After the Mohawks had honored him with the title of sachem, he married one of their women and came to be a brother of the whole confederacy.[8] Old Hendrick, probably the most influential sachem of the Mohawks, and apparently a very discerning individual, had a high regard for Warraghiyagey.[9] In Hendrick's own words:

. . . . he has Large Ears and heareth a great deal, and what he hears he tells us; he also has Large Eyes and sees a great way, and conceals nothing from us.[10]

Hendrick favored both Johnson and Governor George Clinton of New York because they were the source of many personal gifts. Though he seldom took a share of the public gifts from the province, Hendrick refused, as did most of the Iroquois sachems, to do any business until solid marks of friendship in the form of goods were in his hands. The shrewd observer, Thomas Pownall,[11] described Old Hendrick as ". . . . a bold artful intriguing Fellow & has learnt no small share of European Politics, [he] obstructs & opposes all [business] where he has not been talked to first . . . ."[12] Pownall further relates that the old diplomat had secured more than one hundred dollars from Clinton at various times.

The Stockbridge Christian Indians, the inseparable companions of the famed Robert Rogers, shared the Mohawk's high regard for Johnson. They pictured Warraghiyagey as a stalwart oak with friendly protecting limbs. They were well aware of the fact that Johnson had co-operated willingly with the Stockbridge missionaries and had aided them in establishing schools for the Iroquois children to attend.[13] Because he was known as a friend to the whole Northern confederacy the versatile agent was able to make his

---

[7] George Clinton to William Johnson, September 7, 1749, *ibid.*, I, 247–48.

[8] *Wraxall's Abridgement*, p. 246.

[9] There are several ways of spelling Johnson's Indian name. Peter Wraxall spells it Warraghiyagey. See LO 1144. It is elsewhere recorded as Warraghygagey. See LO 1687. However, the more common spelling seems to have been Warraghiyagey.

[10] *Sir William Johnson Papers*, I, 339–44.

[11] Thomas Pownall's "Notes on Indian Affairs," LO 460.

[12] *Ibid.*

[13] Joseph Dwight to William Johnson, October 13, 1751, *Sir William Johnson Papers*, I, 353–54.

presents count as ". . . . simbols & pledges of Friendship."[14] A gift from
Warraghiyagey signified more than a mere donation of goods from the
assembly, even though it might go through the hands of an interpreter or
an Oswego trader. In other words, Johnson was one of the members of the
confederacy, and he seldom shirked the expected obligation of presents. One
might even say that his gifts were the spearhead of friendship with the Iroquois; for they served to nullify the ". . . . frauds abuses & deceits . . . ."
experienced by the natives at the hands of greedy profiteers.[15]

In addition to his knowledge of native custom, the Mohawk sachem of
British heritage had a fundamental understanding of the character of goods
to be used for Indian trade and presents. His store at Mount Johnson
developed into a popular center for the exchange of Indian goods and
Oswego furs.[16] Beaver pelts, deerskins, and raccoon pelts, the cream of the
Oswego trade, found a place in Johnson's warehouse. From here the goods
were sent to Samuel and William Baker for sale in London. In return,
shirts, blankets, halfthicks, flints, lead, powder, knives, guns, ruffled shirts,
and a hundred other items were sent to Mount Johnson for trade and gifts.[17]
Johnson knew the Indians and what they wanted. His memorandum for
presents shows a high correlation with goods to be used for trade. In fact,
they were one and the same thing; and both were sent from Samuel and
William Baker, George Libenrod, and other merchants.[18] A possible exception to this generalization lies in the fact that Johnson often sent the
Indians such articles of food as cattle, hogs, corn, sugar, and rum.[19] Well
did Johnson know that food to eat was more suitable than castor hats or
ruffled shirts when the northern winds began to howl and game was scarce.
Johnson's gifts were practical from all points of view; his skill as a business-
man insured as rapid delivery as was possible under the prevailing circumstances; and his knowledge of Indian custom enabled him to choose appropriate gifts such as kettles, food, and blankets for the women, and powder,
arms, or ridiculous mirrors to please the vanity of the warriors.

Through the fur trade of the new world Johnson had come to be a man
of power and influence. Shiploads of furs to please the expensive fashion
tastes of the eighteenth century had made this Irish immigrant a rich man.[20]

---

[14] Thomas Pownall's "Notes on Indian Affairs," LO 460.

[15] *Ibid.*

[16] *Sir William Johnson Papers*, I, 294–95.

[17] Samuel and William Baker to William Johnson, July 23, 1750, *Sir William
Johnson Papers*, I, 291–92.

[18] "Account of the Proceedings at Oswego," February 17, 1748, *ibid.*, I, 133–38, and
also LO 1369.

[19] *Sir William Johnson Papers*, III, 23.

[20] Samuel and William Baker to William Johnson, July 23, 1750, *ibid.*, I, 291–92.

And with these riches came Mount Johnson and greater facilities for the distribution of gifts. About sixty miles, as a bird flies, from the conjunction of the Mohawk and Hudson rivers, lies today's city of Johnstown, New York, close to the former site of Mount Johnson. It was here, in the 1740's, that this remarkable man carved a comfortable home and fortress out of the wilderness. In 1760, General Jeffery Amherst, expressing the military man's point of view, described Mount Johnson as a ". . . . House badly situated commanded entirely by hills . . . ." where the Indians lived off Johnson.[21] But the place was more than that; it was the second home of the Mohawks, and even of the whole confederacy, a place where they could be sheltered and fed in time of threatened or actual French attacks.[22] Here they received the gifts of the colony of New York as well as supplements from Johnson's own personal stores. Indeed, when expenses showed a tendency to increase, the assembly lost patience with Johnson's seeming extravagance.[23]

Interspersed with orders for presents we find invoices mentioning lumber, screws, pictures, and microscopes, all of which enabled Johnson to move into his new home in January 1750. Johnson built with an eye to his environment, establishing a home designed to meet the rigid requirements of frontier life. A blockhouse was built to provide protection for his family and his native friends. A sheephouse, a mill, and a bakehouse were constructed to provide necessary foodstuffs; an aqueduct yielded water to drink. Johnson also maintained a stable in which to lodge horses of visiting Indians and a storehouse to protect their presents. In addition, small shelters were made for visitors; and a council house was erected for meetings and the distribution of presents.[24] Truly, Mount Johnson was the home of the Indians as well as the Johnson family. The leader of this household was not charitable to the point of being foolhardy, however; for over a period of years Johnson's presents were paid for by the assembly or the Crown, and he died a rich man.[25]

It was not the Indians and traders alone who recognized Johnson's combination of business, diplomatic, and military talents. The colony of New York also realized his ability. Despite the fact that his alliance with the Germans in Albany against the Anglo-Dutch in the scramble for Indian lands made it impossible for him to be a neutral agent in distributing presents,[26] the colony of New York delivered an extraordinary series of com-

---

[21] Webster, *op. cit.*, p. 202.

[22] William Johnson to George Clinton, May 4, 1751, *Sir William Johnson Papers*, I, 276.

[23] William Johnson to George Clinton, May 31, 1747, *ibid.*, I, 96–97.

[24] See the sketch of Mount Johnson reproduced in *ibid.*, I, 260–61. The drawing was made by Guy Johnson, Sir William Johnson's nephew.

[25] *Ibid.*, I, 339–44.   [26] Thomas Pownall's "Notes on Indian Affairs," LO 460.

missions to the young trader, commissions which greatly increased his facilities for the disbursing of gifts.

Governor George Clinton, the council, and the more progressive members of the assembly soon came to recognize the incompetence of those commissioners of Indian affairs who seldom left their comfortable homes in Albany or in New York to travel north in order to visit the Iroquois and to distribute their gifts. As was to be expected, the French took advantage of this situation to extend their influence with the Senecas through such agents as the Joncaire brothers.[27] With a war raging and French Algonquian Indians ravaging the frontier with their scalping parties, some capable person was urgently needed to take charge of Indian affairs.[28] So it was that William Johnson stepped into prominence. In a conference held with the natives in August 1746, William Johnson began his series of counteractions by presenting a large war belt and demanding the alliance of the Iroquois against the French.[29] His commission as commissary of the stores and provisions for the Indians, dated August 27, 1746, authorized him to furnish as many warriors as were needed to go against the enemy.[30] Furthermore, he was instructed to reward those Indians who were successful in returning with scalps of the enemy.[31] Indeed, Governor Clinton instructed Johnson to reside with the Mohawks, for the Governor felt he could serve the king much better in this capacity than if he had a military command.[32] Success brought its own reward, however; and the young commissary received his first actual commission in the forces of New York in May 1748, at which time he became colonel of the Militia Foot, for the city and county of Albany.[33] With this new honor came more supplies for the Albany militia. Many of these supplies were military stores, which could be transmuted into presents for the Indians if such necessity should arise. In consequence, Johnson brought pressure to bear on the assembly so that funds were supplied; and the flow of presents from Oswego and Mount Johnson began.[34] Moreover, his growing correspondence with Clinton reveals the energetic young colonel making the first of a series of journeys with presents to the great council at Onondaga.[35]

---

[27] The Six Nations to Governor Clinton, July 25, 1748, *Sir William Johnson Papers*, I, 174.

[28] *Wraxall's Abridgement*, pp. 36–37.

[29] *Ibid.*, p. 246.

[30] George Clinton to William Johnson, August 27, 1746, *Sir William Johnson Papers*, I, 59–60.

[31] George Clinton to William Johnson, August 28, 1746, *ibid.*, I, 60–61.

[32] *Ibid.*

[33] Commission from George Clinton to William Johnson, May 1, 1748, *ibid.*, I, 166.

[34] John Catherwood to William Johnson, October 19, 1747, *ibid.*, I, 118.

[35] George Clinton to William Johnson, March 18, 1748, *ibid.*, I, 151–52.

SIR WILLIAM JOHNSON

Kelly and Samuel and William Baker and George Libenrod. Whether it was door knobs and latches for Mount Johnson, or blankets and kettles from Amsterdam for the Indians, Johnson had the responsibility of ordering the specifications for quality and quantity of goods; and in theory, the agent was to be compensated by the assembly in the form of warrants.[43]

When the goods arrived in New York, Johnson's difficulties began anew. The merchandise had to undergo the complications of harbor red tape and be transferred from the ocean vessel to a river sloop before it could be started on its journey up the Hudson to Albany.[44] Despite these difficulties, however, Robert Saunders, mayor of Albany, in collaboration with the dynamic George Clinton of New York, kept a constant flow of presents moving up the Hudson to Albany, and from there up the Mohawk River to Mount Johnson.[45]

Johnson's correspondence during this period indicates that George Clinton, then lieutenant governor of New York, devoted most of his time to acting as Johnson's agent in order to secure goods for Indian presents. Once this sailor-governor had set his mind to a thing, he followed it wholeheartedly. Indeed, as far back as June 20, 1743, while still in London awaiting to embark for his new post, Clinton was preparing a gift for the Iroquois and their allies.[46] Such a man was no mean helper. Clinton thought Indians, lived Indians, and shared Johnson's every problem regarding the Indians, including the distribution of presents. And when goods were scarce in New York because merchant ships were late, he searched every shop within his reach to obtain merchandise for Johnson. The favorable results secured by gifts to the natives even motivated Clinton to lend his friend fourteen hundred pounds on a single note, without any security or interest,[47] agreeing to wait for payment until Johnson should receive his appropriations from the assembly.

Together these men worked out the problems and expenses of sending gunsmiths to live with the Onondagas and of preventing unscrupulous individuals from taking the costly arms and clothing away from the native warriors.[48] Whether it was a question of pleasing the forceful William Shirley with an Indian conference, of sending a needed sloop of goods, or of

---

[43] George Clinton to William Johnson, June 16, 1751, *Sir William Johnson Papers*, I, 316–17.

[44] George Clinton to William Johnson, March 25, 1747, *ibid.*, I, 83–84.

[45] Robert Saunders to William Johnson, November 28, 1745, *ibid.*, I, 43–45.

[46] George Clinton to ———, June 20, 1743, HM 9846.

[47] George Clinton to William Johnson, January 16, 1751, *Sir William Johnson Papers*, I, 316.

[48] George Clinton to William Johnson, February 6, 1749, *ibid.*, I, 211–13. See also George Clinton to William Johnson, March 12, 1747, *ibid.*, I, 77–79.

Such restless energy and ambition could not be denied. Men like
Schuckburg, surgeon of the New York Regiment; John Catherwoo[d]
tary to Clinton; and Governor Clinton himself were all working fo[r]
son's promotion.[36] Catherwood, while he was in London liquidatin[g]
of Clinton's accounts, wrote that he had given high recommendation[s]
proper authorities in the hope of securing the appointment of Johnson
council of New York; he was to replace the late Philip Livingston, [as]
commissioner of Indian affairs.[37] A second letter, written on May 26,
conveyed the glad tidings of his appointment to the upper house [to]
Albany colonel. Catherwood added that he hoped that Johnson woul[d]
his good offices among the Indians so that they would not weaken in
loyalty to the Crown, a loyalty which had cost vast sums to secure.[38]
was a wise move for the Crown. New appropriations which could be
tained from the assembly by reason of Johnson's being on the council w[ould]
take the financial burden from the shoulders of the Crown. It proved t[hat]
Johnson himself, however, who bore this burden until he was later fo[rced]
to resign, lest the expense of Indian presents ruin him financially.[39] N[ot-]
withstanding the importance of this commission, Johnson did not take his
oath of office until 1751, because the Indians would expect larger presents
from him as a member of the upper house of the legislature.[40]

If Colonel Johnson had been free to distribute gifts in the most expedient
manner, he would have avoided many of the complications that he encountered. The procedure for securing and distributing gifts was long, tedious,
and required careful advance planning. The first step in this long process
was to secure goods from England. Johnson had to plan well in advance,
for it took from four to six months even to get a reply concerning the goods;
and it was indeed seldom that a convoy of goods actually arrived within this
time.[41] An illustration of the importance of the time element may be found
in one of his letters to George Libenrod, merchant in London. Johnson's
message of August 4, 1752, reads: "Your punctual and Speedy Compliance
will be the greatest inducement to continue and enlarge our dealings."[42]

The correspondence of the administrator of Mount Johnson is filled with
letters, invoices, and lists of goods from London merchants such as William

---

[36] John Catherwood to William Johnson, April 2, 1750, *Sir William Johnson
Papers*, I, 269–70.

[37] Lords of Trade to George Clinton, April 10, 1750, *ibid.*, I, 273.

[38] John Catherwood to William Johnson, May 26, 1750, *ibid.*, I, 282.

[39] *Ibid.*, I, 339–44.

[40] *Ibid.*

[41] "Invoice from Samuel and William Baker to William Johnson," April 26, 1[7]
ibid., I, 220–23.

[42] William Johnson to George Libenrod, August 4, 1752, *ibid.*, I, 372.

undertaking a dozen other tasks, the co-operative Clinton was at Johnson's side.[49] Both men realized that presents were the key to Indian friendship and trade. One cannot help but sympathize with the tireless Clinton when the ungracious assembly refused to make appropriations for gifts which Johnson had long since delivered to the Indians, especially when the Iroquois agent was bombarding the Governor with demands for cash and threats of resignation. Little wonder that Clinton referred to the assembly as ". . . . them & their Crew."[50]

After the blankets, wheat, ruffled shirts, and rum arrived in Albany, they were moved on to Mount Johnson under the direction of Robert Saunders and John Henry Lydius, trader and agent of William Shirley.[51] Since Lydius was experienced in dealing with Indians, he sometimes took the liberty of giving presents to them, informing Johnson later of his actions. Moreover, he had a thriving business in the Albany fur trade and so was well acquainted with many of the headmen in the confederacy.[52] Hence, Lydius, first as a personal advisor to Shirley and later as a commissioner of Indian affairs in Albany, was a competent aide to Johnson.[53] As his interests had good reason to conflict with those of Johnson, however, he would bear watching.

At Albany the goods were transferred to clumsy, flat-bottomed batteau boats; and under the leadership of the Oswego trader, John Van Eps, husky arms propelled them up the Mohawk.[54] When the merchandise was floated up to Johnson's wharf, part of it was unloaded there; but the remainder was sent on to Oswego, for Johnson had been commissioned to supply this post with goods for trade and presents.[55]

Oswego, located on the eastern bank of Lake Ontario, was the sharpest thorn in the side of the French traders of the North. As early as 1743, it was reported to have sheltered twenty men who were distributing the

---

[49] George Clinton to William Johnson, March 25, 1747, *ibid.*, I, 83–84. See also Charles Henry Lincoln (ed.), *Correspondence of William Shirley, Governor of Massachusetts and Military Commander in America, 1731–1760*, I, 429–37.

[50] George Clinton to William Johnson, September 24, 1750, *Sir William Johnson Papers*, I, 301.

[51] Robert Saunders to William Johnson, March 6, 1749, *ibid.*, I, 215–16. See also John H. Lydius to William Shirley, June 20, 1746, LO 27.

[52] John H. Lydius to William Johnson, February 13, 1747/8, *Sir William Johnson Papers*, I, 132–33. See also *ibid.*, I, 313.

[53] John Stoddart to John H. Lydius, May 26, 1747, *ibid.*, I, 90–92.

[54] John Van Eps to William Johnson, December 15, 1747, *ibid.*, I, 123. See also John Van Eps to William Johnson, July 4, 1749, *ibid.*, I, 287.

[55] Teady Magin to William Johnson, July 11, 1750, *ibid.*, I, 287.

superior goods of the English to the Six Nations.[56] When Johnson took over the burden of Oswego, he sent his trusted interpreter, Arent Stevens, there in order to prevent the Indians from going on to Canada with their furs.[57] Where others had failed, Stevens achieved favorable results with gifts and all but neutralized the influence of the French, who often clothed the Indians from head to foot. He was ably aided by the scheming commandant, Walter Butler, whose gifts to the natives apparently came in showers, and included even such unexpected items as grindstones, which had to be shipped from New York, a distance of almost three hundred miles. By such activities, Stevens and a host of traders gradually acquired the allegiance of the confederates.[58] With this friendship to aid them, Thomas Butler, son of the commandant, Teady Magin, John Van Eps, and many others fattened their purses from the exchange of furs and goods.

As the Indian merchandise moved up the Mohawk from Mount Johnson to Lake Oneida and down the Oswego River, the volume of trade and exchange in presents increased, and cutthroat competition became the rule. This was similar to the picture on the Ohio frontier.[59] At the western post at Oswego there was seldom a lack of wampum belts and other goods, as had been the situation when the commissioners of Indian affairs had directed the destiny of this important artery of trade. Still, the disbursers of gifts had to be cautious not to overdo their friendly, expensive custom; for the assembly might refuse to compensate the donors. This happened in the case of both Walter Butler and William Johnson.[60] Perhaps these two men could have learned a great deal had they been able to watch the progress of the famous old Hudson's Bay Company of the north, where regulation of licenses, trade, and presents worked for the long-time benefit of all concerned.[61]

In reconstructing the above picture of William Johnson's convoys of goods as they followed the long, tortuous trail from Europe to his fireside, and from there to Oswego or the council chambers at Onondaga, an attempt has been made to present the difficulties most frequently encountered by the young agent. In comparison with the troubles that Johnson had with the

---

[56] "State of the British Provinces on This Continent of America with Respect to the French Who Surround Them, 1743," LO 39; reprinted in the *New York Colonial Documents*, VI, 226–29.

[57] Arent Stevens to William Johnson, July 11, 1750, *Sir William Johnson Papers*, 1, 288. Arent Stevens was employed by Johnson as a distributor of presents.

[58] Captain Rutherford to Lieutenant Walter Butler, June 11, 1745, *ibid.*, I, 32–33.

[59] Benjamin Stoddart to William Johnson, July 16, 1749, *ibid.*, I, 235–36.

[60] Captain Rutherford to Lieutenant Walter Butler, July 11, 1745, *ibid.*, I, 32–33.

[61] "Abstract of the Hudson's Bay Company Charter Granted 1670 By Laws Made November, 1739," HM 1718.

New York Assembly, however, those difficulties turn out to be minor concerns in the complicated business of distributing gifts.

The power of the purse has influenced the policy of government officials in any age. This policy, in turn, influences individuals. A man in Johnson's position, who was forced to donate presents to the sachems who visited Mount Johnson or to the warriors who returned from French settlements, was at the mercy of the assembly.[62] Influenced by Shirley's letters to England, British officials on the Board of Trade combined with Clinton to urge the assembly to compensate Johnson. In the past, it had been the general policy of the opposition in the assembly, led by James De Lancey,[63] to deliver presents and to protect the families of the Iroquois.[64] Thus, assuming that the assembly would approve accounts for gifts, Johnson supported the warrants of Walter Butler from Oswego and of John Ayscough, Sheriff of New York County. Clinton then laid the accounts of Johnson before the assembly.[65] Although the provincial treasury contained sufficient funds to cover the warrants of Oswego and Mount Johnson,[66] the assembly, logically enough, often refused to consider these warrants. Such action resulted because Johnson was a member of the disliked upper house and because the legislators had no actual proof that goods had been delivered to the Indians. Time and time again Clinton begged Johnson to appear before the assembly to justify his expenses. Clinton's letter of September 24, 1750, states:

I am surprised you don't come down & look into ye large concerns depending, I cannot assist you for I don't know one Syllible of what passes but what I see of their Votes, ... they are at underhand hatching Some vile action, but they have used me so much in their Billingsgate language that I am prepared & shall only dispise them & their Crew.[67]

When Clinton's pleas failed, and Johnson had declared himself too ill with a cold to appear, John Ayscough finally begged the agent to come down from Mount Johnson to put on an actual demonstration for the tidewater legislators. The purpose of this exhibition was to show how strouds and

---

[62] Other Colonial administrators who distributed gifts to the Indians also had trouble with the assembly in obtaining funds. This was especially true in Pennsylvania and Virginia.

[63] James De Lancey was active in New York politics first as a member of the council, then as chief justice, and finally as lieutenant-governor. He presided over the Albany Congress in 1754.

[64] "Report of James De Lancey to Governor Clinton," February 29, 1748, *Sir William Johnson Papers*, I, 139–42.

[65] John Ayscough to William Johnson, September 8, 1750, *ibid.*, I, 298.

[66] George Clinton to William Johnson, September 24, 1750, *Sir William Johnson Papers*, I, 301–2.

[67] *Ibid.*

stockings were given to the Indians and why it was absolutely necessary to do so.[68] To the disappointment of all, the independent Johnson refused to appear before that critical body; and, amid the loud objections of the Iroquois sachems, who demanded their brother's reinstatement, he resigned his commission.[69] It was only at the demand of the sachem, Hendrick, that Johnson troubled himself to appear at a meeting with the council and the Indians in order to straighten out the affair. When he refused to continue because the assembly owed him over thirteen hundred pounds, that obstinate body of legislators appointed a group of Indian commissioners from their own midst.[70] For the most part, these men represented the political enemies of Johnson; and only one of them could claim any experience in dealing with the Indians. These were the Anglo-Dutch traders of Albany who took the French-English rivalries with the Indians lightly indeed.[71] This marked the beginning of a brief decline in the prestige of New York among the Six Nations, for Johnson was no longer the distributor of gifts for that province.

While the Iroquois were acquiring an attitude of contempt for their new managers, Johnson submerged himself in private affairs. In 1754, the former commissioner again rose to brief prominence when he and Hendrick were called upon to aid Benjamin Franklin at the Albany conference.[72] Johnson's suggestions for solving Indian problems arising out of the Ohio tension again demonstrated his capabilities, and Hendrick once more pleaded his case. Hendrick's request that the former Iroquois commissioner be reinstated as the high superintendent for the whole North, free from the domineering New York Assembly, represented the wishes of the whole confederacy.[73] This action pleased even the critical William Shirley.[74]

But what were these expensive presents which concerned the assembly so much? William Johnson's obligations to the Indians in the form of gifts were numerous. A gunsmith was needed to reside with every tribe of the confederacy and their allies in order to keep weapons in repair. Moreover, in addition to being a man who could live with the Indians and speak their language, the smith was highly paid.[75] Certain items were required for a warrior's equipment before he could set out on a raid. For example, Indian shoes or sandals[76] were only one article in many that were essential. A

---

[68] John Ayscough to William Johnson, May 18, 1751, *Sir William Johnson Papers*, I, 333   [69] *Ibid.*, I, 339–44.

[70] *Ibid.*

[71] George Clinton to William Johnson, November 5, 1752, *ibid.*, I, 383.

[72] Governor Hamilton to William Johnson, March 19, 1754, *ibid.*, I, 396–98.

[73] *Ibid.*, I, 339–44.

[74] William Shirley to William Johnson, December 9, 1754, *ibid.*, I, 426.

[75] William Johnson to George Clinton, November 16, 1750, *ibid.*, I, 307.

[76] William Johnson to George Clinton, August 13, 1747, *ibid.*, I, 107–10.

memorandum sent to Clinton on August 13, 1747, stated that each warrior must be supplied with blankets, cottons, strouds, linen, vermilion, light guns, pistoles,[77] cutlasses, long knives, axes, bullet molds, red gimps for binding the hair, Indian awl blades, powder, lead, shot, flints, kettles, looking glasses, scissors, and razors.[78] It seems impossible that one man could carry all of these things, much less go to war with them; but we must remember that each warrior had a family which could use flints, kettles, strouds, gimps, cottons, and linens. A warrior might be vain, but he would not let his family starve. This is illustrated by the Iroquois' frequent demands that forts be built to protect their old men, women, and children in time of war.[79] As might be expected, the Indians also requested that they be clothed and fed after they had been released from the French as prisoners.[80] Such demands as these made it impossible to please the Indians and the assembly at the same time; their interests were in direct opposition. William Johnson favored the Six Nations; and while he was in power, they received their gifts.

It is important that the relationship between the English and these six united tribes be considered. From the British point of view, the Iroquois were the subject allies of Great Britain, although the British were never in a position to impose their will on these independent people until the end of the French and Indian War.[81] After King George's War, in 1748, Clinton wrote to the governor of Canada stating that ". . . . the subjects of the Five Nations of Indians . . . . are indisputably the vassals of the King of Great Britain."[82] Nevertheless, in the minds of the Indians, who recognized their position as a balance of power, friendship could be bought only through a favorable exchange in trade, presents, or military success. Johnson's prestige in securing the allegiance of the Indians was based primarily on presents and trade.[83] It was the gifts that he used to secure immediate services from them.

Soon after Johnson's appointment as colonel of the forces to be raised among the Iroquois, numerous entries appear in the *New York Colonial Documents*, in 1747, concerning the fierce raids of the Iroquois on French

[77] A pistole was a gold coin varying in value, used formerly in Europe.

[78] William Johnson to George Clinton, August 13, 1747, *ibid.*, I, 107-10.

[79] William Shirley to General Abercromby, June 27, 1756, P.R.O., C.O., 5/46 L.C. 521-40.

[80] Anthony Van Schaick to William Johnson, October 14, 1749, *Sir William Johnson Papers*, I, 251-52.

[81] Theodore Calvin Pease, *et al.* (eds.), *Anglo-French Boundary Disputes in the West 1749-1763*, French Series, II, 124-25 (*Collections* of the Illinois State Historical Library).

[82] George Clinton to the Governor of Canada, October 10, 1748, *New York Colonial Documents*, X, 191.

[83] It should be noted that Johnson was accepted as a sachem among the Mohawks. This fact considerably enhanced his prestige.

settlements.[84] True, the official council at Onondaga had declared the confederacy to be neutral; but the Mohawks, under the influence of Colonel Johnson and his presents, made raids on the French and took scalps from men, women, and children.[85] From 1747 to 1748, men such as Thomas Butler personally led parties of murdering Indians on the quest for scalps, promising rewards of castor hats and metal buttons.[86] Hendrick of the Mohawks established a high standard in raiding parties by taking eleven scalps and eighteen prisoners.[87] Johnson's preparation for these raids on the French is revealed in a letter to Clinton, dated March 18, 1747. Here he declared:

I am of opinion We shall make the French Smart this Spring by taking Sculping, & burning them, & their Settlements, but I shall be ruined for want of Blankets, linnen, paint, Guns, Cutlashes, &ca. for I am almost out of all those & Cannot get them in Albany . . . .[88]

It was on this issue, and with ample justification, that the assembly questioned the ethics of paying savages to go out and kill women and children.[89]

After peace came in 1748, the Albany colonel was still working to keep the friendship of the confederates. For example, in April 1748 he undertook a strenuous journey to Onondaga, where he renewed good will with presents and a speech that recalled their ". . . . First Brothership."[90] It is no wonder that William Shirley wrote to him in December 1754, stating:

I am persuaded, his Majy hath not a Subject, who knows so well how to gain the hearts of the Indians, and an Absolute Influence over them, as yourself, and who hath exerted his distinguish'd abilities for his Majys service . . . .[91]

This excerpt from one of Johnson's strongest critics clearly shows the high regard that prominent contemporaries had for the importance of his work.

After reviewing Johnson's activities during the early days of his fruitful distribution of presents, one is forced to the following conclusions. First, Colonel William Johnson's presents were one of the most powerful conciliatory influences on the Iroquois, the greatest Indian confederacy of the eighteenth century.[92] Second, Johnson's avenues of disbursing gifts were through Mount Johnson, Oswego, and the Onondaga Council. Third, Johnson's

---

[84] *New York Colonial Documents*, X, 86, 91, 101.

[85] *Ibid.*, X, 162.

[86] William Johnson to George Clinton, May 30, 1747, *Sir William Johnson Papers*, I, 93–96.

[87] *Ibid.*

[88] William Johnson to George Clinton, March 18, 1747, *ibid.*, I, 80–81.

[89] George Clinton to William Johnson, April 26, 1747, *ibid.*, I, 86–87.

[90] "Indian Council at Onondaga," April 24, 1748, *ibid.*, I, 155–65.

[91] William Shirley to William Johnson, December 9, 1754, *ibid.*, I, 426.

[92] Pease, *op. cit.*, pp. 124–25.

friendship with the Six Nations, largely acquired through the use of presents, was a powerful bulwark against the French in the North.[93] Fourth, and last, all the provinces exposed to the Iroquois were greatly concerned over the friendship of their neighbors.[94]

When we turn to a consideration of the important events on the Ohio, we find this to be the new center of rivalry for the affection of the Iroquois and their allies. The confederacy claimed the Ohio Valley by right of conquest, and already many of their members had made this fertile hunting ground their permanent home. Logically enough, since the forks of the Ohio were said to be the key to the whole Mississippi Basin, Anglo-French rivalry in trade with and in presents to the Indians shifted from Oswego to this new point of tension. It was not unusual, then, that Johnson's correspondence with the governors and Indian diplomats of the middle provinces increased. Johnson had won security in the North with presents, and now Pennsylvania Indian commissioners and traders were following the same policy to fortify the Ohio frontier against the French. The Iroquois of the North were brothers to the Iroquois on the Ohio, and the remaining tribes in this locality were the subjects of the Six Nations.[95] For this reason, Oswego and Mount Johnson were of paramount importance as a center for the distribution of presents during the years 1748–1753.

The Ohio region now takes the stage when the final conflict begins; for the Indians, whether Iroquois or their subjects, had to be bought with presents. Their services were essential as warriors, scouts, or merely neutrals until the danger had passed. This came when Fort Duquesne fell in November 1758.

---

[93] *Sir William Johnson Papers*, I, 662–65.

[94] William Johnson's correspondence with William Shirley, James Glen, Benning Wentworth, and James Hamilton shows that these governors were quite concerned over the friendship of the Iroquois. Their letters appear in *ibid.*, I and II.

[95] The Iroquois claimed that they held the Ohio Valley by right of conquest. Hence such tribes as the Delawares were regarded as a subject people and referred to as "children."

VI. INDIAN DIPLOMACY IN THE OHIO VALLEY, 1748–1751

Throughout the history of Indian diplomacy from 1748 to 1751, presents were regularly employed by both the French and the English as a measure of securing the friendship of the Ohio tribes. This period, which is opened by the culmination of one war and closed by the beginnings of another, is essentially the story of competition for Indian allegiance by means of presents. It is the story of the development of the British alliance with the powerful Miamis after the peace of Aix-la-Chapelle in 1748. When the French failed with presents, they resorted to force. Although it was the goods of Pennsylvania that dominated the shifting alliances of native settlements during the early part of this period, the colony of Virginia emerged on the changing scene by the year 1750. Finding that they could not compete successfully with these two colonies in giving presents, the French, after 1751, turned to killing those Indians who opposed them.[1]

The rise and fall of influential native leaders also changed Indian allegiance during this era. With the death of the wise old Shikalamy[2] in 1749, the Quaker colony suffered the loss of a staunch ally. This old sachem had received presents for many years from the hand of Conrad Weiser, provincial interpreter. In 1750, Pennsylvania lost another friend when the influential Canasatego of the Onondagas died, leaving that branch of the Iroquoian confederacy to the mercy of French presents and a consequent loss of British prestige.[3]

British influence recovered, however, when Monacatoocha,[4] frequently

---

[1] See the accounts of the massacre at Pickawillany: Draper MSS, W.S.H.S. Nos. 1 JJ 3–1 JJ 6, pp. 3–6 (photostat); P.R.O., C.O., 5/1327, L.C. 415–24, C.O. 531–36; P.R.O., C.O., 5/1327, L.C. 431–47, C.O. 549–69. The last citation is the journal of William Trent, Virginia trader who visited Old Briton's town shortly after the French raid.

[2] Conrad Weiser to James Hamilton, April 22, 1749, *Pennsylvania Archives* (1st series), II, 23–24.

[3] *Pennsylvania Colonial Records*, V, 467.

[4] The famous Oneida sachem, Monacatoocha, who occupied such an important place in native politics during the French and Indian War is very easily confused with other Indian leaders because of the problem of Indian names. Monacatoocha was also known as Scarrooyady. The fact that Scarrooyady and Monacatoocha are one and the same Indian is established in the *Pennsylvania Archives* (1st series), II, 114. It is more confusing that Monacatoocha was also called Half King; however, this sachem is not to be confused with the Seneca sachem Half King who was also known as Tanacharisson. *Vide*, note 5. Monacatoocha was an Oneida sachem.

It appears that Monacatoocha became prominent among the Ohio Iroquois, or Mingoes, in the 1740's. He presided, as a representative of all the Ohio "nations," at

called Scarrooyady, and Half King,[5] leaders of the Six Nations and recipients of British presents, resumed the leadership among the Ohio tribes. Another ally was Old Briton, leader of the insubordinate branch of the Miamis which rebelled against the French. Old Briton, often called La Demoiselle, encouraged his Lake Erie tribesmen in the exchange of presents with the British.[6] These presents were furnished by the traders of Pennsylvania, who undermined French prestige by doling out goods at a cheaper rate of exchange.

Although oftentimes unruly, the traders[7] were courageous men who spearheaded the fierce competition for native allegiance on the side of the British by delivering presents. In this business of distributing gifts, the traders were led by the able George Croghan. Aided by his assistant, the half-breed interpreter Andrew Montour, Croghan helped the overworked Conrad Weiser in his many duties as interpreter for the Quaker province. Eventually, when the increased distribution of goods became too much for Weiser, Croghan and Montour took over many of his duties. Not only did the latter two men serve Pennsylvania, but they were also called upon to assist Virginia in the allotting of gifts to the Ohio Indians. The Virginia

---

the important Treaty of Lancaster in 1748. See *Pennsylvania Colonial Records*, V, 307–19. Monacatoocha was one of the eight Indian guides who accompanied Braddock in the historic march toward Fort Duquesne. See chapter vii. Monacatoocha was also present at the death of his close friend Tanacharisson at Harris' Ferry in October 1754. See *Pennsylvania Colonial Records*, VI, 184. Following Braddock's defeat, Monacatoocha, as the leader of the loyal British Ohio Iroquois, went north to reside in the Mohawk country. In 1756, he was influential in bringing peace between Pennsylvania and the Delawares and Shawnees. For references on this remarkable sachem see *Pennsylvania Colonial Records*, V, 665–70, VI, 566; *Sir William Johnson Papers,* II, 438–40, 442–46. It must be pointed out that Monacatoocha should not be confused with the sachem Scaiohady, who also received presents for his services. See *Pennsylvania Colonial Records*, V, 147. Unfortunately Professor Albert T. Volwiler, in his scholarly study *Greoge Croghan and the Westward Movement, 1741–1782*, p. 97, has mistakenly identified Monacatoocha and Scarrooyady (who are one and the same person) as being two separate Indians.

[5] Half King, or Tanacharisson, was a Seneca sachem who resided for many years among the Ohio Iroquois. He, like his close friend Monacatoocha, was a steadfast friend of the British. Half King accompanied Washington on his famous expedition to Venango and Le Boeuf in December, 1753, and was Washington's guide in the Jumonville encounter of May 1754. See chapter vii. It appears definite that Half King died October 1754, his leadership among the Ohio tribes devolving to Monacatoocha. See *Pennsylvania Archives* (1st series), II, 114, 117; *Pennsylvania Colonial Records,* VI, 178, 184.

[6] *Pennsylvania Colonial Records*, V, 298; *Illinois on the Eve of the Seven Years' War*, pp. 105–6, 110, 120–21.

[7] For a list of the licensed traders of Pennsylvania in 1748, see *Pennsylvania Archives* (1st series), II, 14.

government found an additional Indian agent in the capable Christopher Gist, who laid the groundwork for the Ohio Company by his explorations and by his offerings to the natives. Above all, however, the early history of this period centered around the astute Conrad Weiser whose thirty-four years of experience in dealing with the Indians had made him well-acquainted with their appetite for presents.[8]

Weiser dominated Pennsylvania's policy of friendship. He was consulted on almost all matters relating to the Indians. Thus, in the years immediately preceding 1748, his influence was a potent factor in the shaping of Pennsylvania's policy toward the Indians. Weiser's recommendations usually reached the Pennsylvania government through Richard Peters, the secretary and clerk of the provincial council.[9] The numerous letters exchanged between Weiser and Peters, recorded in the *Pennsylvania Archives* and the *Pennsylvania Colonial Records*, give a general picture of Indian affairs in the Ohio Valley. During the years 1748 to 1751, at which time Virginia entered the scene, the donation of goods was a vital factor in Indian politics.

Presents even formed the basis for a dispute between the Pennsylvania Assembly and the proprietaries. In the early years following the initial grant to William Penn, the Quakers had dominated the legislative body; and their influence had been aimed at keeping the frontiers peaceful through the expedient of presents. Although their influence was still in evidence at the beginning of the period now under discussion, other elements were taking control. Despite the increasing crescendo of expenses for goods, however, the government still regarded ". . . . a valuable Present [as] . . . . the most substantial Mark that can be given of the great affection which this Province bears to their Friends the Indians . . . ."[10]

On the other hand, the proprietaries followed a policy of land-grabbing, recompensing the tribes by paltry strouds and shirts. Most painful to the Indians of all of these so-called "purchases" was the memory of the Walking Purchase of 1737.[11]

Disregarding the expenses borne by the proprietaries in the so-called land

---

[8] Conrad Weiser to Richard Peters July 20, 1747, *ibid.* (1st series), I, 761–62.

[9] Richard Peters was appointed secretary and clerk of the provincial council on June 6, 1747. See *Pennsylvania Colonial Records*, V, 68. The correspondence between Weiser and Peters is found in this volume and the *Pennsylvania Archives* (1st series), Vols. I and II.

[10] *Pennsylvania Colonial Records*, V, 293. The Governor was in constant trouble with the Quakers over the question of who was to dominate Indian affairs. See *New York Colonial Documents*, VI, 708; *Sir William Johnson Papers*, III, 940.

[11] "Indian Deed for Lands on the Delaware, 1737," *Pennsylvania Archives* (1st series), I, 541–43. The Indians ". . . . for large Quantities of Goods . . . ." bargained to sell this land, although the succeeding generations disputed the title of Pennsylvania for many years afterward.

"purchases," the provincial legislature appealed to the former for aid in pay-ing for the numerous presents to the Ohio tribes.[12] In answer, the Penn family stated that they felt no obligation toward contributing to such outlays because of the expenses that they already had incurred concerning Indian affairs. In all justice to the proprietaries, it must be noted that they did pay the salary of Conrad Weiser, the interpreter, and even supported his son and a tutor in order that the boy could live in the Indian country and learn the native language. Furthermore, the Penn family, as has been noted, did bear the charges for such cheap presents as were used in the "purchase" of land from the natives.[13]

Apparently the proprietaries believed that the large costs for presents incurred by the provincial government were somewhat impractical, espe-cially in view of French pressure on the Ohio frontier by the year 1751. In dismissing the request of the legislature for aid in financing gifts, the Penns asked that a fortified trading house be erected among the Ohio tribes as a measure of security.[14] This fort was to have thick walls of stone, protective bastions, and a cabin within the fortification. The proprietaries suggested that one of the leading Indian traders be appointed to command the fort, and he was to keep four to six men on duty. The cabin inside the fort was to serve as the storehouse for goods. It was estimated that £400 currency would cover the original construction costs, and £100 would be needed an-nually for upkeep.[15]

The assembly's answer to such a proposal was prompt and to the point. Isaac Norris, speaking for that august body, delivered the following words in justification of the policy of bestowing presents rather than building forts in order to attain the friendship of the Indians:

We have seriously considered the offer made by our Proprietaries of contributing toward building such a House; but as we have always found that sincere, upright Dealing with the Indians, a friendly Treatment of them on all occasions, and particularly in re-lieving their Necessities at proper Times by suitable Presents, have been the best means of securing their Friendship, we could wish our Proprietaries had rather thought fit to join us in Expence of those Presents, the Effects of which have at all Times so manifestly advanced their Interest with the Security of our Frontier Settlements.[16]

In the ensuing dispute over the building of a fort, Governor James

---

[12] *Pennsylvania Colonial Records*, V, 487.

[13] Some uncertainty exists as to whether the assembly or the proprietaries paid the salary of the interpreter. Apparently both contributed. See *ibid.*, V, 487, 546; *Penn-sylvania Archives* (1st series), II, 33.

[14] *Pennsylvania Colonial Records*, V, 546.

[15] *Ibid.*, V, 515. Despite the objections of the assembly to this fort, Croghan was asked to "feel out" the Indians on a project of this kind. See *ibid.*

[16] *Ibid.*, V, 547.

Hamilton was by no means neutral. Though not adverse to the use of donations to the Indians, the Governor, even as late as 1753, pleaded in vain for the erection of defensive forts.[17] Despite an eloquent appeal on the part of Hamilton, the house still "cheerfully" voted presents for Indian allies to the tune of £800, stating that a present was the best answer to the Indians; they held that it symbolized the peaceful intentions of their government. In further reviewing this dispute—although the time element reaches beyond the limits set in this chapter—it is interesting to note that Robert Hunter Morris, who succeeded Hamilton, was able to erect forts in the year 1756.[18] It is also noteworthy that during his administration the most devastating Indian attacks of the entire French and Indian War took place on the Pennsylvania frontier.[19] Thus, it would seem that presents, after all, were the best method of "dominating" the Indians. In short, it was a contest between ruling the Indians by friendship or by fear. In the long run the assembly lost out, but the settlers on the frontier paid for this change in policy with their very lives.

Another problem which perplexed the Quaker colony was the eternal series of disputes that arose between the Indians and private individuals. Conrad Weiser, veteran interpreter, threatened resignation unless the Indians received justice in these cases arising chiefly out of disputes between the natives and traders.[20] Weiser maintained that it was the duty of the province to give satisfaction to the Indians in the form of presents. He stated that ". . . . Rather than the poor Indians should be wronged, the public ought to make satisfaction, If not Reamedy [sic] can be found to prevent it." In the case of John Armstrong, who was murdered by tribesmen because he had cheated the natives,[21] Weiser actually defended the Indians. What on the surface appeared to be an outrage was merely the Indians' way of securing justice; and the interpreter reasoned that the murdered man had been warned, but his greed had made him ignore the handwriting on the wall.[22]

Weiser made persistent complaints regarding this case, pointing it out as an example of what might happen to others if justice were not done to the Indians. These complaints were not futile, and Richard Peters finally notified Weiser that at long last his efforts had been rewarded. The assembly had appointed Weiser as magistrate for a court to be held in Lancaster.

---

[17] *Pennsylvania Colonial Records*, V, 609. James Hamilton, who arrived as the new governor in 1748, took over executive affairs which had been cared for by Anthony Palmer, president of the council. See *ibid.*, V, 363–64. Colonel Thomas Lee in Virginia occupied the same position as Palmer while waiting for the arrival of Governor Robert Dinwiddie. See Lee's letters on Indian affairs in the *Journals of the Board of Trade*, IX, 82, 97.   [18] *Pennsylvania Archives* (1st series), II, 547.

[19] *Sir William Johnson Papers*, II, 446–47, 458.

[20] *Pennsylvania Archives* (1st series), I, 750–51, 761–62.

[21] *Ibid.*   [22] *Ibid.*, I, 751, 758–59.

Here presents were to be handed out to the Indians in order to satisfy injuries brought about by traders and other individuals.[23] The attorney general of the province was authorized to draw up indictments, with prosecutions to follow. Even though the defendants were proved innocent of cheating the Indians, the latter were to be paid regardless. It is remarkable, indeed, that Weiser was able to set up such a court of justice; a tribunal of this kind certainly was never paralleled in the other colonies.[24]

Mention should also be made of Weiser's influence in shaping the policy of Pennsylvania toward the council of the Six Nations at Onondaga. As is well known, these Six Nations were, and remnants of them still are, located mainly within the limits of present-day New York. Still, certain leaders of the various Iroquois tribes settled in the Ohio region;[25] and these Ohio Iroquois, called Mingoes, were within the reach of Pennsylvania's influential presents. However, the management of the Iroquois in the North had been left primarily to the colonies of New York and Massachusetts. Up to the year 1748, the Quaker province had always respected the wishes of the Onondaga council and had sent occasional presents to such influential sachems as Canasatego of the Onondaga tribe. In other words, during King George's War, Pennsylvania, with due decorum, observed the neutrality of the supreme council. This "detachment" does not hold for William Johnson, who represented New York, or for John Lydius, Indian agent for Massachusetts.

William Shirley, the dynamic governor of Massachusetts, wished to gain the financial support of the prosperous Quaker province to help pay the Indians who were working for both Johnson and Lydius. In 1747, Shirley wrote to Anthony Palmer, president of the Pennsylvania council, and acting executive until the arrival of James Hamilton, reporting in enthusiastic terms the success that Johnson and Lydius had achieved through inducing

---

[23] *Ibid.*, p. 771.

[24] Conrad Weiser discusses the crimes of two traders who cheated the Indians, namely, one John Powle and one James Dunning, in a report relating to Indian affairs. See *Pennsylvania Colonial Records*, V, 87–88. For an early act regulating traders see *Pennsylvania Archives* (1st series), I, 254–55. The traders were to give only enough rum to the Indians to "cheer" them after hunting.

[25] For the number of Iroquois and other tribes in the Ohio region Weiser's journal of 1748 gives exact information: "The Senecas 163, Shawonese 162, Owendaets 100, Tisagechroanu 40, Mohawks 74, Mohickons 15, Onondagers 35, Cajukas 20, Oneidos 15, Delawares 165, in all 789." Students of Indian history also point out that in the Southern department there were two more Iroquois tribes—the Tuscaroras (many of whom migrated North about 1722 to join the Five Nations, and thus make the Six Nations) and the Cherokees, related by language to the Iroquois (who never did migrate North). See *Pennsylvania Colonial Records*, V, 351. Also see *New York Colonial Documents*, VII, 883.

the Six Nations to go to war.[26] According to Shirley's figures, it cost from
£600 to £700, in New York currency, to equip one hundred warriors for a
war.[27] Furthermore, the Massachusetts executive stated that his colony had
expended a total of £7,000 for presents to raise the fighting spirit of the
Iroquois. This amount included all of the goods given to the Indians since
the beginning of King George's War.[28] Such a magnificent spirit on the part
of the Indians, Shirley argued, would ". . . . by the blessing of God prove
of unspeakable Benefit for the Safety of his Majesty's colonies in North
America."[29] For this reason he asked for Pennsylvania's immediate support.

Shirley's optimistic message was turned over to the council, and later to
the Pennsylvania lower house. This body, in turn, recommended that
Conrad Weiser be consulted.[30] Immediately Weiser set forth to confer with
his friend Shikalamy, the Oneida sachem at Shamokin, by the forks of the
Susquehanna.[31] After a prolonged consultation with the wise old sachem,
the interpreter informed the council of the following facts. First, the Onondaga Council did not approve of the actions of New York and Massachusetts
in giving presents to the Mohawks and other Iroquois warriors who were
raiding French settlements. Second, Shirley had been sadly misinformed.
As a matter of truth, only a few warriors were aiding the Mohawks in these
raids, not the whole confederacy as Shirley had been led to believe.[32] Third,
Weiser stated that Johnson and Lydius might lose their own "scalps" as a
result of having used such poor judgment as to go against the wishes of the
supreme council. In conclusion, the provincial interpreter stated that he

---

[26] *Pennsylvania Colonial Records*, V, 72–73; *Pennsylvania Archives* (1st series),
I, 746–47. William Shirley was much occupied with military affairs in preparation for
an invasion of Canada. This campaign no doubt took much of his time, possibly preventing him from being as well versed in Indian affairs as he might otherwise have been.
See *Pennsylvania Colonial Records*, V, 140–42.

[27] *Pennsylvania Archives* (1st series), I, 740–41. This evidence was in the form
of an extract of a letter from Colonel John Stoddard to William Shirley, dated May
13, 1747.

[28] *Ibid.*, I, 746–48.

[29] *Ibid.*

[30] *Pennsylvania Colonial Records*, V, 72–73. For a summary of the whole affair, see
ibid., V, 97.

[31] For the advice that Shikalamy gave to Weiser, the latter in return handed out
ten stroud matchcoats and twelve shirts. See *ibid.*, V, 85.

[32] Weiser apparently had respect for Shirley though he disliked Lydius. The interpreter said of the Massachusetts Governor: "I am sorry that Governour [*sic*] Shirly
[*sic*] is Deceived, but it is Like (although he is a Capable and Honest Gentleman,) he be-
lives [*sic*] what he wishes to be True, like the rest of our fellow Creatures." See *Pennsylvania Archives* (1st series), I, 761. There was, however, quite a bit of activity on the
part of the Mohawks and their brethren against the French. See *ibid.*, I, 756; *New York
Colonial Documents*, X, 84, 159.

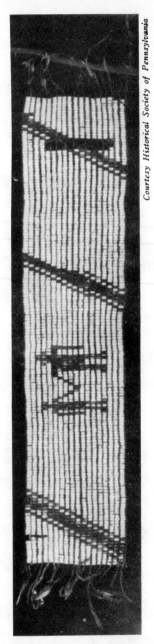

PENN WAMPUM BELT

thought that a whole shipload of merchandise would not induce the Onondaga council to go to war against the French, so highly did the Iroquois at this time regard their neutrality.[33]

As a logical consequence of Weiser's sage advice, the assemblymen, after carefully considering the matter, decided not to risk offending the Six Nations by sending bribes to the Mohawks or the "straggling fellows" who were aiding them.[34] Instead, they decided to offer a present to other Indian "friends" of Pennsylvania.

Conrad Weiser depended mostly upon his good friend Shikalamy for intelligence. This discerning old Indian had been the steadfast friend of the Quaker colony for many years.[35] Weiser had helped Pennsylvania workmen construct the "present" of a cabin at the sachem's home at Shamokin. This cabin, which had a shingle roof, was forty-nine feet long and seventeen feet wide.[36] Indeed, it became an automatic duty for Weiser to feed and clothe this sachem and his family. Periodically Shikalamy made the three-day journey to the interpreter's home,[37] where he and his sons loaded all the wheat meal they could carry on horses to be taken back to their settlement.[38] During the old man's frequent illnesses, Weiser was at his bedside, administering gifts of medicines which enabled the sachem to regain his lost strength.[39] For protection against the winter snows, the Pennsylvania government sent matchcoats, strouds, blankets, powder, and lead to keep Shikalamy and his large family alive.[40] In spite of this care, however, two of the sachem's sons died. At such times of mourning, condolence presents were always sent with expressions of sympathy.[41] Three of the sachem's sons survived their father, and one of these assumed his name and continued to rule at Shamokin.[42] At the death of the great old man, in 1749, once more strouds, matchcoats, wampum, shirts, and "sundry small things"

---

[33] *Pennsylvania Archives* (1st series), I, 761–62.

[34] *Ibid.*; *Pennsylvania Colonial Records*, V, 102.

[35] *Pennsylvania Archives* (1st series), II, 24–25.

[36] *Ibid.*, I, 661. The Moravian missionaries also made visits to Shamokin. See *ibid.*, I, 772; and for the journal of Count Zinzendorf who accompanied Weiser to Shamokin in 1742, see Reichel, *op. cit.*, Vol. I.

[37] Weiser's home was located just west of Reading, Pennsylvania. See *Pennsylvania Colonial Records*, V, 470; Paul H. W. Wallace, *Conrad Weiser, 1696–1760 Friend of Colonist and Mohawk*, p. 138, for a map of the Shamokin Trail.

[38] *Pennsylvania Archives* (1st series), I, 758.

[39] *Pennsylvania Colonial Records*, V, 136–37.

[40] *Ibid.*, V, 138.

[41] *Pennsylvania Archives* (1st series), II, 24. For the death of his son, Unhappy Jake, see *ibid.*, I, 655–56, and for the death of his son-in-law, see *Pennsylvania Colonial Records*, V, 13.

[42] Shikalamy's eldest son probably took his name. See *ibid.*, V, 213; VI, 420.

amounting to some fifteen pounds were sent to his children and grand-children to indicate the sorrow of the Quaker province.[43]

The Pennsylvania Assembly had sufficient reason to regret the death of their loyal friend. Shamokin had been the center of all news relating to the entire Iroquoian confederacy, and native express had even carried dispatches from distant Lake Erie to Shikalamy. When important news came, Shikalamy himself would journey to Weiser's home to deliver facts firsthand and to receive presents in return. In addition, the wise old sachem's advice on important issues had reached Richard Peters through Weiser's letters. Actually there is scarcely a letter pertaining to Indian affairs in which Weiser does not mention his dependence upon this old friend.[44]

Notwithstanding such loyalty, Weiser was not extravagant with his presents to the sachem, as William Johnson undoubtedly would have been. Though the old interpreter could hardly be called stingy, he took to Shamokin only the articles that his friend would need.[45] In comparison with William Johnson's outlays of gifts, however, Weiser's presents were indeed meager.[46] As a matter of fact, the assemblymen had such confidence in Weiser's frugality that they sought his advice concerning amounts that should be spent upon goods as well as the type of article needed for pres-ents. Although the interpreter's answer was usually a conservative esti-mate, it conformed with the situation at hand.[47]

An additional issue that frequently confronted both Weiser and the Pennsylvania government was the problem of delivering goods to the various Ohio tribes. From the government's standpoint, it was much easier to have the Indians come to designated places such as Philadelphia or Lancaster to claim their goods.[48] Here the Indians could be housed and entertained, and comfortable quarters could be had for the various Indian commissioners as well.[49] On the other hand, such an arrangement was not

---

[43] *Pennsylvania Archives* (1st series), II, 23–24.

[44] See Volumes IV and V of the *Pennsylvania Colonial Records* and *Pennsylvania Archives* (1st series), Vols I and II.

[45] *Ibid.*, I, 673.

[46] Weiser thought that William Johnson was too extravagant with presents. See *ibid.*, II, 45. For lists of Sir William Johnson's presents see *Sir William Johnson Papers*, Vols. I, II, and III.

[47] As an example see *Pennsylvania Archives* (1st series), I, 762, where Weiser considers a gift for the Lake Erie Indians.

[48] Lancaster was preferred by the Indians as a meeting place because of its location and the lack of sickness that so frequently visited the people of Philadelphia.

[49] Prominent colonial gentlemen were selected as Indian commissioners and could hardly be expected to undergo rigors of frontier life. Benjamin Franklin, William Fairfax of Virginia, Richard Peters, and William Byrd are examples. Franklin's

so agreeable to the natives. Many difficulties might arise. At one time, for example, three noted Iroquois men died during the journey to Philadelphia.[50] Often this city was dangerous to the health of the aborigines because of the prevalence of diseases during the "sickly season."[51] The physical handicap of age also had to be considered. Since it was the older men who were the sachems, it was they who would be required to make the long journeys; and often their health would not permit such exertions. In addition, the Indians found it difficult to carry their presents home. Thus, in spite of the heavy costs of transportation (costs that sometimes equalled the total outlay of the presents), it became the policy of Pennsylvania, as well as other colonies, to deliver the presents to the Indians.

Condolence gifts were always carried to mourning relatives. In 1750, however, the death of the influential Canasatego provided an exception to this rule. In view of the fact that a large present had already been given to the Six Nations in the previous year, the Pennsylvania government now merely sent Weiser northward with a message of condolence.[52] The legislature of the Quaker province felt that New York had reaped the benefit of the Six Nations' fur trade; therefore, it was only right that this province, instead of Pennsylvania, should bear the expense of any condolence present. Finally, however, under pressure from Governor Hamilton, the assembly did vote a £100 condolence present that was not ". . . . suitable to the importance of the occasion."[53]

Occasionally, when some other colony would "cover the dead" with gifts, Pennsylvania would evade the bestowing of presents; but the Quaker province never shirked offering presents when the responsibility truly rested upon that colony. Events in connection with the arrival of Governor James Hamilton, in 1749, illustrate the Quaker colony's policy of meeting her obligation of presents.[54]

When the Ohio Indians heard of the new Governor's arrival, small groups trekked to Philadelphia to congratulate him. As news of the movement of the Indians reached that city. Weiser was dispatched to tell the natives to return home.[55] Finding that he could not discourage the tribes-

---

interest in native politics prompted him to publish a series of treaties which have been edited by Carl Van Doren and Julian P. Boyd, entitled *Indian Treaties Printed by Benjamin Franklin, 1736–1762.*

[50] *Pennsylvania Colonial Records*, V, 475. The names of these noted Indians were Tocanihan, Caxhayion, and Soterwanachty.

[51] *Pennsylvania Colonial Records*, V, 299.

[52] *Ibid.*, V, 486–87.   [53] *New York Colonial Documents*, VI, 708.

[54] James Hamilton arrived on January 4, 1749. *Pennsylvania Colonial Records*, V, 367–68.

[55] *Ibid.*, V, 398. The Indians did some damage to Weiser's fields for which he was compensated. See *ibid.*, V, 396.

men's progress without offending them, Weiser communicated this news to Philadelphia. At first the assembly contented itself with voting a one-hundred-pound gift for the unwelcome Senecas. When the entire assemblage of natives had arrived, however, they were found to number 280, enough for a major conference. Having no alternative, the reluctant legislators had to vote an additional £500 for gifts.[56] As a result, happy Indians left the conference; their grievances had been satisfied; and they had accepted the Governor's gifts of strouds, duffles, halfthicks, vermilion, plain and ruffled shirts, guns, powder, lead, kettles, hatchets, knives, flints, awl blades, gartering ribbon, bed lace, scissors, earrings, stone rings, morris bells, brass thimbles, beads, brass jews'-harps, handkerchiefs, pipes, and tobacco.[57] Such articles illustrate the increasing dependence of the Ohio Indians upon manufactured goods.

Pennsylvania's merchants certainly must have profited by the constant purchase of this merchandise. Thus, it is not improbable that these merchants actually encouraged the giving of large presents. Thomas Lawrence, dealer in this type of merchandise, was, interestingly enough, a member of the upper house of the provincial legislature.[58] He was also one of the chief merchants who furnished George Croghan with merchandise.[59] In fact, in order to supply the traders with blankets and strouds, Lawrence had to have a great deal of goods on hand.

George Croghan was one who figured prominently in the Indian diplomacy of this period. Facing the competition of other traders. Croghan's orders for goods and French confiscations eventually forced him into financial ruin. Despite these factors, however, Croghan's trading organization, which included inland storehouses, many horses, and a variety of equipment and men, was the largest of its kind.[60] Of importance was

---

[56] *Pennsylvania Colonial Records*, V, 403. The Indians gave a present in return. See *ibid.*, V, 390.

[57] *Ibid.*, V, 406. It is interesting to know that Weiser carefully prepared notes for his speeches and made lists of which Indians received certain goods. See HM 3038; HM 3037; HM 3036. Weiser's writing is most difficult to read, while Croghan's letters are written in a beautiful hand. See HM 22453; Abercromby Papers 300, Henry E. Huntington Library. Hereafter cited as AB.

[58] For a list of the council members, see *Pennsylvania Colonial Records*, V, 306.

[59] See George Croghan to Thomas Lawrence, September 18, 1747, *Pennsylvania Archives* (1st series), I, 770–71. Many of the traders also bought goods from Edwin Shippen, another merchant. Weiser found his merchandise good for presents. See *ibid.*, I, 673. Later Shippen and Lawrence merged into one firm. A third partner was James Burd (1726–1793). For the activities of these men, see Thomas Balch (ed.), *Letters and Papers Relating Chiefly to the Provincial History of Pennsylvania*; Julian P. Boyd (ed.), *The Susquehanna Company Papers*, II.

[60] *Pennsylvania Colonial Records*, V, 294–95. Mention should be made of Professor Albert T. Volwiler's scholarly studies on George Croghan. See Albert T. Volwiler,

George Croghan's encampment at Pennsborough, five miles west of Harris' Ferry. After 1753 his home was at Aughwick, located at the confluence of Aughwick Creek and the Juanita River.[61] From this central location, the trader easily could transport presents in any direction. According to a distance computation made in 1754, Aughwick was some fifty miles, by road, from Carlisle.[62] A little over thirty-five miles to the west (a good day's journey) was the Indian town known as Shawnese Cabins.[63] From the Shawnese Cabins, Croghan needed only to travel westward to reach Shanoppin's Town and Logstown, both located near the forks of the Ohio River. Here Croghan was in the center of the major Indian settlements in the Ohio region.[64]

Since Croghan was an honest and trustworthy man, at least in Weiser's eyes, the trader was the logical person to transport presents.[65] As early as 1747, his men had been far out in the Lake Erie region, trading with the powerful tribes heretofore allied with the French. Knowledge gleaned from these activities caused Croghan, in 1747, to inform Richard Peters and his business partner, Thomas Lawrence, also a member of the council, of the need of ". . . . a Present of powder & Lead . . . ." to keep the friendship of these Lake Erie tribesmen.[66] After having received this news, the assembly appropriated ". . . . £30 or £40 . . . . in Powder Lead, &c., for a Present to go with Mr. Croghan, the Trader, to the Indians seated on Lake Erie."[67] Since no move relating to Indian affairs was made without Conrad Weiser's approbation, Richard Peters asked his advice on the matter. Immediately the provincial interpreter contacted Shikalamy so he could gain the latest information available concerning this new British Lake Erie ally. Then the amazing intelligence came through—some three hundred Indians allied to the Six Nations had cut off the French traders around Lake Erie![68]

The assembly decided to take no chances of losing the friendship of this powerful tribe, which might be forced back into the arms of the French.

George Croghan and the Westward Movement, 1741–1782; George Croghan and the Development of Central New York, 1763–1781, reprint from the *Quarterly Journal* of the New York State Historical Association for January 1923.

[61] See map in Wallace, *op. cit.*, p. 265.

[62] *Pennsylvania Colonial Records*, V, 750–51.

[63] Conrad Weiser frequently traveled thirty to thirty-five miles a day through the forest.

[64] *Pennsylvania Colonial Records*, V, 750–51.

[65] *Ibid.*, V, 518. Weiser stated that some of the traders distrusted Croghan but that he was satisfied with Croghan's honesty.

[66] *Pennsylvania Archives* (1st series), I, 742–43, 770.

[67] *Ibid.*, I, 748, 771.

[68] *Ibid.*, I, 750–51.

Furthermore, Weiser recommended that a "handsome present" be sent to these Indians.[69] Having determined to send the present, the assembly next had to decide on a method of transportation; but

. . . . since none were acquainted with the Indians or the Road to them but the Indian Traders, & there was a necessity to make use of them, it was therefore resolved that a Letter shou'd be wrote to Mr. Croghan, letting him know that the Council had determin'd to make a handsome Present to those Indians to the value of £200, that they wou'd bear the Expence of their Carriage to the Indian Country, & therefore that he wou'd provide a Waggon [sic] to carry them to Harris' Ferry, & Horses to carry them thence; and further, that he wou'd either go himself & take Charge of the Present & be answerable for the Delivery, or recommend some proper person.[70]

By October 1747, one of Croghan's teamsters had appeared for the goods, and the large present was on its way.

In the meantime, however, a delegation of the Canayiahaga Indians from the Lake Erie region had come to Philadelphia. As these delegates, and the Ohio Indians who accompanied them, were ignorant of the large present which had already been provided, they asked for arms because ". . . . the French have hard Heads, and that we have nothing strong enough to break them."[71] Thus, in order to please the delegates two additional presents of munitions and arms were given to the Indians. They were further informed that another assortment of goods, amounting to £850:15:3½, was to be delivered by Croghan, although it was temporarily stored at Harris' Ferry.[72] At this time, the government also promised that Weiser would visit the Ohio Indians, the Canayiahagas, and other Lake Erie tribes in the spring of 1748.

George Croghan, who had proceeded without Weiser, delivered the present in the spring of 1748. When the trader laid his bills before the assembly, the total charges for transportation, wages and food for the men, plus incidentals such as wampum and tobacco amounted to £55:5:0.[73] To the dismay of the legislators, however, Croghan's accounts included an additional £224:5:0. This sum represented personal goods that the trader had used to supplement the provincial gift. In justification of this expenditure, Croghan declared that he had found 1,500 natives in need of arms for

---

[69] *Pennsylvania Colonial Records*, V, 121–23.

[70] *Ibid.*

[71] *Ibid.*, V, 147. At times the Indian metaphorical manner of speaking was humorous, especially when the natives tried to emphasize an issue. The speech made by a representative of the Nantycoke tribe illustrates this point: "We speak in behalf of all our People, the old men and the old women, the young men and young women, the Children of both Sexes, and those who are yet in the belly." See *ibid.*, V, 544.

[72] *Ibid.*, V, 150–51.

[73] *Ibid.*, V, 294.

hunting purposes. Therefore, these natives had been given powder, lead, knives, flints, brass wire, and tobacco, though the last two items could hardly be construed as hunting implements.[74] In acknowledgment of these gifts, the Indians declared that they had 730 men of the Six Nations living on the Ohio and they would go to war at the bidding of Brother Onas (Pennsylvania). The colony's assembly, however, had no intention of making presents to encourage the Indians to go to war. The gifts were merely to be regarded as "necessaries" to "brighten the chain of friendship."[75]

Conrad Weiser did not accompany Croghan on his spring journey of 1748, to deliver the large present to the Ohio Iroquois and to the Canayiahaga tribesmen of the Lake Erie region. Weiser's attention was absorbed in the new developments of the Twightwee confederacy, which had made an application for alliance with the Iroquois and the Quaker colony. The Twightwees, often called the Miamis, were a powerful tribe with many fighting men. The possible friendship of this tribe, also located on the banks of Lake Erie, could not be overlooked.[76] So in July 1748 a conference at Lancaster was called with these Indians, presents were voted upon, and commissioners were appointed.[77]

This treaty was important for two reasons. First, the Twightwees, as recommended by the Six Nations, were to be inducted into an alliance— a move which greatly annoyed the French. Second, the Iroquois sachems also spoke on behalf of the Shawnees, bringing them back as friends, after they had deserted the British by accepting the gifts of Peter Chartier, a Frenchman.[78] Thus, a solidarity of friendship among many of the major Ohio tribes was brought about at this all-important treaty.[79] As a result, Pennsylvania's frontiers would continue to be peaceful though the Treaty of Aix-la-Chapelle, made in April 1748, would not be permanent.[80]

---

[74] *Ibid.*, V, 295. There was an additional carriage fee of £50 for taking the goods from Philadelphia to the Ohio.

[75] *Ibid.*, V, 185. The Virginia government consented to aid in the expense of this gift. See *ibid.*, V, 189–90, 221–22, 224.   [76] *Ibid.*, V, 299.

[77] *Ibid.*, V, 300. It was usually the custom for the assembly to call in Conrad Weiser who deliberated with the legislators on the amount and type of present to be given the Indians. See *ibid.*, V, 197. Thomas Lawrence and William and James Logan also helped in the purchase of goods. James Logan resigned from the council in 1747, and William was, in the same year, nominated to succeed him.

[78] See *Pennsylvania Archives* (1st series) II, 61.

[79] The Six Nations were thanked for their loyalty during the late war. The friendship of the Ohio Iroquois was a significant factor in keeping Pennsylvania's frontiers peaceful during King George's War.

[80] *Pennsylvania Colonial Records*, V, 331–32. Pennsylvania recognized the treaty on May 5, 1748.

At the Lancaster Treaty, the representatives of the Twightwees, Ciquenackqua, Assepausa, and Natoecqueha delegated their authority to Scarrooyady. (Scarrooyady is the same person previously referred to as Monacatoocha. These names are used interchangeably throughout this text, as they are found in the source material.) This Oneida sachem was residing in the Ohio region at this time.[81] The appearance of Scarrooyady as a representative of all the Ohio tribes on the Ohio frontier marked the beginning of a long and sincere friendship with the British. At this time, however, the Oneida sachem, who later became one of the eight Indian guides for Braddock, was injured in an unfortunate accident. Therefore, Andrew Montour replaced him as spokesman for the Indians, while Conrad Weiser represented the Pennsylvania commissioners.[82]

When Andrew Montour consented to speak for the Indians at the treaty in July 1748, he had already consulted with Scarrooyady in order that he might conform to the wishes of the tribesmen. Montour also had conferred with the provincial council a month previous to the treaty. At that time, Montour was introduced by Weiser as being ". . . . a Person who might be of Service to the Province in quality of an Indian Interpreter & Messenger. . . . " as he had been found ". . . . faithful, knowing, & prudent . . . ."[83] Because Montour had his home ". . . . amongst the Six Nations between the Branches of the Ohio and Lake Erie . . . ." he was in a key position to give needed information regarding the size and strength of the Twightwees.[84] Upon being informed of the "vast importance" of the Twightwee delegation, the council, acting on the strength of Montour's advice, had decided to treat with the Lake Erie Indians at Lancaster. Montour was paid for the expenses involved in this service to the council, and he was also asked to meet the Western native delegation at Logstown.[85]

Because Andrew Montour played such an important part in the distribution of presents during the entire French and Indian War it is relevant that a comment be made upon his appearance, talents, and ancestry. He was one of the most colorful of the frontier characters who appeared during the Anglo-French conflicts. When the German missionary, Count Zinzendorf, accompanied Weiser on a journey to Shamokin in 1742, the Count was impressed by the half-breed's unusual appearance. Writing in his journal, the missionary said that

Andrew's cast of countenance is decidedly European, and had not his face been encircled with a broad band of paint, applied with bear's fat, I would certainly have taken him

---

[81] *Supra*, note 5.

[82] The commissioners were Benjamin Shoemaker, Thomas Hopkinson, Joseph Turner, and William Logan. See *ibid.*, V, 307.

[83] *Ibid.*, V, 290–91.   [84] *Ibid.*

[85] Montour knew these delegates personally. See *ibid.*

for one. He wore a brown broadcloth coat, a scarlet damasken lappel-waistcoat, breeches, over which his shirt hung, a black Cordovan neckerchief, decked with silver bubles, shoes and stockings and a hat. His ears were hung with pendants of brass and other wires plaited together like the handle of a basket.[86]

Montour's appearance was extraordinary, to say the least; but the headmen among the Six Nations regarded him as their brother, and the native sachems placed a great deal of confidence in him. This made Montour an invaluable agent for allotting presents. During the course of his relations with the whites, he also gained their confidence. Important colonials such as Conrad Weiser, the Maryland trader Thomas Cresap, George Croghan, Robert Dinwiddie, and Sir William Johnson placed great trust in Montour. Johnson even employed him as an officer in the Northern Department of Indian Affairs.[87] Andrew Montour's rare talents as a linguist were needed wherever presents were handed out. Besides being proficient both in French and English, he had a wide knowledge of Indian languages.[88] Honest interpreters were rare, and those with Montour's linguistic abilities were few and far between.

Following the example of his famous mother, Madam Montour, who received presents for her services as an interpreter, Andrew, too, sought compensation for his duties.[89] In return for his actions at the Lancaster conference, Montour had already asked that the government of Pennsylvania build him a house and ". . . . furnish his family with necessarys [sic] . . . ."[90] Such demands seemed very extravagant to the conservative Weiser. Montour's work at the Treaty of Lancaster marked the beginning of an active career as an agent for the British colonies. This career was later rewarded by donations of valuable lands.

According to the minutes of the Lancaster conference, all went in

---

[86] Reichel, *op. cit.*, I, 95–96. It is noteworthy that the Count was impressed with the warm personality of Montour. This is no doubt the reason why he was so popular with the Indians as well as with the provincials. Croghan at one time stated that Montour was not too adept at business, and Weiser thought that the half-breed was too bold in asking for such high wages.

[87] For an example of Montour's work under Johnson, see George Croghan to William Johnson, December 3, 1757, LO 4940. For Thomas Cresap's recommendation of Montour, see Palmer, *op. cit.*, I, 245–47. The half-breed's Indian name was Eghnisara; for a glowing account of the confidence that the Indians placed in Montour, see "Journal of the Virginia Commissioners at the Treaty of Logstown, May, 1752," *Virginia Magazine of History and Biography*, XIII (October 1905), 154–74.

[88] Reichel, *op. cit.*, pp. 96–98.

[89] There is some question as to whether Madam Montour was Canadian or Indian. Some accounts state that she married a Canadian, while others state that she was the wife of an Iroquois chief.

[90] *Pennsylvania Archives* (1st series), II, 12.

accordance with previously laid plans. Montour's diplomatic speeches, combined with the soothing effect of Pennsylvania's presents, brought about the needed Twightwee alliance. The Lake Erie Indians and the commissioners made mutual presents to each other and smoked the calumet pipe as the sacred seal of friendship.[91] The Pennsylvania government's acceptance of the calumet pipe as a gift from the Twightwees was an ancient custom which made agreements valid and cemented alliances.[92] The Western Indians bestowed a present of deerskins, amounting to £39:2:8, as further evidence of their sincerity. In return, the province gave a total of £189:0:0 worth of goods to the tribesmen. George Croghan sold the merchandise for this gift to Weiser who complained that the charges were too high.[93] Even more noteworthy was the fact that additional expensive outlays were made so that medical attention might be given to those native delegates who became sick.

Yet more donations of matchcoats, shirts, knives, and powder had to be handed out to the Mingoes who had guided their Western allies to the conference. Weiser, in exasperation, completed this total outlay of merchandise by giving some seventy-five pounds of powder to the Nantycoke Indians, who merely came along in order to get a reward in goods. These poor natives ". . . . stood and looked very dull, because they got nothing," but their faces lifted when they received a gratuity.[94]

Following the Lancaster Treaty Conrad Weiser, aided by George Croghan and Andrew Montour, made a belated journey to the Ohio, loaded down with presents. Weiser inquired about the actions of the French, and he soothed the frightened Shawnees, Owendats, Delawares, and Mingoes as best he could with "civil and brotherly" presents from the Quaker province.[95] The provincial interpreter's journal bristles with stories of his twenty- to thirty-mile daily journeys along the old Allegheny Path. Over a period of two months, covering the period from August to September 1748, during which time he went over the "Allegheny hill" and onward to Logstown, Weiser handed out strouds, shirts, and thousands of wampum beads. In addition, he left presents for the "council bag" of two key Indian sachems, Half King and Scaiohady.[96] These donations of strouds, powder,

---

[91] *Pennsylvania Colonial Records*, V, 317. The commissioners and the Twightwees smoked the calumet, which was given to the former as part of the actual contract of alliance. It is also noteworthy that the commissioners explained to the Indians that the white man's treaties were signed in writing.

[92] *Ibid.*, V, 313.　　[93] *Pennsylvania Archives* (1st series), II, 11–12.　　[94] *Ibid.*

[95] See Weiser's journal in *Pennsylvania Colonial Records*, V, 348–58, covering the period from August to September, 1748.

[96] *Ibid.*, p. 358. Scaiohady is not to be confused with Scarrooyady (also called Monacatoocha and Half King) or Half King (Tanacharisson). See notes 4 and 5.

knives, and vermilion were to be handed out later at the discretion of the two sachems, long friends of Brother Onas.

Weiser's actions and the new alliance with the Twightwees at the conference of Lancaster were not to go unchallenged by the French, however. By June 1749, the French governor general had sent one of his most capable officers to distribute gifts to the Ohio and Lake Erie Indians and to assert French ownership of the Ohio Valley. Céloron de Blainville,[97] who was in charge of this expedition, had commanded several French forts; and he had a long and brilliant record in handling refractory Indians. He had even dealt with the Chickasaws in 1739.[98] To aid him in bestowing presents, Céloron procured the help of the alert Philip Thomas Joncaire, past master in the art of using goods to inveigle the natives to accept the French point of view.[99]

Céloron's party traveled south down the St. Lawrence River, passed the picket fort of Abbé Piquet, and reached Fort Niagara by July 1749. From this point, the party moved swiftly southward, burying lead plates at strategic locations along the way.[100] The Senecas, curious about the "piece of writing" on the plates, dug up one which had been buried along the Ohio River, and sent it to the Cayugas. The Cayuga sachems, at a conference held in 1750, made William Johnson a present of this ". . . . leaden Square Plate."[101] When translated, the substance of the inscription on this extraordinary "gift" stated that France, by virtue of force of arms and the treaties of Ryswick, Utrecht, and Aix-la-Chapelle, took possession of the Ohio Valley.[102]

Céloron pushed southwest, continuing to deposit his lead plates. When he arrived at Logstown, he made a large present to the Mingoes and to other tribes which were in attendance. It seems that Céloron attempted to use his presents of goods to overcome the Ohio Indians' objection to the high rates charged by French fur traders.[103] However, the Indians showed so much hostility on this point that Philip Thomas Joncaire frequently

---

[97] *Vide*, chapter ii. Céloron's last name was also spelled Bienville.

[98] "Report of M. Boisherbert on Indian Affairs," November 1747, *New York Colonial Documents*, X, 84.

[99] See Céloron's journal in the *Wisconsin Historical Collections*, XVIII, 36-37. Philip Thomas Joncaire is not to be confused with his brother Daniel. See *New York Colonial Documents*, X, 38-75, for an account of their activities.

[100] For example, Céloron buried one plate at the River Le Boeuf, at the site of present-day Franklin, Pennsylvania. See *Wisconsin Historical Collections*, XVIII, 40.

[101] *Pennsylvania Colonial Records*, V, 508.

[102] For an exact translation of the inscription on the plate, see *ibid.*, V, 510-11.

[103] *Wisconsin Historical Collections*, XVIII, 42-43. Céloron wrote a letter of protest to Governor James Hamilton regarding the Pennsylvania traders. See *Pennsylvania Colonial Records*, V, 508.

had to go ahead to soothe the natives in preparation for the commander's gifts. Finally, in August 1749, the party arrived at the mouth of the White River, headquarters of the main Miami towns. After the preliminary greetings, the Indians gave supper to their French visitors, even though a shortage of food existed. Afterward all smoked the calumet.[104]

After leaving these friendly Miamis, the French party moved northward toward their main objective, the village which was called Twightwee Town or Pickawillany, located on the west side of the Great Miami River. This village, which was under the leadership of the bold sachem, Old Briton (or La Demoiselle) had been the center of rebellion during the year 1747; and the French were well aware of the fact that English wampum belts had been officially accepted by this rebel.[105] Knowing that Old Briton was conspiring to assassinate their officers, the French government still tried to keep the allegiance of the sachem's obstreperous tribesmen by distributing expensive presents.

For purposes of clarification, it must be noted that there were three branches of the Miamis. In the 1740's, La Demoiselle's tribe on the Great Miami had left the main segment of the confederacy under Le Pied Froid, who was the head sachem.[106] By means of presents, the French commandants both at Fort Miami and Detroit managed to keep Le Pied Froid under their control. Unfortunately for the French, however, the dynamic La Demoiselle refused to heed their gifts; even worse, he was successfully using gifts of wampum belts to corrupt the third branch of the Miamis, who were located on the Tippecanoe River.[107] The French were greatly enraged because Le Gris, the young chief of the Tippecanoe Miamis, had received several valuable gifts from the commandant at Detroit; then he had the effrontery to wear one of the French king's medals that he had received in token of alliance![108]

In view of this situation, it is no wonder that Céloron gave La Demoiselle "magnificent presents" in an effort to get him to return to Le Pied Froid and his old village.[109] Offering branches of porcelain[110] as he spoke, the French commander pleaded with Old Briton to cease trading with the

---

[104] *Wisconsin Historical Collections*, XVIII, 48–49.

[105] "Occurrences in Canada During the Year 1747–1748," *New York Colonial Documents*, X, 139.

[106] Captain Charles de Raymond to La Jonquière, October 11, 1749, *Illinois on the Eve of the Seven Years' War*, pp. 120–21.

[107] *Ibid.*

[108] *Ibid.*

[109] *Wisconsin Historical Collections*, XVIII, 50.

[110] Céloron refers to what the English called a string of wampum. *Vide*, chapter i, for a discussion on "strings" as they differed from "belts."

English and to notify them that the British traders were no longer welcome. Following Céloron's speech, the sly La Demoiselle retired to his quarters with the French presents. On the next day, the sachem, with every appearance of sincere friendship, smoked the traditional calumet with his visitor and promised friendship with Father Ontontio, the French governor.[111] After this conference Céloron shrewdly guessed that he could not trust Old Briton, and he carefully examined the old men in the camp. The suspicions of the French commander were justified when he talked to Le Pied Froid, the head Miami sachem, ten days later at Fort Miami (called Kiskokou by the French).[112]

Céloron had hardly vanished from the scene before Governor-General La Jonquière was bombarded with a series of communications from Charles Raymond, commandant at Fort Miami, telling of the dangerous symbolic gifts being made by La Demoiselle. Secret flags, belts, pipes, strings of red wampum, and blankets of red and black cloth were being carried to all the tribes of the Miami confederacy.[113] A general conspiracy was afoot!

British traders were now sweeping some eighty Ohio and Lake Erie villages with forty horse loads of goods at a time. Seeking to halt this flow of British gifts, the French Governor-General again resorted to the use of presents.[114] He sent Louis Coulon de Villiers[115] to the Miami post to replace the excited Raymond. Instructions for Sieur de Villiers stated that as a last resort in his effort to bring the rebellion to a close, he was to give Le Gris, Le Pied Froid, and La Demoiselle a "complete chief's costume." These instructions further ordered Villiers to see that La Demoiselle left his village and returned to his old settlement. The French fear of La Demoiselle was revealed in the orders which declared that young Le Gris and Le Pied Froid were to guide Villiers safely to see the rebellious chieftain. Villiers was to promise La Demoiselle that the Governor-General would send goods for all his needs.[116] Thus the French hoped to halt the rebellion. Notwithstanding all of these presents—and promises of still more presents—La Demoiselle continued to be faithful to the alliance

---

[111] *Wisconsin Historical Collections*, XVIII, 53–54.

[112] *Ibid.*, XVIII, 56. Céloron made his way to Canada by way of Detroit, Fort Frontenac, and Montreal.

[113] Charles Raymond to La Jonquière, September 4, 1749, *Illinois on the Eve of the Seven Years' War*, pp. 105–6; same to same, September 5, 1749, *ibid.*, pp. 109–10; same to same, October 11, 1749, *ibid.*, pp. 120–21.

[114] Instructions for Sieur de Villiers from La Jonquière, July 10, 1750, *ibid.*, pp. 218–19.

[115] Louis Coulon de Villiers was commonly known as Sieur de Villiers. He is not to be confused with his brothers François, Joseph (Jumonville), and Nicholas. For a clarification on this family, see *ibid.*, pp. xxxii–xxxiv.

[116] *Supra,* note 114.

made with Pennsylvania in 1748. Realizing that any peaceful settlement was out of the question, Jonquière, even as early as October 1751, began secret plans to destroy Pickawillany, and drive out the Pennsylvania traders.[117]

The temporary peace of Aix-la-Chapelle in April 1748 had brought a lull in Pennsylvania's gifts; by 1750, however, the Twightwees once more were visiting Croghan at Aughwick. Using the plea that the French were conspiring to strike them, the Twightwees secured the promise of the Quaker assembly to give them guns, powder, and lead to be used for defensive purposes.[118] Moreover, Hugh Crawford, a trader from Pickawillany, brought word from La Demoiselle that he had refused a large French gift of powder, bullets, bags of paint, needles, and thread. Fearing the worst, the Miami tribesmen had left the goods scattered about, not even picking them up.[119] In addition, the Miamis sent wampum to confirm their message to Pennsylvania, a message which signified a friendship that ". . . . would last whilst the Sun and Moon ran round the World." Shortly after receiving this letter and other intelligence, the Quaker colony finally sent a present to the Miamis.[120]

Faced with the problem of keeping the Ohio Indians in a good humor by protecting their lands from encroaching settlers, the assembly was apt to forget the more distant Twightwees.[121] During this time, the death of Shikalamy focused the attention of Weiser and the legislators upon condolence presents. Still, the assembly found time to vote offerings to the Mingoes for their loyalty during the late war.[122] Subsequently, however, intelligence received from William Johnson, the Western traders, and the Ohio Indians forced the assembly to fix its attention upon the plight of their most loyal friends, the Miamis. News came that the ever active Joncaire was on the Ohio, giving valuable presents to any influential Indians who would accept them.[123] Moreover, when Conrad Weiser returned from Onondaga, he told of the many expensive clothes that were literally lavished upon the Iroquois by the French priests. The crowning blow of all, however, was the testimony of the Pickawillany traders who had been captured by the French. These men related how the French at Detroit gave presents of tobacco to any Indian who would capture Eng-

---

[117] La Jonquière to Céloron, October 1, 1751, *Illinois on the Eve of the Seven Years' War*, p. 384; La Jonquière to Rouille, October 27, 1751, *ibid.*, p. 421.

[118] *Pennsylvania Colonial Records*, V, 436.

[119] *Ibid.*, V, 437.

[120] *Ibid.*, V, 463.

[121] *Ibid.*, V, 441.

[122] *Ibid.*, V, 447.

[123] *Ibid.*, V, 463.

lish traders.[124] John Frazier, a trader who had escaped after undergoing this experience, charged the French with offering a present of one thousand dollars to any Indian who would get the scalp of either George Croghan or James Lowry, another Pennsylvania trader.[125] In his testimony Frazier further related that Joncaire had a present worth £1,500, which he was recklessly using to debauch the Ohio Indians.

With this information at hand, James Hamilton thundered at the penny-pinching assembly in an effort to get a worth-while present for the Twight-wees and their allies. In answer, the recalcitrant legislators stubbornly pointed out that it was they, and not the neighboring colonies, who were bearing the expense of these gifts.[126] Isaac Norris, the speaker, declared that the assembly would vote one more gift for the Miamis and their Ohio allies; but he urged that the proprietaries again be petitioned to share in this outlay. In consequence of this decision, Montour and Croghan were notified to prepare to take the goods westward in the spring of 1751.[127]

What a present it was! Transportation costs alone were estimated at two hundred fifty pounds, while the total cost of the goods amounted to seven hundred pounds.[128] The careful instructions given to Croghan and Montour reveal the legislators' concern over the outcome of their huge financial investment. Some of these instructions follow. Part of the present could be given to sachems who aided in the speeches, but they must stick to the subject, lest the policy of the assembly be misunderstood. Croghan was cautioned to use prudence and skill in proffering the bequest so that the goods would have an effect in strengthening previous alliances.[129] As might be expected, separate speeches to each of the Ohio tribes and the Twightwees were written out previously and included in the instructions. Montour was ordered to make himself "master" of these speeches so that he could express in detail the will of the assembly. Finally, the agents were told to accept as allies two more Miami tribes, the Waugh-haughtanneys and the Pyankeskees.[130]

It is at this time that presents from the colony of Virginia enter the scene of action. As far back as the spring of 1748, under pressure from the Quaker assembly, Governor William Gooch had secured an appropriation

---

[124] *Ibid.*, pp. 482–83. Céloron captured several traders at a later date. See *Wisconsin Historical Collections*, XVIII, 112.

[125] *Pennsylvania Colonial Records*, V, 482–83. See *Pennsylvania Archives* (1st series), II, 14, for a list of Pennsylvania traders active in 1748.

[126] *Pennsylvania Colonial Records*, V, 486–87.

[127] *Ibid.*, V, 488.

[128] *Ibid.*, V, 498, 519.

[129] *Ibid.*, V, 519.

[130] *Ibid.*, V, 520.

to supplement the large present to the Ohio and Lake Erie Indians.[131] It must be remembered that Virginia's interest in Ohio Indian affairs dated back to the treaty at Lancaster in 1744. At this time the Iroquois in return for presents, had acknowledged the right of Virginia colonists to use the lands that settlers had previously occupied.[132] It was at this time also that the Virginia commissioners came to appreciate the importance of the Onondaga sachem Canasatego, who was one of the chief representatives of the Six Nations at this treaty. Thus it was that Conrad Weiser acted on behalf of the province of Virginia, rather than Pennsylvania, when he carried wampum for the condolence of Canasatego's relatives after his death in 1750.[133]

The colony of Virginia had a special reason for obtaining the friendship of the Western Indians. In the fall of 1750, Virginia, on behalf of the Ohio Company, an ambitious land project headed by a number of distinguished gentlemen, [134] was interested in purchasing lands from the Ohio Indians.[135] It was for this reason, apparently, that Colonel Thomas Lee, president of the Virginia council and a member of the Ohio Company, had taken a great interest in native politics.[136] Christopher Gist, the Maryland surveyor, and an able frontiersman, was employed to prepare the way for the proposed occupation of Indian lands. Gist was to explore the area of the Ohio Company's land grant and to invite the Indians to come to Logstown to receive a present. Upon his arrival in Logstown on November 25, 1750, the Marylander found the Indians to be hostile; they feared that he had come to take their lands.[137]

Handicapped by his lack of ability to speak Indian languages, Gist joined George Croghan and Andrew Montour, who were delivering a small present to the Twightwees at Pickawillany in preparation for a large Pennsylvania conference to be held at Logstown in the spring of 1751.[138] Thus

---

[131] *Pennsylvania Colonial Records,* V, 224.

[132] See *Indian Treaties Printed by Benjamin Franklin,* pp. 43, 49; *Pennsylvania Archives* (1st series), I, 656–58.

[133] See Conrad Weiser's journal to Onondaga, *Pennsylvania Colonial Records,* V, 470–80.

[134] See the scholarly study on the Ohio Company, Kenneth P. Bailey, *The Ohio Company of Virginia and the Westward Movement 1748–1792. A Chapter in the History of the Westward Movement,* pp. 33–61, for a discussion on the personnel of the company.

[135] Colonel Thomas Lee to the Board of Trade, October 18, 1749, *Journals of the Board of Trade,* IX, 97.   [136] *Ibid.,* IX, 82, 97.

[137] William M. Darlington (ed), *Christopher Gist's Journals with Historical, Geographical, and Ethnological Notes and Biographies of his Contemporaries,* pp. 34–35.

[138] *Ibid.,* pp. 34–35, 45. Hamilton sent Croghan and Montour with a present for the Miamis as an emergency measure against the French. This was done before the assembly voted the large present. See *Pennsylvania Colonial Records,* V, 485.

the Virginia agent had protection as he accompanied the Pennsylvania agents through the villages of the Delawares, Shawnees, Wyandots, finally arriving at the Twightwee village of Old Briton.[139] Gist had apparently been in great danger from the French before he had joined the company of Croghan and Montour. In renewed efforts to ally the Indians, Philip Thomas Joncaire had been sent southward with five canoes of presents, which he was handing out to the Ohio tribes.[140]

Upon the return of Croghan and Montour in the spring of 1751, Gist left his guides and returned to Virginia to relate his success in preparing for the Virginia treaty with the Indians. This meeting was planned for 1752, and was to be held at Logstown. In the meanwhile, Croghan and his half-breed companion had been given complete charge of the £700 gift to be distributed at this Indian town. Weiser was absent because there was no treaty to be made with the Indians. Thus all matters were left to Croghan and Montour.[141]

Although these two gentlemen had only to deliver the provincial gift to the Twightwee delegates and their allies on the Ohio, the interpreters were handicapped at every turn by the presence of Joncaire. Nevertheless, Croghan was equal to the situation; and despite the actions of the Frenchman, he allotted preliminary favors of strouds, matchcoats, and stockings to the head tribesmen.[142] Later, the orations of Montour were so effective, especially when accompanied by gifts, that the Indians severely reproached Joncaire.[143] Although Croghan does not indicate any humor in his journal, it must have been a most unusual sight to see the tribesmen dancing around the outwitted Frenchman, pointing their fingers to his nose. Anxious to follow up the diplomatic defeat of Joncaire by not overlooking any opportunity of pleasing the Indians, Croghan had their guns, kettles, and hatchets mended.[144]

What complete success the resourceful Croghan had in delivering the £700 gift is revealed in his enthusiastic comments to Governor Hamilton.

I took all the Pains I could to make the Present have its full Force and Weight with the Indians, and I have the Pleasure of assuring your Honour [James Hamilton] that the Indians were all unanimously pleased at your Honour's Speeches, and likewise acknowledged it was a great Present . . . .[145]

In addition, the trader told how the sachems of the Six Nations had aided

139 *Ibid.*, V, 522–24; Darlington, *op. cit.*, pp. 49–50.

140 *Pennsylvania Colonial Records*, V, 497.

141 *Ibid.*, V, 517–18.

142 *Early Western Travels*, I, 58–69. Herein is contained Croghan's journal.

143 *Ibid.*

144 *Ibid.*

145 *Pennsylvania Colonial Records*, V, 539.

him in dividing the goods so that each tribesman was fully satisfied with his share. Such complete victory over the French, and the Indians' open declaration of their contempt for the Canadians set the stage for the Virginia conference called by Christopher Gist in 1752.

Despite these British diplomatic victories, however, the French were not to be underestimated. They were still active. For instance, before the Twightwees had time to accept another present, a swift force of Canadians and Indians swept down upon La Demoiselle in June 1752 and destroyed his entire village. Not content with wreaking this vengeance, the raiders boiled the famous Miami chief and ate him before the very eyes of his confederates.[146]

In exasperation, the French had finally resorted to violence to stop the flow of British presents. In part, they were successful; but this massacre at Pickawillany culminated the period of peaceful competition for native allegiance which dominated the Ohio Valley from the last peace in 1748 to the year 1751. From this time forward, the gifts were to be used for securing warriors in preparation for the eventual conflict. Presents to the Indians had helped to crystallize the conflict between the British and the French.

---

[146] *Supra*, note 1.

VII. PRELUDE TO THE FRENCH AND INDIAN WAR, 1752–1754

Anglo-French competition in giving presents to the Iroquois and their allies had been carried on peacefully from the time of the Treaty of Aix-la-Chapelle in 1748 through the year 1751. From this time on, however, certain events transpired to bring to an end this period of peaceful competition. A new governor, Robert Dinwiddie, energetically took over the reins of leadership for the colony of Virginia and made extensive plans for new treaties and presents for the Ohio tribes.[1] Furthermore, the Ohio Company's far-reaching scheme for the settlement of Western lands became a part of Virginia's plan for the "purchasing" of native lands with gifts of merchandise. These factors combined with the activities of the traders to bring increasing pressure upon the French.[2] As a result, the French, with their backs against the wall, were forced to use more aggressive measures in dealing with the Indians.

This period of force began with the fall of Pickawillany in June 1752, and ended with the capitulation of Washington at Fort Necessity in July 1754.[3] Violence began this era in the contest for the control of the New World—violence which finally resulted in the Seven Years' War. From the beginning to the end of the period, huge British gifts of textiles, hardware, and munitions were poured upon the Ohio Iroquois and their confederates. The French, on the other hand, unable to compete with such large gifts, simply resorted to force as a method of subduing the Indians—and not without success.

The first step necessary to restore French prestige among the Ohio Indians and those of Lake Erie was to crush the budding British-Miami alliance. According to the enthusiastic reports of Robert Dinwiddie, the new lieutenant governor of Virginia, the Miamis (called Twightwees by the English) were a vast confederacy capable of mustering ten thousand fighting men.[4] In 1748, at Lancaster, the Twightwees had consummated

---

[1] For a scholarly study on Robert Dinwiddie, see Louis Knott Koontz, *Robert Dinwiddie, His Career in American Colonial Government and Westward Expansion.* Dinwiddie's activities in connection with the Ohio Company are well covered in Kenneth P. Bailey, *The Ohio Company of Virginia and the Westward Movement 1748–1792. A Chapter in the History of the Colonial American Frontier.*

[2] See *Wisconsin Historical Collections*, XVIII, 114.

[3] For an account of the terms of the capitulation see *Pennsylvania Archives* (1st series), II, 146–47.

[4] Robert Dinwiddie to the Board of Trade, October 5, 1752, P.R.O., C.O., 5/1327,

an alliance with the British; and by the early part of 1752, La Demoiselle openly declared that he was against the French and for the British alliance.[5] French representatives along the Ohio stated that by 1752 all the Indians along what they called the Beautiful River were sympathetic to the English. In fact, it had become dangerous for the French even to venture near Pickawillany. The French had found this situation to be true when two soldiers were scalped for their carelessness in exposing themselves near the Twightwee town.[6] Such was the state of affairs that had been brought about by the factor of British goods being handed out competitively as gifts and being utilized as articles of trade.

A French attack upon Pickawillany would have a twofold significance. Valuable British goods could be confiscated and La Demoiselle's Indian village could be eliminated as a center of conspiracy.[7] Even as the trader William Trent tramped over the dry stream beds during the summer's heat of 1752 to bring a present of goods to Old Briton's village, the French decided to act. Virginia's present reached Pickawillany, but Old Briton was not alive to receive it. The astute French had deceived the Twightwees by bestowing on them a French coat and some wampum as a token of good will.[8] Then, after the natives had relaxed their vigilance and the majority of the warriors had gone out hunting, a force of two hundred forty French and Indians swooped down upon the defenseless village on June 21, 1752.

The attacking party of French Indians had received a present of two belts of wampum from the governor of Canada and instructions to confiscate English goods and to kill the Indians allied with the English; but they were told not to murder the English traders if this could be avoided. These instructions were observed in part. In their plundering after the victory, however, the attacking Algonquian Indians exhibited great savagery.[9]

L.C. 383–86, C.O. 497–502. For Andrew Montour's estimate of the importance of the Twightwees, see Palmer, *op. cit.*, I, 245–47.

[5] For the Treaty of Lancaster in 1748, see *Indian Treaties Printed by Benjamin Franklin*, pp. 109, 113, 122. For the state of the Twightwee alliance in 1752, see *Wisconsin Historial Collections*, XVIII, 104.

[6] *Ibid.*, XVIII, 110.

[7] One of the main objectives of the French offensive was to confiscate British Indian goods. See Minister to Duquesne, May 15, 1752, *ibid.*, XVIII, 121.

[8] Twightwees to Robert Dinwiddie, June 21, 1752, P.R.O., C.O., 5/1327, L.C. 449–50, C.O. 561–62.

[9] The brutality of the French Indians showed that the French either were unmindful of such conduct or unable to control their savage allies. Only two of the traders escaped, namely Thomas Burney and Andrew McBryer. See the journal of William Trent, June 21, 1752, P.R.O., C.O., 5/1327, L.C. 431–47, C.O. 549–69. Fourteen of the Indians were killed and only one trader was wounded. The attacking Indians fell upon

When William Trent arrived, he found the village in deep mourning; Old Briton, the Piankashaw "king," had been boiled and eaten only a few yards away from the settlement.

As an expression of the sympathy of the Virginia government, Trent bestowed a scarlet cloak upon Old Briton's young son. A complete outfit of clothes was prepared and presented to the widow of the slain chief. In distributing the remainder of the goods, Trent allotted hats, shirts, stockings, and jackets to the young Piankashaw "king," to the Turtle or Musheguanockgue, and to two other Twightwee leaders.[10]

William Trent expected an Iroquois declaration of war as a result of this massacre.[11] Even the *Maryland Gazette* reported that the Six Nations were exasperated and that those tribes living on the Ohio had declared war on the attacking French Indians, vowing not to leave one of them alive. Tomahawks and black wampum were passed among the Indians, and nothing was heard but talk of "blood and revenge."[12] Despite such rumors, however, the Iroquois did not declare war. Thus the French had successfully punished the rebellious Twightwees.

After receiving the sad news of the massacre from Thomas Burney, one of the two traders who escaped from Pickawillany, both Virginia and Pennsylvania made condolence presents to their faithful allies. When Robert Dinwiddie received this "intelligence," which was confirmed by William Trent's journal, the Virginia Governor immediately wrote to the Board of Trade. Enclosing a tentative list of goods to be used as presents and a copy of Trent's journal, he pleaded the urgency of appropriating money from quit-rents to cover the costs of gifts.[13] The Virginia Governor gave the ordering of presents the same attention that characterized this administration in other matters. This is illustrated in his "Sketch of goods suitable for a Present."[14] Here proportions of each item, from strouds and halfthicks to bed lace and linens, were specified. True to his Scot ancestry, Dinwiddie even divided

---

the trader, stabbed him, scalped him, and, according to the best accounts, ate his heart. See *ibid.* The traders who were captured were carried to Canada and later to France, where they were released and sent to England. For a reference regarding the traders, see *Pennsylvania Colonial Records*, V, 600–601. Charles Sieur de Langlade, who led the attack, had great influence among the Canadian Indians and married a native woman. See *Wisconsin Historical Collections*, XVIII, 128–31.

[10] *Supra*, the journal of William Trent, note 9.

[11] Draper MSS, W.S.H.S. Nos. 1 JJ 3–1 JJ 6 (photostat).

[12] See the *Maryland Gazette*, November 9, 1752, Draper MSS, No. 1 JJ 1–1 JJ 2 (photostat).

[13] Robert Dinwiddie to the Board of Trade, December 10, 1752, P.R.O., C.O., 5/1327, L.C. 415–24, C.O. 531–36.

[14] "Sketch of Goods Suitable as a Present for the Indians," December 10, 1752, P.R.O., C.O., 5/1327, L.C. Tr., C.O. 565–66.

the various "pieces" of garlix into fractions to be used to fashion shirts for men and women.

Dinwiddie's correspondence also partially reveals how the new Governor became further acquainted with the needs of the Indians. Shortly after Dinwiddie's arrival in Virginia, Thomas Cresap,[15] the Maryland frontiersman, wrote to inform the new Governor of the method of giving wampum and of inviting the Indians to a council. At this time, Cresap also recommended Andrew Montour as a person of good character and a capable interpreter, who was much beloved by the Indians.[16] It was, therefore, a well-informed governor who dispatched the trader, Thomas Burney, to the Twightwees with a wampum message stating that Virginia would send presents of arms, powder, and clothing in the spring of 1753. So great was Dinwiddie's faith in presents that he declared that he knew of no better method of securing the friendship of the Indians than by the use of gifts.[17]

The Board of Trade, fully aware that the powerful Twightwee confederacy was important for the security of the colonies and for the protection of trade and commerce, voted a sum, not to exceed £1,000, to be used for gifts.[18] This amount was to be taken out of the revenue received from the tax of two shillings per hogshead of tobacco exported. In Dinwiddie's own words, the Board of Trade acknowledged that the most effectual way to

---

[15] Thomas Cresap was born in England about 1700 and came to America while still in his teens. He became acquainted with the Washington family after renting a farm from them. Later he moved to an area on the Susquehanna River opposite the present city of Columbia, Pennsylvania. This land was disputed by Pennsylvania and Maryland. It was at this time that he took the part of the proprietaries of Maryland and incurred the subsequent wrath of the Pennsylvanians who eventually set his home afire. After this experience, he moved to a place called Old Town, on the Maryland side of the Potomac just above the South Branch of the same river. Among other things, his establishment was designated as a tobacco inspection warehouse. See J. Hall Pleasants (ed.), *Archives of Maryland*, L, *Proceedings and Acts of the General Assembly 1752–1754*, pp. 318, 324. Here at Old Town, Cresap met the warriors who were traveling north and south during the perpetual feuds between the Northern and Southern Indians. The house was surrounded by a log fort, where Cresap, the ". . . . Rattle Snake Colonel, and a vile rascal . . . ." handed out goods to the Indians. See the "Morris Journal," Sargent, *op. cit.*, pp. 372–73. Braddock had a very low opinion of Cresap. See *Pennsylvania Colonial Records*, VI, 400. Despite the references to Cresap's character, he enjoyed the confidence of Dinwiddie and Washington. For further information regarding this interesting frontier personality, see Kenneth P. Bailey, *Thomas Cresap, Maryland Frontiersman*; see also a brief sketch in *Dinwiddie Papers*, I, 10.

[16] Thomas Cresap to Robert Dinwiddie, December 27, 1751; Palmer, *op. cit.*, I, 245–47. See also Robert Dinwiddie to Thomas Cresap, January 23, 1752, *Dinwiddie Papers*, I, 17–19.

[17] P.R.O., C.O., 5/1327, L.C. 415–24, C.O. 531–36.

[18] See Munro and Fitzroy, *op. cit.*, IV, 200–203; P.R.O., C.O., L.C. 4–5, C.O. 6–7.

gain the friendship of the Indians was by ". . . . making them presents . . . ."[19]

Meanwhile, Thomas Burney had also informed Pennsylvania authorities of the disaster that had befallen La Demoiselle and his band. Bearing a small gift of one scalp and three strings of wampum, Burney delivered the courageous Twightwee message, ". . . . before we will be subject to the French, or call them our Fathers, we will perish here."[20] After the letter and the scalp had been laid before the assembly, the legislators generously contributed a sum of £200 for a gift to be used for the "Necessaries of Life."[21] To supplement this generous outlay, the Quaker colony also donated six hundred pounds to be spent on the other tribes which were in alliance with Pennsylvania.

Many factors were at work to prevent the immediate delivery of these presents. The dangers from the French in transporting the Twightwee gift over such a great distance and the lack of responsible persons to carry such a large cargo caused a long delay in the delivery of Pennsylvania's present. Governor Hamilton was not able to send the goods until later;[22] and it was indeed unfortunate that they were not delivered to the Twightwees and their Iroquois allies until the time of the Carlisle conference in September 1753, more than a year after the attack on Pickawillany![23] Moreover, weather conditions prevented Dinwiddie from delivering an immediate gift; and his present was given to the natives at Winchester in the spring of 1753.

The situation became more serious when Thomas Burney, who was to advise the Twightwees of the Virginia present, delayed his return to Pickawillany. Consequently, the discouraged Twightwees had no word from their allies. Indeed, more than a year had passed after the attack by the French and the Canadian Indians, and the Twightwees had received no presents from the British. It is no wonder that these loyal Miami tribesmen finally broke under the strain of French pressure and a part of them deserted the English.[24]

Lack of immediate and suitable gifts had broken up the powerful Twightwee chain of friendship. Only a fraction of the Miami confederacy still espoused the English cause; and this group was eventually alienated by the rapacious land policy of the Virginians at the treaties of Logstown in 1752, and Winchester in 1753. Dinwiddie's dreams of building a mighty native

[19] *Supra*, note 18.

[20] *Pennsylvania Colonial Records*, V, 600.

[21] *Ibid.*, V, 616, 617.

[22] *Ibid.*, V, 639.

[23] *Ibid.*, V, 658, 666–86.

[24] Robert Dinwiddie to Captains Cresap and Trent, February 10, 1753, *Dinwiddie Papers*, I, 22–24.

auxiliary force were shattered. He no longer had the aid of the Miamis and the Southern confederacies. James Glen[25] of South Carolina prevented the latter Indians from aiding Braddock, while the French had broken the back of La Demoiselle's faction at Pickawillany. When Dinwiddie attempted to secure the help of the loyal faction of the Twightwees in 1754, the natives told the Virginia Governor that they would fight only if paid as auxiliaries.[26] This was a far cry from the spirit of Old Briton, who had vowed friendship with the British until the end of time.

With neither powder nor lead from Virginia, the Twightwees had no alternative but to turn to their former enemies, the French.[27] Therefore, only a small representation from the Twightwees actually attended the three important Indian conferences that took place between June 1752 and September 1753. Rumors were spread that the Twightwees had even taken up arms against the English.[28]

Another cause for the Indians' eventual distrust of the English was the Logstown Treaty of 1752. As a result of this treaty, the Indians lost vast native hunting grounds to the Ohio Company, all for the price of a present in goods. It was the object of the members of the Ohio Company to secure from the Indians at Logstown a clear title to a large area of land centering around the forks of the Ohio River. Christopher Gist had been sent to explore this area in 1750–1751.[29] At this time, Gist was directed to invite the Indians to come to Logstown to receive the king's present. But the Indians, fearing that he had come to take their lands, were hostile to Gist on this first expedition.[30] Although satisfied with the findings of Gist, the company sent him on a second expedition in the early part of 1752. This time he was to explore the southern portion of the Ohio and return with additional information. When he was questioned by friendly natives, Gist again found it expedient to conceal his objectives. So he told the Indians that he had come

. . . . to invite all the great men of the Indians to a Treaty to be held at Loggs Town the full moon of May next, where a Parcel of Goods, a Present from the King of Great Britain would be delivered by the proper Commissioners. . . . .[31]

During the months before the treaty took place, Gist was occupied in laying the groundwork for a successful meeting. He had the responsibility

---

[25] For the trouble between Glen and Dinwiddie in 1755 relating to Indians for Braddock, see chapter viii.

[26] *Dinwiddie Papers*, I, 94–95.

[27] *Ibid.*, I, 109.

[28] *Ibid.*

[29] Darlington, *op. cit.*, p. 31.

[30] *Ibid.*, pp. 34–35.

[31] *Ibid.*, p. 71.

of hiring Andrew Montour as interpreter, and he urged the latter to make the best possible agreement with the Indians for the later distribution of goods.[32] Montour was appointed head interpreter when Dinwiddie found that Conrad Weiser's services could not be secured.[33] With Weiser unavailable, the Virginia Governor wrote Thomas Cresap to urge Montour to make his home in Virginia and to be present at Logstown when the gift for the Indians arrived.[34] Little wonder that the Governor was concerned about the king's present, for it was said to be the largest gift ever bestowed upon the Indians.[35] If he succeeded in driving a shrewd bargain for the Ohio Company, Montour was to receive a large portion of company land.[36]

As a member of the Ohio Company, Dinwiddie had the affairs of that organization "much at heart." He wanted to make certain that the goods, amounting to some seven hundred pounds, would redress the grievances of the Indians.[37] In addition to his other activities in connection with this present, the Governor appointed three commissioners to represent Virginia at the Logstown Treaty[38] and checked on the delivery of the gift at each point on its journey from Winchester to Logstown.[39]

James Patton,[40] one of the three commissioners, was ordered to see that the goods were deposited at Winchester.[41] As some of the luxurious items sent over by the king were not suitable for Indians, the Virginia council called upon Patton to set a just value on the articles so that they might be

---

[32] Darlington, op. cit., pp. 234–35.

[33] See Robert Dinwiddie to Conrad Weiser, December 12, 1752, Dinwiddie Papers, I, 6–7.

[34] Robert Dinwiddie to Thomas Cresap, January 23, 1752, ibid., I, 17–19.

[35] The fact that the gift was the largest ever offered to the Indians is mentioned frequently in the printed text of the treaty. See "Treaty of Logg's Town," Virginia Magazine of History and Biography, XIII (October 1905), pp. 154–74.

[36] Darlington, op. cit., pp. 234–35.

[37] Ibid., p. 167. Dinwiddie was well aware of native complaints regarding the Treaty of Lancaster in 1744. Six months before the Logstown meeting he wrote to the Board of Trade on January 20, 1752, declaring: ". . . . these Indians I hear make some objections to Treaty of Lancaster, they say they do not understand Pen and Ink work, and that their Interpreter did not do them Justice. . . . ." See P.R.O., C.O., 5/1327, L.C. 347, C.O. 453.

[38] The commissioners were James Patton, Lunsford Lomax, and Joshua Fry. See Dinwiddie Papers, I, 7–10.

[39] See ibid., I, 9–10.

[40] Colonel James Patton (1692–1755), was a former naval officer. He was appointed commander-in-chief of all military forces in Augusta County in July 1752, after the Logstown Treaty. See Draper MSS 1 QQ 68 (film). In following this command he was killed on the Augusta County frontier on July 30, 1755. See Draper MSS 1 QQ 83 (film). For an additional sketch, see Dinwiddie Papers, I, 8–9.

[41] The early name for Winchester was Frederick Town.

exchanged for other goods which the Indians would rather have.[42] Patton's orders from the council further specified that this exchange was to be made in Fredericksburg.[43] The merchandise was then taken to Winchester. At this settlement Thomas Cresap contracted to deliver the whole present to Logstown on the Ohio, by May 15, 1752, at a price of one pistole[44] per hundred pounds, avoirdupois.[45]

Patton also had to solve the problem of obtaining the supply of wampum that was to be used at the treaty. He found that he could secure these beads from Cresap, who had plenty of black and white wampum that he regularly used for Indian affairs. It seemed that the Maryland trader generously bestowed wampum, liquors, butter, salt, corn meal, beef, and tobacco upon the Indians in order to build up friendship among the tribes for the Ohio Company. In the past, Cresap had turned these accounts over to James Patton for payment.[46]

With details concerning the delivery of the present left to Thomas Cresap, the commissioners could proceed to carry out the minute instructions given to them. First, they were to take notice that the goods were not damaged. Second, the delegates were to enlarge upon the value of the present, for it was conceded to be the largest ever given to the Ohio tribes. Finally, since the purpose of the gift was to soothe the tribesmen's ruffled feelings, which had been brought about by claims of fraud, instructions called for an explanation of the English title to the Ohio lands. When this had been clarified for the Indians, the tribesmen were to be informed that the gift was in keeping with the promise made by the commissioners at the Lancaster Treaty in 1744, at which time they had promised to bring Indian complaints to the attention of the king.[47]

If any treaty ever revolved around presents, the Logstown Treaty of 1752 is an outstanding example. Everything possible was done to humor the Indians. Even those tribesmen who met the delegation along the route of travel were furnished with wampum to "open their hearts and clear their

---

[42] Council Meeting, March 3, 1752, Virginia Council Journals, typescript copy, pp. 358–59, Virginia State Library.

[43] *Ibid.*

[44] A pistole was a coin worth from about $3.60 to $4.00.

[45] Council Meeting, December 12, 1751, Virginia Council Journals, typescript copy, pp. 356–57, Virginia State Library. Anthony Strothers carried the present from Fredericksburg to Winchester. See *Dinwiddie Papers*, I, 9.

[46] Palmer, *op. cit.*, I, 244–45.

[47] Other instructions were to wipe away bad impressions regarding the company created by Pennsylvania traders; to cultivate the Iroquois friendship; to warn the Indians about the French; to ask about an Indian murderer; to find out whether the Indians would be interested in religious education. See *Virginia Magazine of History and Biography*, XIII (October 1905), 143–52.

eyes."[48] When the delegates arrived at Logstown late in May 1752, the tribesmen were immediately informed of the great present. Andrew Montour, interpreter for Virginia, was extremely busy at this time. He was aided in his various duties by George Croghan, who used his influence to create a favorable opinion toward the Virginia commissioners. Although Croghan was not an official interpreter, Governor Hamilton of Pennsylvania was in complete accord with his participation at Logstown. Thus it was that Andrew Montour and George Croghan worked together in carrying out Governor Hamilton's recommendation that Montour urge the Ohio tribes to accept the king's present in a gracious manner.[49]

One of the first items on the agenda at this meeting was a consideration of the Treaty of Lancaster, made in 1744. The discussion of this treaty was conducted in such a manner that the British did not have to acknowledge any claims of fraud on their part.[50] Refuting the "pen and ink work" of the whites, Half King, speaking for the Indians, exhibited much surprise to understand that the English claimed the whole Ohio Valley by virtue of this former treaty. Staunch ally of the English though he was, Half King showed great reluctance about confirming the early deed. In typical Indian fashion he declared:

. . . . We never understood, before you told us Yesterday, that the Lands then sold were to extend further to the Sun setting than the Hill on the other side of the Alleghany Hill. . . . .[51]

Despite this objection, the whites had their way; and on June 13, 1752, the sachems of the Iroquoian confederacy agreed to ratify the Lancaster Treaty of 1744.[52] The signing of this agreement is part of an old story, often repeated in American history. Time and time again the Indians nullified their agreements in order to obtain new rewards in goods. Using sugary terms that indicated a lack of sincerity, the commissioners induced

---

[48] *Virginia Magazine of History and Biography*, XIII, 154–74. The Indian queen at Delaware Town was given a brass kettle, tobacco, and other trifling articles.

[49] *Pennsylvania Colonial Records*, V, 568. See also Robert Dinwiddie to James Hamilton, December 18, 1751, *Dinwiddie Papers*, I, 15–16.

[50] For an account of the Lancaster Treaty in 1744 where Conrad Weiser handed out strouds, shirts, jews'-harps, halfthicks, guns, and vermilion, see *Indian Treaties Printed by Benjamin Franklin*, pp. 43, 59. Weiser, as interpreter, represented Virginia, Maryland, and Pennsylvania to the Ohio tribes.

[51] *Virginia Magazine of History and Biography*, XIII (October 1905), pp. 154–74.

[52] After the final speeches had been made, the commissioners delivered the goods to Half King and the other chiefs, who gratefully accepted them. Thereupon the sachems appointed some of their warriors to make a fair division of the articles which they did without the ". . . . least noise or disorder." The representatives of each nation then took the goods, which were to be subdivided when they arrived home. See *ibid.*, XIII, 164–65.

the natives to sell their hunting grounds for what Dinwiddie termed a "fair purchase."[53]

It should be noted here that the energy of Robert Dinwiddie was not confined to the Northern Indians, but was expended on the Southern tribes as well. He plunged into the thick of native politics, becoming involved in the affairs of almost every tribe along the Colonial frontier. As a consequence of this activity, Dinwiddie incurred the hostility of Governor James Glen of South Carolina, who opposed him at every point possible. For example, Governor Glen made it a point to censure the "purchases" at Logstown in 1752.[54] Glen always tried to keep the Virginia Governor at arm's length from the principal Southern tribes because of the latter's inexperience.[55] As far as Dinwiddie was concerned, however, the South Carolina executive was a "wrongheaded man."

South Carolina's opposition did not prevent the Virginia Governor from handing out goods to the Cherokees, Catawbas, and other Southern tribes.[56] As a matter of fact, in 1752, the "emperor" of the Cherokees journeyed some seven hundred miles through briers and thickets in order to cultivate friendship and trade with Virginia. To please the Cherokee "emperor" and his companions, Dinwiddie ordered a handsome reward of fine clothes and other articles.[57]

Continuing to "converse" with Southern tribes through the friendly medium of presents, the Virginia Governor was especially interested in cultivating the Cherokees and the Catawbas after 1752.[58] Negotiations and messages were kept up during 1753; and by the spring of 1754, Dinwiddie dreamed of bringing about a peaceful settlement of the long-standing feud between the Six Nations and the Southern Tribes.[59] Working toward this

---

[53] Robert Dinwiddie to James Glen, May 23, 1753, P.R.O., C.O., 5/13, L.C. 477–82, C.O. 611–13 (film).

[54] James Glen to the Earl of Holdernesse, June 25, 1753, P.R.O., C.O., 5/13, L.C. 463, C.O. 595 (film).

[55] James Glen to Robert Dinwiddie, June 1, 1754, P.R.O., C.O. 5/14, L.C. Tr., C.O. 489 (film).

[56] It had been the practice, even before Dinwiddie's arrival, for Virginia to dole out goods to the Southern tribes. For instance, in August 1751, the president of the Virginia council gave the emperor of the Cherokees a gift worth £200. See Council Meeting, August 9 and 10, 1751, Virginia Council Journals, typescript copy, pp. 326–28, Virginia State Library.

[57] Robert Dinwiddie to the Board of Trade, December 10, 1752, P.R.O., C.O., 5/1327, L.C. 415–24, C.O. 531–36.

[58] The Catawbas, staunch British allies, were very poor and did not hesitate to ask for presents. See Palmer, op. cit., I, 248–49.

[59] Hoping to unify all the Southern tribes for the benefit of the English cause, Dinwiddie warned them about French aggressions. For the cause of unity, he also sought the co-operation of neighboring governors. See Pennsylvania Colonial Rec-

goal, Dinwiddie invited representatives of the Catawbas to meet with the Iroquois, Twightwees, and the Ohio Indians in order to partake in a present from the "father" of the Indians, the king of Great Britain.[60] The Virginia Governor promised the Catawba warriors gifts of arms and supplies,[61] and painted a bold picture of a completely unified force of British native auxiliaries, which would include the Cherokees, the Chickasaws, and the Ohio Mingoes. This was the force which would go against the French.

By furnishing the Southern Indians with gifts, Dinwiddie was hoping to secure a larger force of native allies than even the Iroquois could muster. It has been observed previously that the Governor first attempted to organize the large Miami confederacy into a potential native army because their warriors approached the ten thousand mark. When part of the Twightwees turned to the French allegiance in 1753, however, Dinwiddie began to concentrate upon the Southern tribes because ". . . . the Soe'ern Indians are more to be courted than the five Nat's being ten Times their Number. . . . ."[62] Indeed, the energetic work of Dinwiddie was beginning to bear fruit; the Catawbas and Cherokees promised one thousand warriors to defend the Ohio against the French, in case of an invasion. Although encouraged by his work with the Southern tribes, Dinwiddie did not forget the other Indians; and he still maintained hopes that the promise of a "handsome present" would enable him to lure Twightwee auxiliaries.[63]

The meeting at Winchester in 1754, however, was doomed to failure. In spite of the promises of goods, no tribesmen came to meet the Governor during the sixteen days that he waited. The Ohio Indians sent messages saying that they were obligated to defend their lands against the French. As they had joined the forces of Colonel Washington, however, they asked that the king's present be sent to them on the frontier.[64] Neither did the

---

ords, V, 630–34; *Dinwiddie Papers,* I, 11, 12–13, 15–16. For the Indian correspondence, see Robert Dinwiddie to the Cherokees, May 31, 1753, P.R.O., C.O., 5/1327, L.C. 549–50, C.O. 655–56; Robert Dinwiddie to the Catawbas, May 31, 1753, P.R.O., C.O., 5/1327, L.C. 547, C.O. 653–54. The governors of New York had tried unsuccessfully to bring about a unified Indian policy. See *Pennsylvania Colonial Records,* V, 632. The most successful attempt at unifying the Indian policy of the Northern colonies came at the Albany conference of 1754. The selection of William Johnson as Colonel of the Six Nations was the groundwork for the later superintendency. Dinwiddie declared that the Virginia government could not afford the expense of sending commissioners to the Albany meeting because of a projected conference with the Ohio Indians at Winchester in 1754. See *Dinwiddie Papers,* I, 81, 99.

[60] *Dinwiddie Papers,* I, 60–61.
[61] *Ibid.*
[62] *Ibid.,* I, 99.
[63] *Ibid.,* I, 94.
[64] *Ibid.,* I, 201–5, 205–7.

Southern tribes come up to accept the king's present.[65] Nor did the Cherokees and Catawbas send warriors to defend their hunting grounds on the
Ohio. They stayed at home, having been advised to do so by James Glen.[66]
In summary, it might be said that the Winchester conference of 1754, the
purpose of which was to unify all the Ohio and Southern tribes, failed for
two reasons: the hostility of James Glen, who resented Dinwiddie's presents
to the Southern confederacies;[67] and the French crisis on the frontier, which
kept the Indians away from the conference.

Thus the scene of action is carried back to events on the Ohio. To meet
the French threat here, Dinwiddie had the privilege of spending some
£10,000, part of which was to be used for presents to secure native warriors.[68]
With such sound financial backing, it would seem that the Virginia Governor could have organized a formidable native fighting unit. Yet, despite
his efforts, failure resulted. In order to follow the chain of events that led
up to Washington's capitulation at Fort Necessity, it is necessary to pick
up the affairs of the Ohio Indians after the Treaty of Logstown in 1752.

By virtue of the fact that the tribesmen at this treaty had turned over
some 200,000 acres of land to the Ohio Company, the way was prepared
for British settlement of this princely domain. There was only one difficulty

---

[65] See Robert Dinwiddie to "King Head men and Warriors of the Catawbas," April
19, 1754, *Dinwiddie Papers*, I, 131–32; Robert Dinwiddie to the Emperor King of Chote,
and the Warriors of the Great Nation of Cherokees, April 19, 1754, *ibid.*, I, 132; Robert
Dinwiddie to Wayhocke, Kehowe, Telefowe, Kehowe, Corronah Toxso, Skyonaco
Kehowe, Warriors of the Cherokees, *ibid.*, I, 133 (no date).

[66] Robert Dinwiddie to James Glen, August 5, 1754, *ibid.*, I, 272–76; same to same
October 25, 1754, *ibid.*, I, 377–79.

[67] Glen prevented Dinwiddie from securing the aid of the Cherokees and Catawbas for Braddock in 1755. *Vide*, chapter viii, notes 16, 17. Despite Glen's opposition, the Virginia Governor continued to negotiate with the Southern Indians
and to give them presents. In July 1754, he sent the Augusta County trader, Abraham
Smith, to the Cherokees and Catawbas with medals, powder, blankets, and lead. This
gift was apparently the one that the Southern tribes had failed to accept at Winchester
in 1754. See *ibid.*, I, 231–32. After Braddock's defeat, the energetic Dinwiddie still
sought the favor of the Southern Indians with gifts. At a treaty held at Catawba
Town on the Broad River, he sent a gift designed to form the Cherokees and
Catawbas into a permanent league of friendship. See LO 870 for the treaty. For a
discussion involving the expenses of the commissioners, William Byrd and Peter
Randolph, see their memorial to the Lords of the Treasury, P.R.O., C.O., 5/1329,
L.C. 107–9, C.O. 135–39. For negotiations that Dinwiddie carried on with Old Hop
of the Cherokees, see LO 1380.

[68] See Thomas Robinson to Robert Dinwiddie, July 5, 1754, P.R.O., C.O., 5/211,
L.C. 49–51, C.O. 91–96. Dinwiddie was directed to give part of this fund to Glen.
The South Carolina Governor promptly asked for, but did not receive, £6,000. See
Dinwiddie Papers, II, 282. Most of the fund was apparently to be used for building
a fort in the Cherokee country.

—the French had already taken possession of the area. For this reason, it was Dinwiddie's design to offer presents to the Ohio tribes in order to get them to defend the very land that had recently been "purchased" from them by means of goods.[69] In order to accomplish this, Dinwiddie arranged for a meeting at Winchester in September 1753. (This meeting is not to be confused with the previously mentioned Winchester Treaty of 1754, which was chiefly concerned with the Southern Indians.)

Although the allotment of merchandise, which consisted mostly of blankets, arms, and powder, was not a large one, it presented much difficulty in transportation.[70] After some deliberation on this problem, the Virginia council decided to hire a vessel to transport the goods northward to Falmouth, opposite Fredericksburg on the Rappahannock River.[71] At this point, William Fairfax,[72] who had been selected as commissioner for the scheduled conference, assumed the responsibility of seeing that the goods were delivered to Winchester. Here in September 1753, Fairfax, aided by William Trent, George Croghan, and Andrew Montour, was prepared to tempt the Indians with gifts in order that he might gain his ends.[73]

The foremost of all the Ohio tribesmen came forward to accept Virginia's presents of arms, and the influential Monacatoocha of the Oneidas was the principal Indian spokesman. A total of ninety-eight Indians, including the women and children, attended the meeting. Sachems present included the feared Shingis,[74] who represented the Delawares; Neuchyconer, a "king," and Tomenebuck, who spoke for the Shawnees; Big Kettle, a spokesman for the Wyandots; and the young "king" called Raccoon and his chief warrior, the Turtle, who composed the loyal faction of the Twightwees.[75]

Since the French invasion of the Ohio had put the Indians in an "unsettled" frame of mind, little could be done to substantiate the Ohio Com-

---

[69] Robert Dinwiddie to Captain Cresap and Trent, February 10, 1753, *Dinwiddie Papers*, I, 22–24.

[70] P.R.O., C.O., 5/1328, L.C. 15–40, C.O. 27–44.

[71] Council Meeting, April 21, 1753, Virginia Council Journals, typescript copy, p. 2, 1st Lot, Virginia State Library.

[72] William Fairfax, grandson of Thomas, the fourth Lord Fairfax, was a representative of an aristocratic Virginia family. He had been in Spain, the East Indies, New England, and finally had moved to Virginia where he cared for the large estates of his kinsman, Lord Fairfax. For an enlarged sketch, see *Dinwiddie Papers*, I, 20–21.

[73] See William Trent's account of the meeting in P.R.O., C.O., 5/1328, L.C. 15–40, C.O. 27–44. For William Fairfax's journal see P.R.O., C.O. 5/1328, L.C. 43–72, C.O. 47–72 (film).

[74] Shingis or Singis was an important leader among the Delawares. During the latter part of the French and Indian War, he proved to be a terror along the frontier.

[75] *Supra*, note 73.

pany's land claims.[76] Accordingly, the speeches at the meeting were composed of rather long harangues concerning the deceit of the French and the advisability of building an English fort.[77] Pipes were smoked; wampum was exchanged; and the traditional toasts with liquor were made. Once more the familiar chain of friendship legend[78] was developed by Monacatoocha in an eloquent speech; and, finally, the present was divided. Leaving the allotting of the arms and blankets to the delegates of the Six Nations, William Trent set apart one-fifth as a condolence gift for the Twightwees. Following the division of the merchandise by the Iroquois, each "nation" turned its goods over to Trent, who carried it as far west as Logstown.[79]

Inasmuch as all the major Ohio tribes had sent delegates to the meeting, Fairfax seized upon the opportunity to invite all the Indians back to a conference at Winchester in the "full moon of May next" to receive a large present from the king.[80] This projected meeting in 1754, as has been noted, was a part of Dinwiddie's plan to reconcile the differences between the Northern and Southern tribes by means of the soothing medicine of the king's present.[81]

After leaving Winchester in 1753, the sachems requested that the dignified Fairfax send a belt of wampum to James Hamilton to announce the fact that the Ohio Indians wished to meet at Carlisle with the Quaker colony.[82] This meeting at Carlisle offered an excellent opportunity for Hamilton to bestow the long-delayed £200 condolence gift to the Twightwees and the additional £600 to the Ohio tribes.[83]

Although the French occupation of the Ohio indicated a strong possi-

---

[76] The Indians were hurried and wished to be back on the frontier as soon as possible. Yet they did not want to miss an opportunity to meet with their old friend, Brother Onas (Pennsylvania), at Carlisle. This meeting took place directly after the one at Winchester in the summer of 1753. See *Pennsylvania Colonial Records*, V, 657, for a letter from Fairfax to Hamilton arranging for the meeting. It was apparent that the Indians preferred the friendship of Pennsylvania to that of Virginia despite Dinwiddie's numerous gifts. The Virginia Governor had hoped to save the whole Ohio region for the British by means of a few gifts at Winchester but he did not count on the excited state of mind of the Indians who wanted military assistance. See William Trent to Robert Dinwiddie, August 11, 1753, Etting Collection of Ohio Company Papers, I, 1753–1755 (folio); *Early Western Travels*, I, 94.

[77] P.R.O., C.O., 5/1328, L.C. 15–40, C.O. 27–44.

[78] See chapter i for a discussion of the legend regarding the chain of friendship.

[79] *Ibid.*

[80] P.R.O., C.O., 5/1328, L.C. 43–72, C.O. 47–72 (film).

[81] See Robert Dinwiddie to the Board of Trade, November 17, 1753, P.R.O., C.O., 5/1328, L.C. 13–14, C.O. 21–24.

[82] William Fairfax to James Hamilton, September 14, 1753, *Pennsylvania Colonial Records*, V, 657.

[83] *Supra*, note 23.

OLD HENDRICK, SACHEM OF THE MOHAWKS

bility of war, the Pennsylvania Assembly continued to insist that "necessaries" be given as presents rather than munitions.[84] For example, when
the Shawnees pleaded for arms to avenge French attacks made on the
Twightwees during the winter of 1751–1752, Hamilton wrote to Croghan
and declared with emphasis that it was against the sentiments of those who
had charge of "Publik Money" to make gifts of arms for such purposes.[85]
At the Carlisle meeting, therefore, although they had full knowledge of the
French advances, the commissioners aimed solely at pleasing the Indians
with ample goods as a measure of friendship.[86] During the meeting, where
Monacatoocha again was the main Indian spokesman, the commissioners
were told of Half King's three messages to the French, ordering them out
of the Ohio region. In reply to these messages, the French commander had
told Half King, in no uncertain terms, that

I do not like your selling your Lands to the English, they shall draw you into no more
foolish Bargains. I will take care of your Lands for you and of you. The English give
you no Goods but for your land. We will give you our Goods for nothing.[87]

As a matter of fact, the French were now going all out for a military occupation of the Ohio. In order to feed French soldiers native warriors were
employed at a specified sum per month to hunt for meat.[88]

In order to meet the French advance, Virginia, at the preceding conference at Winchester, had appointed Christopher Gist, Andrew Montour, and
William Trent as a kind of committee to select a location where arms could
be readily distributed to the Indians should they need them. Now, at Carlisle, Weiser advised that the commissioners have available additional
merchandise to supplement the arms which could be given to the Indians.
As a result of this suggestion the original lists of goods were examined and
additional quantities were ordered and bought from John Carson, a merchant
of Philadelphia.[89] The presents were then transported at the usual rate of
carriage.

Pennsylvania commissioners accepted calumet pipes, shells, wampum,
and skins from the numerous Indians congregated at Carlisle. In return,

---

[84] See the instructions given the commissioners, Benjamin Franklin, Isaac Norris,
and Richard Peters, *Pennsylvania Colonial Records*, V, 658–59.

[85] For the correspondence on this matter see *ibid.*, V.

[86] For the report of the commissioners on the Carlisle meeting, see *ibid.*, V, 655–
86. In order to check on the Iroquois' attitude toward the new French fortifications,
the Quaker colony sent Weiser to Onondaga. His instructions are printed in *ibid.*,
V, 636, and his journal may be found in *ibid.*, V, 642–47. Weiser was instructed to
tell the Six Nations that if they were attacked, Pennsylvania would send ". . . . Cloathing [*sic*] and so forth. . . . ."

[87] *Ibid.*, V, 667.

[88] *Ibid.*, V, 623.   [89] *Ibid.*, V, 669.

with great dignity, the commissioners bestowed a beautiful wampum belt upon the Six Nations' delegates. Depicted on this belt were six figures, holding hands. The first five figures represented the Five Nations,[90] while the sixth denoted the government of Pennsylvania cementing a close union between the Iroquois tribes and the Quaker colony. Special attention was given to condolence gifts for the Twightwees and other nations which had lost warriors during French incursions.

After they had received handkerchiefs and strouds with which to wipe their eyes, and apologies for not having had their weapons mended, the tribesmen were ready to journey back to the Ohio. Horses were provided to aid in carrying their goods.[91] Because of the crisis upon the Ohio, however, part of the goods were left with George Croghan, who was to deliver the merchandise when it was "safe and reasonable" to do so.[92] These goods were held up because of the threat of confiscation by the French; apparently, however, the Indians had faith in the Pennsylvania government and were satisfied with these arrangements.

From all appearances it would seem that the Indians had forgotten the problems of the Ohio Company and the urgent requests of Virginia's William Fairfax to defend the Ohio against the French. Except for the few tribesmen who were to aid Washington under Half King and Monaca-toocha,[93] the majority of the Ohio Indians were to succumb before the French threat of force. One report had it that the great Half King was reduced to tears when the French told him that he was an "old woman." Furthermore, the French threatened to put the sachem in irons if he did not go home and cease his objections to the French occupation of the Ohio.

It remained for Dinwiddie to force the French to a showdown. In the fall of 1753, he sent young Major George Washington to warn the French that they were occupying lands belonging to the English. Washington

[90] The Six Nations for centuries had been composed of the Cayugas, Oneidas, Mohawks, Senecas, Onondagas, and the Tuscaroras, the last tribe having joined the confederacy at a later date. This date is open to question. It was about the year 1722, however, that the Tuscaroras migrated north. It is to be noted that some of the Tuscaroras were still living in the South as late as 1766. See *New York Colonial Documents*, VII, 883.

[91] *Pennsylvania Colonial Records*, V, 680–81.

[92] *Ibid.*, V, 682, 684. Hamilton wanted to know what Dinwiddie's plans were for meeting the French advance. Logically enough, the Pennsylvania Governor felt that the goods could be left with Christopher Gist, Andrew Montour, and William Trent, who already had a consignment of arms to give the Indians whenever the need arose. See James Hamilton to Robert Dinwiddie, *Pennsylvania Archives* (4th series), II, 208–14.

[93] To prevent confusion it must be noted that Half King and Monacatoocha were different Indians, although the latter bore the name Half King at a later date. *Vide*, sketches, notes 4 and 5, chapter vi.

selected Christopher Gist as his companion on this memorable journey to Venango and Fort Le Boeuf.[94] At Logstown, Washington met Monacatoocha and the later infamous Shingis of the Delawares. The young Major gave Monacatoocha a twist of tobacco and a string of wampum and asked that a runner be sent for Half King, who was to act as Washington's guide.[95]

After Half King and several other Indians had joined the small party, they met Chabert Joncaire at Venango in early December 1753. A typical illustration of the fierce courtship of the Ohio Indians occurred at this frontier post following this meeting. Greeting Half King and his tribesmen with extreme friendliness, the Frenchman plied liquor and presents so fast that the Indians were soon rendered "incapable of business."[96] The alert Washington was almost confounded by the aggressiveness of Chabert Joncaire. Fortunately for Washington, however, he had the assistance of the capable Christopher Gist, who was able to fetch the Indians when the young Major was prepared to leave for Le Boeuf. This was not an easy task, for the constant favors that the French lavished upon the native guides in order to prevent them from going farther with the English caused Gist great difficulty in prevailing upon the Indians to continue with Washington.[97]

At Le Boeuf, where Legardeur de St. Pierre politely refused Washington's request to withdraw from the Ohio,[98] Half King received presents and rewards and was the object of ". . . . every Stratagem the most fruitful Brain could invent. . . . ."[99] More French liquor and promises of presents followed, thereby forcing Washington to watch Half King closely in order to hold him to his agreement to guide the English party back home. The Virginia commander later stated that the French methods would have prevailed at any other time, but his determined insistence finally resulted in Half King's keeping his promise. It is to Washington's credit that he was thoroughly alert to the situation and warned Half King against the flattering advances of Joncaire. Remarkable indeed is the fact that an Indian attempted, by firing from ambush, to kill young Washington.[100] It is a matter for conjecture whether this attacker had been bribed with liquor and goods to assassinate the young officer. Yet, this incident, as well as Washington's entire journey, serves to illustrate the dependence both of the French and of the English upon the aid of the Indians. It was Half King

---

[94] See Louis Knott Koontz, *The Virginia Frontier, 1754–1763,* for a well-documented account of this journey.

[95] *George Washington's Diaries,* I, 46.

[96] *Ibid.,* I, 56.

[97] *Ibid.,* I, 56–57.

[98] See *Pennsylvania Archives* (8th series), V, 3642–43.

[99] *George Washington's Diaries,* I, 61.

[100] *Ibid.,* I, 64.

and Monacatoocha who were with Washington on his return mission to the frontier in the spring of 1754, but their assistance had been obtained solely by generous gifts for the sachems themselves and their families.[101]

Noting that the French had acquired the assistance of the Ottawas and the Chippewas and were using presents to court other Indians, Washington was in complete accord with Dinwiddie's undertaking of organizing the Cherokees, Catawbas, and the Chickasaws as a supplement to the friendly Ohio Indians.[102] No one realized more fully than Washington that wampum, spirits, and treaty goods were a necessity when dealing with the tribesmen. Among other things, the Dinwiddie-Washington correspondence during the spring and summer of 1754 is filled with discourses relating to the use of gifts to keep the "Indians in the British interest."[103] The Virginia Governor co-operated with Washington to the fullest extent. He not only sent food, medals, and other Indian goods, but he also made sure that Washington had the able assistance of Montour and Croghan.[104]

Finally, when Washington attempted to find the small party of French under Jumonville in May 1754, he was completely dependent upon his native guides. Before reaching the near-by Indian camp, the English party had been ". . . . frequently tumbling one over another, and so often lost that 15 or 20 minutes search would not find the path again."[105] When Monacatoocha and Half King joined the party, however, the Indians followed the tracks and found the obscure French hiding place in short order. Then ensued the historic encounter in which Jumonville was killed. Particularly gratifying to Washington was the capture of Monsieur La Force,[106] who, aided by Joncaire, had caused the young commander so much concern in corrupting Half King with bribes at Venango in late 1753.

After July 3, 1754, when Louis Coulon de Villiers avenged the death of his brother Jumonville[107] by forcing the capitulation of Washington at Fort

---

[101] *Dinwiddie Papers*, I, 189–90; Palmer, *op. cit.*, I, 249.

[102] See George Washington to Robert Dinwiddie, April 25, 1754, *Writings of Washington*, I, 42; George Washington to Horatio Sharpe, April 27, 1754, *ibid.*, I, 44.

[103] For example see *Dinwiddie Papers*, I, 169–70, 186–87, 189–90, 191–93; *Writings of Washington*, I, 48, 51, 55, 72, 75, 77.

[104] *Writings of Washington*, I, 74–76.

[105] *Dinwiddie Papers*, I, 179.

[106] Captain Robert Stobo, who was with Washington at Fort Necessity and was later taken to Fort Duquesne, declared that La Force was greatly missed at that fort following his capture. See *Pennsylvania Colonial Records*, VI, 142. Washington described La Force as a ". . . . bold Enterprising Man, ... whose active Spirit leads him into all parts, add to this a perfect use of the Indian Tongue and ye influence with the Indians." *Dinwiddie Papers*, I, 180–81.

[107] Otherwise called Joseph Coulon de Villiers (1718–1754).

Necessity,[108] the prestige of the English colonies with the Ohio Indians dropped to a very low mark indeed. Only Half King and Monacatoocha, with their families and a few other tribesmen, went over to the English when Pennsylvania and Virginia promised to provide food and shelter for the Indian women and children.[109]

Meanwhile, the French had successfully driven Ensign Edward Ward and his small group away from the forks of the Ohio and were lavishly handing out merchandise at Fort Duquesne. So confident were the French of their friendship with the tribesmen, achieved by a show of military force and presents of strouds, guns, gunpowder, bullets, blankets, and fine suits of clothes, that the Indians were allowed the complete liberty of the fort.[110]

British prestige suffered further damage at the hands of the commander at Fort Cumberland. Any of the Ohio Indians who had not already been alienated were bewildered by the inexperienced commander at this post. Colonel James Innes[111] ". . . . so ignorantly conducted . . . ." native treaties that William Shirley, for one, thought that the very security of the colonies was threatened.[112] To the great surprise of Dinwiddie, who carried out the agreement, Innes even went so far as to promise horses to the natives.[113] One of the most striking examples of the commander's exaggerations occurred when he offered wine, rum, and provisions to the Indians and then made a speech telling them of the British capture of the ". . . . great Town Paris, and their [the French] king Prisoner in former years . . . ."[114] Perhaps the crowning blunder of all, however, was the occasion

---

[108] For the terms of the capitulation see *Pennsylvania Archives* (1st series), II, 146–47. The French agreed to hold back their Indian allies and the English were granted the honors of war allowing them ". . . . to march out Drums beating, wth [*sic*] a Swivell Gun. . . . ." Also see *Pennsylvania Colonial Records*, VI, 141–43, 161–63.

[109] Andrew Montour to James Hamilton, July 21, 1754, *Pennsylvania Colonial Records*, VI, 130; George Croghan to James Hamilton, August 16, 1754, *ibid.*, VI, 140–41.

[110] *Ibid.*, VI, 142–62.

[111] James Innes, a native of Scotland, had a varied military career and lived for a time in North Carolina. He served with Lawrence Washington in the unsuccessful expedition against Cartagena under Colonel William Gooch, who was governor of Virginia. Why Dinwiddie selected as a commanding officer at Fort Cumberland a man so much criticized for his lack of military ability and, more important, so inept in dealing with the Indians is a moot question. The fact remains that both Braddock and Dinwiddie had confidence in James Innes.

[112] William Shirley to Richard Peters, May 21, 1755, *Pennsylvania Archives* (1st series), II, 321–22.

[113] *Dinwiddie Papers*, I, 422–23.

[114] P.R.O., C.O., 5/15, L.C. 285, C.O. 397.

when Innes advised Braddock not to take along more than eight Indian guides on the march to Fort Duquesne.[115]

With such a sad state of native politics existing on the Ohio, the only hope for a reorganization of Indian affairs came from the Albany conference, which had been taking place during the summer of 1754. It will be remembered that Dinwiddie was unable to send delegates to this important meeting because he was under heavy expenses in arranging for the projected meeting with the Ohio Indians at Winchester. Without the Virginia commissioners, men such as Benjamin Franklin, Conrad Weiser, William Johnson, Peter Wraxall, and the representatives from most of the Northern colonies went ahead to lay the groundwork for a grand plan of reorganization.[116] The most powerful sachems of the Six Nations spoke their pieces here, and received large presents, one of which was £800 from the New York Assembly.[117] Another gift of £500 in Maryland money was furnished by the delegates of that province.[118] With the approval of the Iroquois sachems, and at the request of the Board of Trade, William Johnson was appointed Colonel of the Six Nations and was to be entrusted with presents for that confederacy.[119] Here was the basis for the superintendency system that was to bear so much fruit in securing Indian allies for Johnson's campaign against Crown Point in 1755.

On the Ohio, however, Indian affairs went from bad to worse. In August 1754 the only Indians in the British alliance were those who were living off Croghan at Aughwick.[120] A powerful military offensive by the French, beginning at Pickawillany in 1752, and ending with the capitulation of Washington and the capture of the forks of the Ohio, overawed the Ohio Indians; and thereafter the dazzling array of French presents forced the bewildered Indians into a French alliance.

In reviewing the British loss of prestige, one must remember that the following factors all played an important part in the loss of native allies. Dinwiddie had been handicapped by Glen, who nullified the effect of Virginia's presents to the Southern Indians. The "purchases" of land by mere presents of goods also worked to the detriment of the British. In addition, the Virginia Governor was not always skillful in his selection of men to hand

---

[115] *Vide*, chapter viii. For the Dinwiddie-Innes correspondence, see *Dinwiddie Papers*, I, 320–22, 396–97, 422–23.

[116] See the "Minutes of the Albany Conference," *Pennsylvania Colonial Records*, VI, 57–133.

[117] *New York Colonial Documents*, VI, 834.

[118] P.R.O., C.O., 5/15, L.C. Tr. (film).

[119] *New York Colonial Documents*, VI, 917–19.

[120] *Vide*, chapter viii for a discussion of the problems of feeding and housing the Indians at Croghan's settlement at Aughwick.

out presents. Colonel James Innes is a prize example here. Surprisingly enough, Half King thought Washington "good natured" but inexperienced. Though he made no complaint regarding the presents that had been given him by the youthful commander, the sachem pointed out that Washington would ". . . . command the Indians as his slaves, and would have them every day upon the Out Scout [sic] and attack the Enemy by themselves, and that he would by no means take Advice from the Indians. . . . ."[121]

Thus had come the crisis in the struggle between Britain and France in the New World. The British campaigns of 1755 were to tell a story that might have been different but for Indian allies. Presents had been used to cultivate the Indians, but disunity and a lack of finesse in treating with the tribesmen had alienated all but a few Ohio warriors and the Six Nations in the North.

---

[121] *Pennsylvania Colonial Records*, VI, 151. It is of interest that Washington's Indian name was Conotocarious. This name had been bestowed on his grandfather and it meant "devourer of villages." See *Writings of Washington*, I, 38–39.

VIII. PRESENTS AS A FACTOR IN THE FRONTIER CAMPAIGNS OF 1755

By the year 1754, the necessity of Indian auxiliaries had become quite apparent to British military leaders; and George Washington, for one, was convinced that this Indian service could only be obtained through the use of presents. Whether the service be scouting, hunting, or any one of numerous jobs the tribesmen could perform, Washington maintained that it was a "standing maxim" that Indian assistance had to be purchased.[1] Washington further concluded that people who were familiar with the nature of the Indians were well aware that the friendship of the aborigines was not sufficiently great to allow them to perform these services gratis.[2] As a matter of fact, the young military leader complained that once he had found it necessary to supply one of his own ruffled shirts to a native in order to secure intelligence.[3]

In turning to the British campaigns of 1755, the principles behind the shrewd analysis by young George Washington may be observed in Braddock's defeat on the Monongahela, William Johnson's successful Lake George campaign, and William Shirley's attempt to organize a force against Fort Niagara. The plans for this threefold onslaught against the French were consummated at the council of war held at Alexandria in April 1755.

It is clear that at the very outset of the conference the problem of securing funds for Indian presents was a matter of prime importance to Braddock as well as to the Colonial governors who attended the meeting.[4] In addition, Braddock was greatly concerned with the appointment of an agent to handle the delicate affairs of the Six Nations and their allies. In answer to this situation, the governors, who formed a good representation of the most important colonies, gave their approval to the appointment of William Johnson as the sole superintendent of the Northern Indians.[5]

---

[1] *The Writings of Washington*, I, 52.

[2] *Ibid.*

[3] *Ibid.*

[4] "Minutes of a Council Held at Alexandria," April 14, 1755, *Documentary History of the State of New York*, II, 378–79; *Pennsylvania Colonial Records*, VI, 364–68; P.R.O., C.O., 5/46, L.C. 29–34.

[5] The following governors were in attendance: William Shirley of Massachusetts, Robert Dinwiddie of Virginia, James De Lancey of New York, Horatio Sharp of Maryland, and Robert Hunter Morris of Pennsylvania. It is significant that James Glen of South Carolina was not invited. His influence with the Cherokees and Catawbas might have enabled Braddock to secure a large auxiliary force.

There were other problems which arose; but the attention of the Colonial representatives was also focused on two issues regarding Indian gifts: the value of presents to be given to the natives, and in what manner these goods were to be supplied. It was finally agreed that the cash should come from a common fund supplied by the Crown. In turn, the colonies would supplement this common fund with amounts determined according to the proportions settled upon at the plan of union in Albany in 1754.[6] The administrators further agreed that the £800 sterling, appropriated for the Northern Indians, would be divided. Five hundred pounds were to be used for the Iroquois and their allies, while the remaining three hundred pounds would be sent to the Western Indians, via Oswego.[7] Concurring further, the governors approved the selection of military leaders. It was decided that Johnson should lead an expedition against Fort Frederick or Crown Point; William Shirley would take command of the forces to move against Niagara; and Braddock himself would initiate the threefold attack by marching on Fort Duquesne. Out of these plans emerged several discords which were to grow in major proportions as deciding issues in the outcome of the frontier campaigns in 1755.

The first discord to be discussed here concerns the conflict between Johnson and Shirley. It is evident that enough money was provided for presents to secure warriors for the two northern campaigns. What Braddock and the other members of the Alexandria conference did not anticipate was the bitter rivalry that was to develop between Shirley and Johnson.[8] Several accounts make it obvious that the Massachusetts Governor expected William Johnson to secure Indians for the Niagara campaign. Moreover, Shirley expected Western Indians to congregate at Oswego, tempted by the £300 present.[9]

The obtaining and handling of native auxiliaries was another major problem in the 1755 campaigns. Braddock might have realized that Johnson, so far to the north, could have had little influence in obtaining immediate native auxiliaries in the Ohio campaign. Indeed, from evidence at hand, it is now clear that Braddock thought that such an extensive military force as he now had made Indians unnecessary. The General's apparent dislike of these unconventional warriors of the forest made him overlook their true

---

[6] *Vide*, note 4.

[7] When William Shirley became convinced that Johnson was not supporting him as far as securing Indians for the Niagara campaign was concerned, he attempted to lure the Indians over to his command by every means possible. See *Sir William Johnson Papers*, I, 644–45, and Lincoln, *op. cit.*, II, 243–48.

[8] See *Sir William Johnson Papers*, I, 644–45.

[9] *Ibid.*, I, 598–99.

importance in frontier warfare.[10] A close examination of Braddock's correspondence immediately after the meeting at Alexandria reveals that he was very much concerned about the necessity of Iroquois' aid for Johnson and Shirley, but not for himself. For instance, he describes in detail all of his preparations in a letter to Thomas Robinson, dated April 19, 1755.[11] He reiterated plans relating to gifts for the Northern Indians, as was discussed in the meeting five days before; but nowhere does he mention his own native scouts and warriors or the presents necessary to secure their services. From outward appearances it would seem that this European General was naïve enough to believe that he was capable of defeating the French without assistance from the Indians. Actually this could hardly have been the case, for Braddock had been promised four hundred Southern Indians by Lieutenant Governor Robert Dinwiddie of Virginia.[12]

Upon his arrival in the Old Dominion, one of the Virginia Governor's first moves was to attempt to secure the friendship of the Southern tribes, mainly the Catawbas and the Cherokees. Unfortunately for Dinwiddie, his plans were consistently opposed by Governor James Glen of South Carolina, who bitterly denounced almost every move made by the government of Virginia.[13] Thus Dinwiddie's frequent presents to the Southern tribes were of no avail in securing warriors so long as Glen's co-operation was wanting.[14] Braddock was unaware of this feud; and when the prom-

---

[10] It is apparent from contemporary journals that Braddock was so absorbed in the complications of his command that he paid relatively little attention to the Indian guides after leaving Fort Cumberland. It was not until July 3 and 4, when the great forest surrounded his army, making it obvious that he was dependent upon the Indians, that the General earnestly pleaded with "presents and promises" to induce the native guides to obtain intelligence. See the journal of Robert Orme, aide-de-camp to Braddock (hereafter cited as "Orme's Journal"), in Sargent, *op. cit.*, p. 348. The other journal printed in this work has been called the "Morris Journal," deriving its name from the former owner, Reverend Francis O. Morris of Yorkshire, England. See *ibid.*, p. 366. The "Morris Journal" was actually the record of events as kept by the seamen who were assigned to the march by Commodore Augustus Keppel.

[11] Edward Braddock to Thomas Robinson, April 19, 1755, P.R.O., C.O., 5/46, L.C. 19–28.

[12] "Croghan's Journal," *Early Western Travels*, I, 97. Robert Orme was under the impression that Dinwiddie had promised the General only three hundred Indians. See "Orme's Journal," Sargent, *op. cit.*, pp. 314–15.

[13] The controversy between Glen and Dinwiddie concerned presents, forts, Indian lands, and Indian policy in general. See, for instance, Robert Dinwiddie to James Glen, August 5, 1754, *Dinwiddie Papers*, I, 272–76. For the controversy on the Cherokee fort, see *ibid.*, I, 484–85.

[14] Glen wrote that Dinwiddie was not experienced in native politics and that New York and South Carolina should deal with the Indians. James Adair, trader, was also in conflict with Glen. Adair criticized the South Carolina Governor for attempt-

ised native auxiliaries did not put in their appearance at Fort Cumberland, he innocently inquired why the government of South Carolina had not been consulted, for these Indians were the natural allies of that province.[15]

South Carolina's indifference was not the only factor that prevented Dinwiddie's Cherokees and Catawbas from coming to aid Braddock. When the Virginia Governor had summoned the Southern tribes, he had chosen Christopher Gist's son, Nathaniel, as his agent. However, Richard Pearis, a trader, who was an agent for the colony of Virginia at this time, but later served Maryland, challenged the right of young Gist to summon the Indians. A confusion of authority followed. Since Pearis had plied the Indians with liquor, however, he was able to divert them from going to Braddock's assistance; and when the inexperienced Gist was unable to produce any sealed document to prove that he was not an impostor, the natives finally returned to their towns.[16] Thus it was that the Ohio expedition was deprived of the assistance of the Cherokees and of the Catawbas, the latter often called the "bravest of Indians."[17] Why Dinwiddie, after spending so much money for presents, allowed an inexperienced man like Nathaniel Gist to assume the responsibility for such an important mission is still an unanswered question.

---

ing to influence the Indians by "kind promises and smooth speeches" when, instead, presents were needed. See *Adair's History of the American Indians*, p. 259.

[15] "Orme's Journal," Sargent, *op. cit.*, p. 316. It should be noted that it was much easier for the Cherokees to negotiate and trade with South Carolina rather than Virginia because of the problem of distance. South Carolina was closer to the Cherokee towns by six hundred miles. See Robert Dinwiddie to the Board of Trade, December 10, 1752, P.R.O., C.O., 5/1327, L.C. 415–24, C.O. 531–36. Moreover, Dinwiddie did not know that Glen was giving the Cherokees and Catawbas presents during the very time when they should have gone to aid Braddock. It seems that the sachems refused to go because they had made previous plans to meet the South Carolina Governor in June 1755. See Robert Dinwiddie to James Glen, July 28, 1755, *Dinwiddie Papers*, II, 125–26.

[16] "Orme's Journal," Sargent, *op. cit.*, pp. 314–15; *Early Western Travels*, I, 98. Dinwiddie was highly displeased with the actions of Pearis. His letter of June 26, 1755 to Pearis reads: "I cannot help observ'g, if it had not been for the unseasonable and disagreeable Difference between You and Gist, I am fully of Opinion they [the Cherokees] w'd, according to their former Promise, have sent some of their Warriors long before now to join our Forces." See *Dinwiddie Papers*, II, 77. At this time the Governor also sent a letter to the Catawbas and Cherokees urging them to join Braddock. See *ibid.*, II, 76.

It is of interest to note that Nathaniel Gist's father, Christopher, joined Braddock's forces and, with Croghan's Indians, performed valuable guide service. At one time he was almost caught by two French Indians who observed him when reconnoitering Fort Duquesne. See "Orme's Journal," Sargent, *op. cit.*, pp. 209, 349. For the later activities of Nathaniel Gist, see Samuel Cole Williams, "Nathaniel Gist, Father of Sequoyah," *The Tennessee Historical Society's Publications*, No. 5 (January 1933), pp. 39–54.

[17] "Orme's Journal," Sargent, *op. cit.*, p. 287.

Such an action does not seem at all consistent with the Indian-conscious Dinwiddie who sent ribbons, cutlasses, and laced hats for the warriors encamped at Fort Cumberland. As a matter of fact, the Virginia Governor sent some six hundred pounds' worth of goods to the Southern Indians in his attempts to enlist their aid.[18]

In the meantime, the scene shifted to the Ohio frontier, where the Quaker colony was making presents of food in order to obtain native support for Braddock. George Croghan, agent for Pennsylvania who later became Braddock's Indian manager, maintained that the basic cause for Braddock's defeat was a lack of Indian support. If anyone ever tried to obtain auxiliaries by means of food, arms, and other gifts, it was Croghan. But let us go back to the beginning of Croghan's story.

After Washington's capitulation at Fort Necessity in July 1754, those Indians, led by Half King (otherwise known as Monacatoocha) went to Virginia.[19] After a brief stay in this province, they joined Croghan at Aughwick,[20] where they were supported by funds from the Pennsylvania government.[21] In September 1754, Conrad Weiser reported that Croghan was feeding and caring for at least two hundred Indians—men, women, and children—who were living in some twenty cabins.[22] On behalf of the Quaker assembly, Weiser assured these Delawares, Shawnees, and Iroquois that they were welcome to stay at Aughwick and that they would be notified of any change in plans.[23] A conference with Croghan followed, at which time Weiser turned over three hundred pounds to the agent to help him in supporting the natives. Weiser noted that Croghan had to supply the Indians with five bags of corn a day—an amount which did not

---

[18] The actual amount was £599:2:3. See P.R.O., C.O., 5/15, L.C. 575–86 (film); Robert Dinwiddie to Thomas Robinson, June 6, 1755, P.R.O., C.O., 5/15, L.C. 587–90 (film).

[19] See the biographical sketch of Monacatoocha and Half King (Tanacharisson), notes 4 and 5, chapter vi.

[20] Aughwick was located at the junction of Aughwick Creek and the Juanita River, the present site of Shirleysburg, Pennsylvania. See Albert T. Volwiler, *George Croghan and the Westward Movement 1741–1782*, p. 48.

[21] *Early Western Travels*, I, 96. See also "Instructions to Conrad Weiser, August 24, 1754," *Pennsylvania Colonial Records*, VI, 147–48.

[22] Conrad Weiser to James Hamilton, September 13, 1754, *Pennsylvania Colonial Records*, VI, 148–50.

[23] James Hamilton was to be succeeded by Robert Hunter Morris as lieutenant governor of Pennsylvania. For this reason the immediate future of Indian affairs was uncertain. See *Pennsylvania Colonial Records*, VI, 148. This confusion prevented Conrad Weiser from accepting the aid offered by the Delawares and Shawnees for Braddock's expedition. The sachems waited until late in the fall of 1754; and when no answer was given them, they went home. See *Early Western Travels*, I, 96–97; *Pennsylvania Colonial Records*, VI, 158.

include the extra grain taken by the natives whenever they felt they needed more. This was a small quantity of food, however, when compared with the large amount of butter, milk, squashes, and pumpkins that the Indians consumed.[24]

Of the two hundred Indians who were at Aughwick in September 1754, only fifty remained to journey to Fort Cumberland with Croghan the following spring. The decrease in the number of warriors was due to the "bloody flux" disease as well as to the consumption of liquor. This liquor, which ruined the health of many, was given to the Indians by Lewis Montour, a half-breed trader, and a brother of the more honorable Andrew Montour, interpreter.[25]

On April 14, 1755, immediately after the Alexandria council of war, Robert Hunter Morris, governor of Pennsylvania, directed Croghan to bring his Indians to Fort Cumberland.[26] A large number of belts and strings of wampum was sent to Croghan, with instructions to use them to the utmost advantage in employing Indians. Morris also pointed out that the greater the number of Indians the trader could procure, the greater would be the amount of credit given to their province.[27]

By the first day of May 1755, Croghan had successfully delivered the Governor's message to the Indians, who approved the suggestion to move on to Fort Cumberland. Since Braddock did not want the women and children in camp, Croghan apparently planned to leave them at Aughwick.[28] Although his accounts were in order, Croghan complained that the assembly probably would not reimburse him for the expense of maintaining the women and children at his place. This plan was not carried out, however; and, much to the disgust of Braddock and Colonel James Innes, commander at the fort, Croghan's warriors arrived at Fort Cumberland accompanied by their women and children.

Braddock's questions concerning the Southern Indians at this time reveal that the General had little or no information regarding his native auxiliaries.[29] Croghan replied that he did not know their whereabouts and referred the General to Captain Andrew Montour. Montour informed Braddock that Dinwiddie's agent had failed in securing the aid of the Southern Indians. To make matters still worse, Colonel James Innes, fearing that the women and children would be too much trouble to feed

---

[24] *Pennsylvania Colonial Records*, VI, 149.

[25] *Ibid.*

[26] Robert Hunter Morris to George Croghan, April 23, 1755 (erroneously printed as 1756), *ibid.*, VI, 372.

[27] *Ibid.*

[28] George Croghan to Robert Hunter Morris, May 1, 1755, *ibid.*, VI, 374–75.

[29] "Croghan's Journal," *Early Western Travels*, I, 97.

and shelter, requested Braddock to send some of the fifty Indians back to Aughwick. Eight of the warriors remained with the British to act as scouts and hunters, and Pennsylvania assumed the burden of paying for the food and shelter of the women and children of these remaining guides.[30] General Braddock now made every effort to please these warriors. He directed Croghan to satisfy their every want, and he personally assured the warriors that their families would have the very best of care at Aughwick.[31] Moreover, the General made a handsome present to the visiting Delawares, urging them to join the march as soon as they could. Regardless of Braddock's extreme kindness to the Delawares, however, they did not join the expedition. Probably, as George Croghan conjectured, the former breaches of faith on the part of the English were the cause of this lack of co-operation.[32]

Near the end of April 1755, Braddock went to Winchester to meet the Indians expected from the south; but when none appeared, he returned to Fort Cumberland. According to a contemporary journal, on May 17, Braddock lavished presents of strouds, rings, beads, linen, knives, war paint, and wampum on the remaining eight Indians in an effort to secure their promise to act as guides and scouts. On the following day, Monacatoocha, speaking for the Indians, vowed their allegiance. Much to the astonishment and pleasure of the natives, the General celebrated this announcement with the firing of three howitzers and several other large guns, whereupon the Indians retired to their own camp to feast on bullock and to perform the war dance.[33]

When the army finally got under way early in June, Croghan and the eight Indians were ordered to march with the advance party. While they were out scouting on June 18, Scarrooyady and his son were captured by the enemy. The prestige of this sachem of the Six Nations was so great, however, that the French Indians themselves refused to allow him to be killed. Later the son escaped while Scarrooyady was tied to a tree. He rejoined Braddock's army, and shortly thereafter Croghan's Indians were able to rescue the sachem himself.[34]

[30] Edward Braddock to Robert Hunter Morris, May 20, 1755, *Pennsylvania Colonial Records*, VI, 398.

[31] *Ibid.*

[32] "Croghan's Journal," *Early Western Travels*, I, 98; "Morris Journal," Sargent, *op. cit.*, p. 380. The Delawares had previously offered their aid to Weiser for this campaign but it had been temporarily refused. *Vide*, note 23.

[33] "Morris Journal," Sargent, *op. cit.*, pp. 377–79. The Indians were quite pleased with the presents that they had received on the 17th of May. To show their approval, they ". . . . made a most horrible noise, dancing all night." *Ibid.*, p. 378.

[34] "Orme's Journal," Sargent, *op. cit.*, p. 336. This boy was killed accidentally on the march. *Vide*, note 40. Scarrooyady was condoled by presents for the loss of

Five days later a delegation of Mohawks visited the British camp. Having realized the inadequacy of his scouting force, Braddock went out of his way to please these natives. In addition, he gave special presents to them in an effort to obtain their assistance. Nevertheless, the Mohawks "deserted" the camp that night, taking with them one of the eight remaining scouts. Later this deserter was found trying to conceal himself along the flanks of the main column, but the Indians would not allow the British to punish him.[35]

As the main column approached Fort Duquesne, the possibility of being ambushed became more and more likely. Surprise attackers could easily conceal themselves in the ravines, which were covered by a primeval forest and a heavy growth of underbrush.[36] The British General now became fully aware of his almost complete dependence upon Croghan's eight Indian scouts. This was definitely hostile territory. Once they discovered the remains of an enemy camp, and these native scouts, making use of signs known only to veterans of forest warfare,[37] were able to ascertain that one hundred and fifty persons had been encamped here. By July 3, the hazards of scouting had become so great that Braddock could not obtain intelligence unless he constantly prevailed upon the Indians with presents and promises.[38] Finally, on the following day, after much persuasion, the natives left to reconnoiter about Fort Duquesne. Three days

---

his son by Pennsylvania after the campaign was over. See *Pennsylvania Colonial Records*, VI, 523. It should be mentioned that Robert Orme frequently calls Scarrooyady by the name of Monacatoocha. This fact is quite confusing and gives the reader the impression that there are two Indians instead of one.

[35] "Orme's Journal," Sargent, *op. cit.*, p. 340. This Indian apparently rejoined the remaining seven scouts. One reason why the Six Nations refused to aid Braddock was because of their traditional feud with the Cherokees and Catawbas who were expected to accompany the British General. See William Johnson to the Board of Trade, July 21, 1755, *Documentary History of the State of New York*, II, 393. This feud was actually not a valid excuse for the Six Nations' (at least the Mohawks') "deserting" the General at such a crucial time, for, as it turned out, the Southern Indians (the Catawbas and the Cherokees) never appeared. *Vide*, note 16. To be perfectly fair to the Indians, it ought to be borne in mind that the natives were, in truth, under neither moral nor legal obligation to come to the aid either of the English or French. To regard the Indians as "deserters" in all such cases is merely following the conventional attitude toward the American Indian—who nearly always has been thought of as a pawn or mercenary, rarely as a member of a sovereign "nation."

[36] For a fuller discussion of this point, see Lawrence Henry Gipson, *The British Empire Before the American Revolution*, Vol. VI, *The Great War for Empire, the Years of Defeat 1754–1757*, pp. 62–98.

[37] "Orme's Journal," Sargent, *op. cit.*, p. 341.

[38] *Ibid.*, p. 348.

later they returned with a French officer's scalp and the report that they had seen only a few men at the fort.[39]

An accident which brought great sorrow to the Indians occurred at this time. Despite the fact that he had given the proper countersign, Scarrooyady's son was mistaken for a hostile Indian and was killed when he approached the British camp.[40] Robert Orme feared that this mishap would alienate the Indians. This was not the case, however, and it should be recorded to the everlasting credit of Edward Braddock that he bestowed the "usual presents" in such an unusual manner that the Indians became even more strongly attached to the British cause.[41]

As the winding force of British troops moved slowly forward, the Indians, encouraged by constant gifts, kept the commanding General informed of French actions and of the number of troops at Fort Duquesne. It was the advance party made up of Croghan and his Indians that first sighted the French forces, which were composed of four lieutenants, twenty cadets, one hundred soldiers, one hundred Canadians, and six hundred warriors.[42] The latter had come solely for the booty—a kind of "present" bestowed by the French.[43] Contrary to long-held belief, the

---

[39] "Orme's Journal," Sargent, *op. cit.*, p. 348. Christopher Gist also performed valuable guide service at this time. *Vide* note 16.

[40] *Ibid.*, p. 350. The inexperience of Braddock in using Indian auxiliaries was very apparent in this incident. To prevent the accidental shooting of Indian allies, William Johnson, on the other hand, ordered his Indians to wear a red filet (net) over their head. See "Instructions for Major General Lyman," July 17, 1755, *Sir William Johnson Papers*, I, 730–32.

[41] "Orme's Journal," Sargent, *op. cit.*, p. 350.

[42] "Relation du Combat du 9 Juillet, 1755," Sargent, *op. cit.*, p. 409. According to the record of Daniel Hyacinthe Marie Lienard Sieur de Beaujeau, who led the French Indians, the party was composed of 600 natives, 72 soldiers, and 146 Canadians. See Jean Marie Shea (ed.), *Relations Diverses sur La Bataille du Malangueulé Gagné le 9 Juillet, 1755, par les François sous m. de Beaujeau, Commandant du Fort du Quesne sur les Anglois m. Braddock, Général en Chef des troupes Angloises*, p. 19. Washington wrote that he was certain the whole number of French and Indians did not exceed three hundred men. See, for example, George Washington to Mary Washington, July 18, 1755, *Writings of Washington*, I, 150–52.

[43] Beaujeau stated that the French Indians came along only as auxiliaries for the booty that they might obtain. See Shea, *op. cit.*, p. 20. As a matter of fact, the Indians had decided not to accompany the French; but at the last moment before leaving, Beaujeau taunted the natives by saying, "Je suis déterminé à aller au devant des ennemis; quoi! laisserez-vous aller votre pére seul? Je suis sur de les vaincre." After this brave speech, the Indians decided to follow their bold leader. See *ibid.* The booty that the French Indians shared amounted to thirteen pieces of artillery, much arms and ammunition, one hundred cattle, and four hundred horses killed or captured. See Shea, *op. cit.*, p. 20; "Equipment taken from the English by the French in the battle of July 9, 1755," Arch. Nat. Col. F3, 14 ff. vo. (Library of Congress photostat).

Courtesy Huntington Library

JOHN CAMPBELL, FOURTH EARL OF LOUDOUN

British were not completely surprised by the enemy attack. After they had been observed by the advance guard, the French spread out to fight Indian fashion, hiding in the dense undergrowth and the ravines along the British flanks. Heavy firing began about 3:00 p.m. on that fateful July 9, with the British advance parties falling back upon the main column and baggage section, causing the greatest confusion.[44]

The story of this massacre is familiar to all and need not be repeated here. The British were left with a dying general and a routed army, which was now under the leadership of George Washington, who had not yet recovered from a serious illness. On the other hand, a victorious enemy claimed all the rich spoils of military supplies.

The eight Indians who had so loyally assisted the Braddock forces were not forgotten. The government of Pennsylvania rewarded these faithful men with warm words of thanks—and presents. At a council held at Philadelphia in August 1755, Governor Robert Hunter Morris expressed sympathy to Scarrooyady for the loss of his son and then spoke to the sachem and the other warriors of the Six Nations in these words:

> Brethren of the Six Nations: You
> that are here, to wit, Scarrooyady,
> Cushuwayon, Froson, Kahuktodon,
> Attschechokatha, Kashwughdaniunto,
> Dyioquario. You fought under General
> Braddock, and behaved with Spirit and
> Valour during the Engagement; we should
> be wanting to ourselves not to make you
> our hearty acknowledgements for your
> Fidelity and Assistance. We see you
> consider yourselves as our Flesh and
> Blood, and fight for us as if We were
> your own kindred. By this Belt we
> return you our hearty thanks.[45]

Shortly after these unmistakable expressions of gratitude, the assembly rewarded Scarrooyady and his brethren with strouds, matchcoats, blankets, halfthicks,[46] garlix, knives, awl blades, bed lace, scarlet garters, sorted rings,

---

It should be mentioned that the French, due to the shortage of presents, hereafter successfully obtained Indian allies by promises and gifts of plunder. This was particularly true at the victories of Oswego in August, 1756 and Fort William Henry in August, 1757. See *New York Colonial Documents*, X, 464, 615–18. It is noteworthy that the gallant Montcalm risked his life to restrain the French Indians from cruelly treating British prisoners. See *ibid.*

[44] Sargent, *op. cit.*, pp. 353, 384–89.   [45] *Pennsylvania Colonial Records*, VI, 524.

[46] For an explanation of the various types of gifts, see chapter iii. A halfthick was a cheap woolen cloth given to the Indians for clothing. It was commonly allotted in "pieces," and dyed with bright colors.

morris bells, gunpowder, lead, tobacco, pipes, and guns.[47] It should also be remembered that the province of Pennsylvania had been responsible for the complete support of the dependents of these warriors. While the eight scouts were at the front, the province had sent flour, Indian corn, and salt to the women and children who had been left at George Croghan's encampment at Aughwick under the care of his brother.[48]

Two years later, when George Croghan wrote out his account of Braddock's defeat, he absolved himself of all blame regarding Braddock's Indians. He carefully pointed out that he had been acting under orders when he sent all but eight of the Indians back to Aughwick. "But I am of the opinion," he bitterly concluded, "that had we fifty Indians instead of eight, that we might in a great measure have prevented the surprise, that day of our unhappy defeat."[49] George Washington defended the courageous Edward Braddock, who had five horses shot from beneath him before he was fatally wounded; but other contemporaries pointed out that the British ". . . . held in too great Contempt the Indian Manner of Fighting. . . . ."[50] It does seem fairly obvious that a sufficient number of native auxiliaries would have changed the outcome of this most significant battle. Enough presents had been used to procure more than the number of warriors needed to avert defeat; but again best-laid plans were ruined by poor Indian management. Unfortunately for the British, control of Indian affairs had not yet been centralized under one capable head.

With the Ohio frontier now rendered defenseless against bold war parties of French Indians, Washington was put in command here and was commissioned by Dinwiddie to distribute presents as he saw fit.[51] Following William Johnson's example, the young colonel sought competent assistance to deal with the Indians. His choice fell on the experienced George Croghan

---

[47] *Pennsylvania Colonial Records*, VI, 566.

[48] George Croghan to Robert Hunter Morris, May 20, 1755, *Pennsylvania Colonial Records*, VI, 398–99.

[49] George Croghan's Statement, August 18, 1757, Sargent, *op. cit.*, pp. 407–8. See also *Early Western Travels*, I, 96–99, for Croghan's journal in 1755.

[50] Robert Hunter Morris to William Shirley, July 28, 1755, *Pennsylvania Colonial Records*, VI, 496–98. Morris refers to the letter that he received from Robert Orme on July 18, 1755. See *ibid.*, VI, 487–89. Dinwiddie also stated that the defeat was due to the French method of "bush fight'g." See *Dinwiddie Papers*, II, 125–26. The official summary of the causes of Braddock's defeat listed, as one of three reasons, "The Want of Indians or Other irregulars to give timely Notice of the Enemy's Approach, having only three or four guides for out Scouts." See Thomas Dunbar and Thomas Gage to William Shirley, October 21, 1755, Lincoln, *op. cit.*, II, 311–13.

[51] *Dinwiddie Papers*, II, 184–87.

and his fellow-interpreter, Andrew Montour.[52] Washington held that one man, Christopher Gist, for example, should be empowered to give presents to all the Indians, using subordinates if necessary, but all working with one policy in mind.[53] Such centralization would prevent conflicting gifts and the wasteful handing out of large numbers of goods to Indians at treaties. In other words, specific gifts were to be made for designated services.[54] This pattern was followed by the Crown in 1756, when Indian administration was reorganized under the energetic direction of William Pitt, and Edmond Atkin was appointed Southern superintendent of Indian Affairs.[55]

There can be little doubt that Braddock's defeat had an unfortunate effect upon the Ohio Indians and the Iroquoian confederacy.[56] Certainly many presents would be needed to restore the prestige of the British. It was a discouraged Croghan who wrote to Johnson stating that the Colonial governments were not taking pains to win over the Indians and that Pennsylvania was actually making the error of treating with the very natives who had fought against the General. Croghan further noted that Virginia was paying courtship to the Cherokees and Catawbas, tribesmen who had failed to aid Braddock.[57] Governor Dinwiddie, however, could see no reason why the fact that the Cherokees and Catawbas had turned a deaf ear to his summons in June 1755 should prevent his giving them additional presents. More important, he maintained that presents without stint should be given the Southern Indians because of their superiority in numbers.[58] Nevertheless it was

---

[52] Dinwiddie sent both Croghan and Montour to help Washington distribute presents and deal with the Indians generally.

[53] George Washington to Robert Dinwiddie, June 12, 1757, *Writings of Washington*, II, 57–59.

[54] Same to same, May 27, 1754, *ibid.*, I, 55.

[55] Edmond Atkin became superintendent over the Southern Indians in 1756. His position corresponded to William Johnson's position in the North; but Atkin did not have either the tact in dealing with, or the ascendancy over, the Indians that Johnson had.

[56] George Croghan to William Johnson, September 10, 1755, *Sir William Johnson Papers*, II, 28–30.

[57] *Ibid.*

[58] *Dinwiddie Papers*, I, 99, II, 289, 306. Though Dinwiddie favored the Southern Indians in the matter of presents, Johnson thought the Northern Indians more important. In a contemporary document, now in the Loudoun Papers, is to be found a good illustration of the latter's position. This manuscript contains, in parallel columns, a comprehensive list of presents for the Northern and Southern Indians. In every case Johnson allows more goods for the Northern Indians in spite of their smaller numbers. For example, he allows four hundred guns for the Northern Indians while he plans to give only three hundred guns to the Southern Indians. See LO 2507.

not until 1756 that gifts were used extensively to renew treaties with the Ohio and the Southern Indians.[59]

The scene shifts now to the North, where preparations were in full swing for the most successful campaign of the year. In order to understand the difficulties encountered in presenting goods to the Iroquois at this time, William Johnson's position after the conference at Alexandria must be clarified. According to the minutes of that meeting, Braddock was commander-in-chief, and William Shirley was second-in-command. Shirley was also in control of the purse strings as far as the giving of presents was concerned.[60] William Johnson held two important offices. He was sole manager of the Six Nations and their allies;[61] and he was commissioned major general, and placed in command of the expedition to Crown Point. These offices gave him complete authority over the distribution of presents to the Northern Indians—with one exception. That exception involved William Shirley. Shirley, who was appointed commander-in-chief after the death of Braddock, interpreted his military commission as giving him authority not only over the Indians, but even over the Indian superintendent himself!

In the ensuing conflict between Shirley and Johnson, the latter's prestige among the Mohawks counted strongly in his favor. Since this tribe was one of the three senior members of the confederacy, its friendship carried much weight.[62] Numerous presents of arms, clothing, vermilion, and textiles had made its members loyal to the British.[63] The Mohawks were especially pleased with the appointment of their old leader as the new manager of Indian Affairs; during the past few years they had acquired an attitude of contempt for the stingy commissioners of New York who had failed to please their expensive appetite for presents.[64] The continued support of the

---

[59] In a letter from Johnson to Lord Loudoun, September 10, 1756 (LO 1759), the former complained that the provinces to the south, through their extensive gifts, were actually drawing the Iroquois away from his influence.

[60] Edward Braddock to Thomas Robinson, April 19, 1755, P.R.O., C.O., 5/46, L.C. 19–28. For a summary of the dispute that developed between Johnson and Shirley over presents, see "Summary of Disputes between Governor William Shirley and General William Johnson," 1755, Stanley Pargellis (ed.), *Military Affairs in North America 1748–1756, Selected Documents from the Cumberland Papers in Windsor Castle,* pp. 153–54; William Johnson to the Lords of Trade, September 3, 1755, Lincoln, *op. cit.,* II, 243–48.

[61] Commission from Edward Braddock, April 15, 1755, *Sir William Johnson Papers,* I, 465–66.

[62] Wraxall's "Notes on Indian Affairs at Mount Johnson," July 4, 1755, *New York Colonial Documents,* VI, 988.

[63] *New York Colonial Documents,* VI, 992–93.

[64] William Johnson to William Shirley, December 17, 1754, *Sir William Johnson Papers,* I, 429–30.

Mohawks was essential to Johnson for the complete success of the proposed campaign.

A study of the *Sir William Johnson Papers* and the *New York Colonial Documents* reveals several problems which arose in connection with the use of gifts to procure the aid of native warriors. These problems, unless solved, threatened the success of the Crown Point expedition. One issue centered around the duplication of presents doled out by Johnson and Shirley. Another difficulty involved funds that were sorely needed for gifts, but which were withheld by Shirley. A third problem was the distribution of rum to the Indians and its resultant sad effects upon the natives. Finally, it was necessary to overcome the odium of Braddock's defeat through the expedient of presents to the Six Nations.

William Shirley, the new commander-in-chief, shrewdly concerned himself with instructing Johnson to congregate as many Indians as possible at Oswego. Here they were to be entertained generously.[65] It is possible that Shirley was hoping to raise a huge force of Indians who would aid him in the construction of vessels with which to attack Niagara. Johnson's correspondence reveals a series of commands, demands for scouts, and orders for presents from the Massachusetts executive.[66] Shirley was even so naïve as to propose that the Indians should be formed into regimented army companies with captains, lieutenants, and ensigns.[67] In answer to this proposal, however, Johnson coldly informed him that the Indian officers had, first of all, to be interpreters. It was the responsibility of these Indian officers to satisfy the wants of the tribesmen as well as to lead them; the Indians simply could not be regimented.

As the time drew near for the great conference at Mount Johnson, where Braddock's present was to be given to the natives, Shirley felt the needed Indian support for his own campaign slipping through his fingers. Consequently, he sent John Lydius,[68] former trader and land purchaser for the notorious Connecticut Land Company, and his assistants to Mount Johnson to swing the Indians over to his Niagara forces. In their attempt to discredit Johnson, Lydius and his subordinates informed even the loyal Mo-

---

[65] "William Shirley's Instructions to William Johnson," December 7, 1755, *New York Colonial Documents*, VI, 1026–27.

[66] For example, see William Shirley to William Johnson, June 15, 1755, *Sir William Johnson Papers*, I, 598–99.

[67] William Johnson to William Shirley, June 19, 1755, *ibid.*, I, 614–17.

[68] John Henry Lydius, 1693–1791, was a successful Indian trader having a headquarters near Fort Edward. Though Shirley displayed great confidence in him, entrusting him with many important assignments, Johnson never seems to have trusted him. Lydius' association with the notorious Connecticut Land Company left a stigma attached to his name.

hawks that Johnson was merely an upstart and that all of his money for presents came from the great Governor of Massachusetts.[69] Shirley's men annoyed Johnson's interpreters and were so rude to Arent Stevens, when they demanded to see his credentials to deliver gifts, that the old man rolled up his sleeves and challenged any of them to a test of fisticuffs.[70] These men also started the rumor that Johnson had more than £5,000 for presents which he was deliberately withholding. This sort of eighteenth-century propaganda caused the diluted loyalty of the Senecas to turn; and it also created ". . . . discord Fractions & riot . . . ." among the Mohawks.[71] A temporary crisis arose when Lydius, without invitation, came into the council house at Mount Johnson on July 3, 1755.[72] This unwelcome entrance caused one of the sachems to demand that the agent of Governor Shirley be removed. The Indians declared they wanted no "snake" such as Lydius in the room; and only after the council house atmosphere had been cleared of all "impurities" with a belt of wampum could the meeting begin.

Conditions were so serious by July 30, 1755, that Johnson, who was now in Albany en route to Lake George, wrote to Governor De Lancey of New York as follows:

Lydius is his [Shirley's] Indian Premier, and [under] him are a Number of Agents, working with Money and by every Kind of Artifice to destroy my Influence, to overset the Measures agreed upon at our Meeting & to turn the Indians from the Crown Point to the Niagara Expedition.[73]

As late as the eve of the battle at Lake George, Hendrick of the Mohawks made a last plea for unity among the native warriors by severely scolding them for accepting the presents from John Lydius.[74]

The financial terms announced by Braddock at the Alexandria meeting gave Shirley still another tool with which to prevent the effective distribution of presents by Johnson. According to the arrangements made at this meeting, the new manager of Indian affairs was to have £2,000 for gifts. From this amount, an immediate cash outlay of £800 was to be supplied; and the rest was to be used later.[75] This fund was to be supplemented with money appropriated by the provincial assemblies. Out of the £800 immediate cash, the Governor of Massachusetts demanded £300 to be used to obtain the

[69] William Johnson to James De Lancey, July 30, 1755, *Sir William Johnson Papers*, I, 794–97.

[70] William Johnson to James De Lancey, August 8, 1755, *ibid.*, I, 841.

[71] *Ibid.*

[72] "Indian Proceedings at Mount Johnson," July 3, 1755, *New York Colonial Documents*, VI, 984.

[73] William Johnson to James De Lancey, July 30, 1755, *ibid.*, I, 794–97.

[74] *New York Colonial Documents*, VI, 9.

[75] "Minutes of the Council at Alexandria," April 14, 1755, P.R.O., C.O., 5/46, L.C. 29–34.

services of Indians for the Niagara campaign.[76] In case Johnson should want more funds, as he did in a very short time, he was supposed to get them through Shirley, who was authorized to draw on the unlimited resources of the imperial treasury.[77] However, when Johnson was forced to appeal to his superior for more funds with which to support the 1,106 Indians who came to the great conference at Mount Johnson, Shirley complained that the colonies had not lived up to their agreement to supplement the money advanced by Braddock.[78] This difference was settled by Braddock, who ordered the Massachusetts executive to turn over the remaining funds to Johnson.

This action is evidence of the fact that, above all else, Braddock wanted harmony. Robert Orme, aide-de-camp to the general, later wrote that had Braddock lived, the news over the bitter rivalry of the two commanders in the North would have distressed him greatly.[79] In fairness to Shirley it must be pointed out that he vigorously sought to obtain provincial contributions for gifts.[80] His own province actually took the lead and granted £600 for its share of the original funds advanced by the Crown.[81] The other assemblies were not so prompt in their actions. The New Hampshire Assembly struggled with Governor Benning Wentworth and then stated that they would contribute nothing until they could consider the grants made for Indian services by other provinces. The New York Assembly conjectured as to the probable cost of guns, strouds, and paint for each warrior.[82]

The slowness of the other assemblies to act in this respect aggravated the situation for William Johnson. Since Shirley decreed that he must wait for provincial reimbursement, it is logical that Johnson would refuse to please the expensive tastes of the warriors by donations from his own pocket.[83] On June 19, 1755, in exasperation, he wrote to Shirley that ". . . . the Inhabitants of these Colonies will reap a thousand fold for their present Expenses and enjoy their Possessions in uninterrupted Security."[84]

The basis for all this provincial bickering over the expense of presents

[76] *Ibid.*

[77] Edward Braddock to Thomas Robinson, April 19, 1755, P.R.O., C.O., 5/46, L.C. 19–28.

[78] William Shirley to William Johnson, May 7, 1755, *Sir William Johnson Papers,* I, 491–93.

[79] Robert Orme to William Johnson, September 2, 1755, *ibid.,* I, 894–96.

[80] William Shirley to William Johnson, May 7, 1755, *Sir William Johnson Papers,* I, 491–93.

[81] Vote of the General Assembly of Massachusetts, June 24, 1755, *ibid.,* I, 656.

[82] Benning Wentworth to William Johnson, May 23, 1755, *ibid.,* I, 536–38.

[83] Johnson resigned his post once before when the New York Assembly refused to compensate him for money advanced to buy presents.

[84] William Johnson to William Shirley, June 19, 1755, *ibid.,* I, 614–18.

seems to lie in conflicting interpretations of the provisions made by the
council of war at Alexandria. For example, Johnson was to be supplied with
funds through Shirley.[85] Thus the logical assumption would be that Johnson
was to be financed for gifts whether the colonies paid their share or not.
Apparently Shirley finally arrived at this conclusion too, for after the great
conference with the Indians at Mount Johnson, he did lay a warrant on the
deputy paymaster in Boston for £3,000 to be used by Johnson.[86] At least
Johnson had money enough to finance the Indian warriors on the campaign,
for he now had a total of £5,000 to be used for presents for the Six Nations
and their allies.[87] One wonders whether these funds might have changed
the results of the Battle of the Monongahela had they been used to secure
warriors and guides for Braddock.

The leaders of the Northern military campaign were confronted with still
another major problem—the devastating effect of liquor on the Indians.
Johnson never turned against liquor for personal use or for general hospitality. Invoices reveal many orders of Jamaica, West Indian, Madeira,
and Vidonia spirits for his storehouses.[88] This alert distributor of presents
well knew, however, that to give the Indians rum in one hand and strouds,
guns, or food in the other meant that the Indians would sell the latter to
obtain more liquor.[89] Despite all that Johnson could do to prevent this sort
of thing, as many as six kegs of rum a day would find their way into the
council rooms during the great conference.[90] Then, to the dismay of all
concerned, great quantities of goods would be gone the next day, while
more rum would be in the hands of the Indians. This underground traffic
seems to have been encouraged by the Anglo-Dutch inhabitants of Schenec-
tady and Albany, who were not seriously concerned with military affairs.[91]

Despite all of these handicaps and difficulties, however, the greatest
Indian conference up to that time was held at Mount Johnson from June 21
to July 4, 1755. If ever the effective use of presents accomplished an end,
it was at this huge meeting. In order to nullify the ". . . . expensive

---

[85] Edward Braddock to Thomas Robinson, April 19, 1755, P.R.O., C.O., 5/46,
L.C. 19–28.

[86] William Johnson to John Watts, July 1755, *Sir William Johnson Papers*, I,
769–71. In Johnson's mind there was some question as to whether this amount was
to be in pounds sterling. He wrote that he assumed that the money would not be in
provincial currency.

[87] William Shirley probably spent a great deal for presents that John Lydius gave to
the Iroquois in addition to the £5,000 used by Johnson.

[88] Colden and Kelly to William Johnson, May 20, 1755, *ibid.*, I, 526–27.

[89] William Johnson to James De Lancey, June 2, 1755, *ibid.*, I, 560–61.

[90] Indian Proceedings at Mount Johnson, June 28, 1755, *New York Colonial
Documents*, VI, 976–77.

[91] *Sir William Johnson Papers*, I, 560.

Bribery . . . ."[92] of the French it was absolutely necessary to observe this native custom, especially since the Indians realized their own importance. In Johnson's own words to Braddock on May 17, 1755,

They [the Iroquois] are a begging . . . . set of People & expect to be denied nothing they ask for, & tho a proper Moderation must be used towards them in these Matters, yet a conduct is necessary till they have heartily entered into Hostilities against the French. They are fully possessed of their own Consequence & the eagerness of the French to debauch them from us is such as they would stick at no Expense to compass & this the Indians well know & often repeat.[93]

Certainly it was "diplomatic" to use presents in a situation like this.[94] It was necessary to finance the journey of the Indians to Mount Johnson, and, at the same time, to provide corn for the women, children, and old men left at home. In addition, the Indians at the conference had to be fed, special gifts had to be provided, and the sachems had to be suitably clothed. Above all, Johnson maintained, the women must be pleased.[95]

In order to negotiate with the more important Indian villages and to arrange for leading the natives to Mount Johnson a well-informed staff of interpreters was employed. An interpreter had to be a man who had lived with the Indians, who had gone with them on their hunts, and who had become well known to them and beloved by them.[96] One such person, the veteran Arent Stevens, has been mentioned already. Apparently Stevens knew the customs of all of the Iroquois Indians. He could start a war dance, take up the war hatchet, deliver a present of condolence, make a wampum belt speech, and obtain desired services for a specified amount of goods.[97] The papers of Mount Johnson's leader reveal a hundred services performed by this underpaid interpreter who often threatened to quit unless his salary was raised.[98] Stevens was assisted by the interpreter Jacobus Clement in his superhuman task of escorting hundreds of Iroquois braves to Mount Johnson.[99] These men were required to buy beef, corn, peas, bread, and pork from the German farmers along the road. They had to put out signs

---

[92] William Johnson to William Shirley, May 16, 1755, *ibid.*, I, 504–8.

[93] William Johnson to Edward Braddock, May 17, 1755, *ibid.*, I, 513–14.

[94] The Indians' change in attitude as revealed in their increasing demands for presents is interesting. The transition can be traced through the Lancaster Treaty of 1744, through the Logstown Treaty of 1752, to the great council at Mount Johnson in 1755. In each instance, the Indians become bolder and bolder in their demands for gifts.

[95] "Some Hints for a Commanding Officer," May 24, 1755, *Sir William Johnson Papers*, I, 539–40.

[96] William Johnson to Thomas Pownall, June 12, 1755, *ibid.*, I, 582–83.

[97] *Ibid.*, I, 288, 588–91, 635–36, 831.

[98] Arent Stevens to William Johnson, July 30, 1755, *ibid.*, I, 755–56.

[99] William Johnson to Goldsbrow Banyar, June 14, 1755, *ibid.*, I, 588–91.

at every outpost of civilization to keep curious inhabitants away from the young warriors, who were apt to take a scalp or ravage a corn field without much notice.[100]

William Printup, another interpreter, who had resided for many years among the Onondagas, had the responsibility of bringing the Indians of the Susquehenna region to the conference. Like all the other interpreters, he knew that the best way to bring the whole tribe to the meeting was to contact the head warriors and sachems first. At the conference, Johnson had Daniel Claus,[101] later his son-in-law, to aid him in distributing presents and in translating speeches. Mydert Wymple, a smith, was dispatched to the Senecas and Cayugas to mend their axes, hoes, and arms.[102] Even the Mohawks, who were noted for their services as scouts, acted as propaganda agents to bring their brethren to the great conclave. These faithful adherents were carefully instructed as to their duties. A speech which Johnson made to these loyal warriors on May 17, 1755, went into some detail to explain the situation to them.

If they [the rest of the Iroquoian confederacy] say they are planting their Corn & if they should come now they will lose their Crops & be in want of Food, You must tell them I will take Care & make up to them what Losses they may suffer hereby ... on this Article you must act with ... promise with Caution.[103]

Perhaps the most important person at the conference, with the exception of Johnson himself, was the competent Peter Wraxall.[104] As a secretary for Indian affairs, as aide-de-camp to Johnson, and as a kind of subexecutive under his leader, Wraxall worked indefatigably until he was so exhausted that he could scarcely copy the numerous letters dictated by Johnson.[105] The secretary's minutes of the conference reconstruct the picture of the distribution of presents to the numerous Indians, who arrived at Mount Johnson in the latter part of June 1755.

---

[100] William Johnson to Arent Stevens, June 7, 1755, *Sir William Johnson Papers*, I, 635–36.

[101] Daniel Claus came to the colonies from Germany in the 1740's. After living among the Iroquois and learning their language he was employed by Johnson as an interpreter in 1755. He later married a daughter of William Johnson and became a deputy superintendent.

[102] "Instructions to Mydert Wymple," July 22, 1755, *ibid.*, I, 765.

[103] Indian Proceedings at Mount Johnson, May 17, 1755, *ibid.*, I, 631–33.

[104] Peter Wraxall, author of the famed abridgment of Indian records, was by birth an Englishman. He came to America in 1754 and secured the position of Indian secretary in New York. When Johnson took over Indian affairs, Peter Wraxall became a most loyal secretary and acted as the former's aide-de-camp in the Lake George campaign. Although he died young, in 1759, at the age of forty, he had married and made a name for himself in frontier life.

[105] *New York Colonial Documents*, VI, 1010–13.

.... William Printup .... arrived from the Susquehanna .... & reports .... a great number of the Indians .... their women & Children .... will be all here tomorrow. .... In the Evening Capt. Stoddart arrived with several Sachems and Warriors .... Col. Johnson .... paid the usual Compliments of welcome (giving each a Dram of Rum, a Pipe & some Tobacco) they said the remainder of their People would be down tomorrow .... The 21. This Morning another Party of Onondagas, Oneidas & Tuscarores arrived to the Amt. of 105. and say more are yet behind. at Dinner time the Sachems & warriors of the hither Mohock Castle March'd to Col. Johnsons with the Revd. Mr. Ogilvie their Missionary & their Chief Sachem at their Head & and made a fine appearance.[106]

Once the Indians had arrived in camp, haggling over presents, intrigue, and confusion ensued. Feeding 1,106 men, women, and children, as Johnson wrote, " .... amounts to a great Expense every day .... they have spoiled my Meadows & .... every Green thing about my Estate."[107] The Indian superintendent realized, however, that he had to put up with this sort of thing if he hoped to procure the aid of the Indians.

Johnson also made note of the many individual conferences which he held with influential sachems in order to prepare for the coming meeting. On June 27, 1755, he wrote the following to Braddock.

Their Sachems & Leading Men I have talked to seperately [sic] in private, & by Arguments, by Promises and by Presents, I think I have given a deep Wound to the French Interest. .... .[108]

These conferences were a heavy drain upon Johnson's energy, but they yielded success. One record tells how he converted an influential Mohawk warrior from the French interest by the use of presents and the promise of making him a sachem.[109] This daily labor from early morning to midnight tired Johnson to the point of illness; and in a letter to Goldsbrow Banyar,[110] dated May 20, 1755, he stated: "Since my arrival here, no Man living has had so much trouble and hurry ...." On June 19, in another message, this time to the merchants in New York, his pen reflects the increased confusion about him. "I am so beset by Ind[ians] & ca. that I declare I have Scarce a Min[ute's] time to take a pen or write a Word. ...."[111] Mount Johnson was evidently a busy center for the distribution of Indian presents during the summer months of May, June, and July, 1755.

---

[106] "Indian Proceedings at Mount Johnson," June 17–21, 1755, *Sir William Johnson Papers*, I, 640–42.

[107] William Johnson to Edward Braddock, June 27, 1755, *ibid.*, I, 662–65.

[108] *Ibid.*

[109] "Indian Proceedings at Mount Johnson," May 20, 1755, *ibid.*, I, 634.

[110] Goldsbrow Banyar, a provincial official in New York, for many years kept Johnson informed on events in that city. Banyar apparently was interested in land acquisition and for this reason wanted the friendship of Johnson. See *Sir William Johnson Papers*, I, 921–22.

[111] William Johnson to Colden and Kelly, June 19, 1755, *ibid.*, I, 612.

On June 21, the great conference opened, with men, women, and children of nine nations (tribes) attending each meeting. In addition to Peter Wraxall, Reverend John Ogilvie[112] (missionary for the Society for the Propagation of the Gospel in Foreign Parts), and Johnson himself, the British were represented by five interpreters; and a competent staff they were.[113] After key warriors had been won over by presents, the promise of Braddock's gifts, and the influence of Abraham and Hendrick, Mohawk leaders of the whole confederacy, the conference ran its expected course.[114] As the smaller New England colonies had looked to Massachusetts for leadership in the granting of funds for presents, so the smaller tribes now looked to the Mohawks, the Onondagas, and the Senecas for leadership in the acceptance of these goods.[115] Thus the senior tribes may be said to have determined the policy for the entire confederacy.

Obviously as a result of Johnson's influence, Hendrick was first nominated as speaker for all the sachems. He wisely declined this nomination in favor of the Red Head, a Seneca sachem whom Johnson had brought over to the British side some time previously.[116] It is apparent, however, that never once during the entire conference did Hendrick's influence cease to be felt.

The conference included three main meetings and exchanges of wampum-belt speeches. On June 21, Johnson's welcoming speech was read and translated by Daniel Claus. Then the customary day was allowed for the Indians to consider their answer. The following day the Red Head arose in council and declared his friendship for the English and his contempt for the French. Two days later Johnson delivered Braddock's speech to the Indians. It is possible that the shrewd superintendent may have edited Braddock's speech here and there to make it more effective, for Warraghiyagey was a master of native metaphor and an eloquent speaker in his own right. This session

---

[112] Reverend John Ogilvie, native of New York and educated at Yale and King's College, was an outstanding missionary for the Society for the Propagation of the Gospel in Foreign Parts. His correspondence reveals a conscientious representative of the Anglican Church whose religious leadership brought many of the Mohawks and other Iroquois to accept Christianity. Examples of his letters relating to the status of missions, and finally to his acceptance of an assistantship at Trinity Church, New York, in 1764, are found in the S.P.G. MSS, Series B, Volume II, Parts I and II (Library of Congress film). Also see John Wolfe Lydekker, *The Faithful Mohawks*, pp. 64, 65, 90–92, 102–4; Frank J. Klingberg, *Anglican Humanitarianism in Colonial New York*, pp. 79, 80 n., 81, 82, 151.

[113] "Indian Proceedings at Mount Johnson," June 21, 1755, *New York Colonial Documents*, VI, 964.

[114] *Ibid.*, VI, 964–66.

[115] *Ibid.*, VI, 988.

[116] *Ibid.*, VI, 966–67.

closed amid high excitement when Johnson made his own speech and presented the war belt to the sachem Abraham, who could be depended upon to accept it.[117] Immediately thereafter Arent Stevens, agile even in his old age, began the war dance and ". . . . Johnson then ordered a large Tub of punch out, for, to drink the King's health."[118]

The last session took place on June 29, at which time there was a renewed presentation of the war belt. Johnson himself started the war dance, and many of the important sachems joined in. A heavy rainstorm prevented the distribution of General Braddock's great present until July 1, however. At this time the goods were laid out upon the ground in the middle of the great council yard, while the sachems and headmen sat in a surrounding circle, as was the custom before gifts were distributed.[119] Shoes, light Indian guns, vermilion, blankets, shirts, strouds, tobacco, pipes, rum, powder, flint, food for the trip home, and wampum were included in this present.[120] The thousands of pounds in money provided for these goods by the Crown had not been in vain, for Johnson was able to write to De Lancey on July 10, 1755, the encouraging news that the Iroquois and their allies had unanimously consented to join against the French.[121]

Certain questions still persist. Two in particular seem to demand an answer. Were the Indians an aid to the Crown Point campaign? Did they help Shirley capture Niagara? The answer to the second question is obvious. Johnson's hostility cost Shirley any assistance he may have counted on from the Indians, and he became hopelessly bogged down at Oswego in the building of galleys for transport.

The Crown Point campaign met with more success. Johnson left for Albany and proceeded northward along the Hudson to the great carrying-place at Fort Edward. His troops consisted of about 3,700 militiamen, commanded by incompetent New England officers who resented Johnson's authority,[122] and three hundred Indian warriors, led by Old Hendrick.[123] Many of these warriors had followed Indian trails across the frontier and joined the troops at Fort Edward in preference to accompanying the tedious transports up the Hudson.

In the meantime, the French had not been idle. Taking the offensive, the swift-moving Baron Dieskau rushed southward with a large force com-

---

117 *Ibid.*, VI, 974–75.

118 *Ibid.*

119 *Ibid.*, VI, 979–80.

120 *Ibid.*, VI, 964–80. See also *Sir William Johnson Papers*, I, 625–42.

121 William Johnson to James De Lancey, July 10, 1755, *ibid.*, I, 706–7.

122 *Ibid.*, I, 542.

123 William Johnson to the Board of Trade, September 3, 1755, *New York Colonial Documents*, VI, 993–97.

posed of French and Abnakis and Iroquois Indians. (The latter Indians were chiefly Cagnawagas, who were related by language to the Mohawks. They had been the recipients of many gifts from William Johnson.) The shadow of defeat once more darkened the path of a European general.[124] The British were better prepared to meet this drive, however. The British Indians, reinforced by a stirring oration from Hendrick, who shamed them for their lack of enthusiasm and their acceptance of gifts from Shirley, were in high fettle. Furthermore, the British were able to use the new road which connected the southern end of Lake George with the western bend in the Hudson River to keep these auxiliaries well supplied with war materials and presents.

Early in September, Dieskau, intent upon destroying Johnson's base of supplies, encamped north of Fort Edward. Believing that he was closing in on the fort, his traitorous Indian guides led him to the road to Lake George, where the surprised French General ran into Johnson's advance Indian scouts. On September 14, 1755, Johnson's militiamen felt the pressure of the superior French forces and retreated to join the main British army.[125] Then the center of Johnson's forces moved up to meet the French advance. At this point the powerful flanks of Iroquoian Indians saved the day by fiercely closing in on the enemy. This action cost the Iroquois many lives; they were particularly unfortunate in losing many of their outstanding leaders.[126] Among these was Old Hendrick, who had been one of the first to die.

The British gained a bloody victory—the only important one of the year.[127] This success could not have been achieved without the aid of the native warriors and scouts. Once more the strength and importance of the

---

[124] "Indian Proceedings," May 28, 1755, *Sir William Johnson Papers*, I, 634–35. See also "Peter Wraxall to Henry Fox," September 27, 1755, Pargellis, *op. cit.*, p. 141, for a discussion of the Cagnawaga Indians under Dieskau. Also see Shea, *op. cit.*, pp. 11, 13–16. For an account of the treachery of the French Indians, see "Baron Dieskau to the Keeper of the Seals," September 14, 1755, Arch. Nat. Col. F3, 14, 144–46 (Library of Congress photostat). Dieskau had the able Legardier de St. Pierre as his Indian manager. Unfortunately for the French, St. Pierre was killed in the Lake George battle. This fact may have contributed to the Indian disorganization and treachery on the French side. See "Account of the Battle that was Fought at Lake St. Sacrament," October 4, 1755, Arch. Nat. Col. F3, 14, 183–88 (Library of Congress photostat).

[125] *New York Colonial Documents*, VI, 1003–4.

[126] *Ibid.*

[127] Mention should be made of the British capture of Fort Beauséjour in the Nova Scotian peninsula in early July 1755. See Arch. Nat. Col. F3, 14, 123–27 (Library of Congress photostat). It is of interest to note that the presents had to be used also to secure the services of the Indians in Nova Scotia. See *Journals of the Board of Trade*, X, 27.

Iroquois had been demonstrated; and once more presents had helped to win a major victory. Johnson reaped personal glory as a great commander and was rewarded with a hereditary title to pass on to his children.[128] Unfortunately the paltry strouds which Johnson gave to the war-weary Indians could not bring back their young men lost in battle, the cream of the Iroquois confederacy.[129] The Mohawks in particular were to feel the loss of their youth, the finest of a declining race of people. The Indians, through their acceptance of presents, were helping to remove the French from the Northern continent. In so doing, they were forfeiting their position as a balance of power. Subsequently, Pontiac was to take up the cudgels of the vanishing race in an effort to restore to the Indian his hunting grounds of old.

[128] *Sir William Johnson Papers*, II, 343–50.

[129] "Conference Between Major General Johnson and the Indians at Lake George," September 11, 1755, *New York Colonial Documents*, VI, 1010–13.

IX. PRESENTS TO THE INDIANS ON THE OHIO AND NORTHERN FRONTIERS, 1756–1763

In the period immediately following the campaigns of 1755, British military prestige suffered a blow among the Indian confederacies from the Iroquois in the North to the Creeks in the South. Colonel George Washington, who was entrusted with the defense of the long Virginia frontier, and Colonel James Innes, commander at Fort Cumberland, were empowered to give presents to those tribesmen who would aid British forces against the French-Indian depredations. Farther north, the more peaceful Pennsylvania frontier suffered the worst Indian attack in its history. One of the chief reasons for this assault by the Shawnees and the Delawares was the British encroachment on Indian land. It remained for William Johnson to bolster the wavering allegiance of the Ohio and Northern Indians by oratory and presents. In the South, the Cherokees were said to be angry because of James Glen's extensive use of presents to "purchase" their hunting grounds.[1]

However, outlays of merchandise from the Virginia treasury at last brought many Catawbas and Cherokees to the defense of the Virginia frontier.[2] Presents served even to bring the Cherokees and Delawares to the assistance of Forbes in his campaign of 1758. This help from the Delawares, former enemies of the English, and the other Ohio tribes was secured only after the Quaker colony had satisfied the shrewd Delaware sachem Teedyuscung.[3] Great quantities of goods, valued at hundreds of pounds,

---

[1] George Croghan to William Johnson, September 10, 1755, *Sir William Johnson Papers*, II, 28–30. Glen made this purchase during the summer of 1755, preventing the Southern Indians from aiding Braddock. According to Dinwiddie, the total area amounted to 40,000,000 acres. See *Dinwiddie Papers*, II, 202. For a description of points of interest in the Ohio area, see A. E. Angl., pp. 126–32, 438 ff. vo. (film). Some mention of the Ohio Company is made in Alvord's classic study of the period. See Clarence Walworth Alvord, *The Mississippi Valley in British Politics, A Study of the Trade, Land Speculation, and Experiments Culminating in the American Revolution.*

[2] Christopher Gist acted as a deputy for the Southern superintendent, Edmond Atkin. For an example of Gist's accounts, see LO 4670. See LO 3990 for Atkin's recommendation of Gist's appointment.

[3] Teedyuscung's name seems to have a varied spelling as in the case of most Indians. He is often referred to as ". . . . Tedisung or King Tediuscung. . . . ." See *Sir William Johnson Papers*, II, 824. Johnson's account of this remarkable sachem is not too flattering. According to the Northern superintendent, Teedyuscung was by birth a Delaware. Before the beginning of hostilities in 1754, he lived with his tribe in the Wyoming area. After Braddock's defeat, he moved to a place called Diahogo. Then he accepted the hatchet from the French at Niagara and led attacks on the frontiers of Pennsylvania and Maryland. Finally, after the peace negotiations

L. J. Mᵠᵘⁱˢ DE MONT-CALM.

LOUIS JOSEPH, MARQUIS DE MONTCALM

had to be expended before this old sachem rested his case concerning land fraud.

After the close of the Indian war in Pennsylvania, the battle-scarred Lake George area again became the scene of conflict between the French and the English. During this contest both sides secured the aid of Indian warriors through the expedient of presents. The brilliant victories of Montcalm, during the years 1756–1758, were nullified by the steady offensive of Jeffery Amherst's armies of regulars, provincials, and native warriors. These warriors were obtained from the recruiting center at Mount Johnson, where thousands of pounds in rewards had been handed out to the Iroquoian tribes and to the Western Indians. Following the victor, as always, the tribesmen gradually deserted their French masters when they saw which way the tide was turning. With this overwhelming strength and power the British at last occupied the Western French posts after the surrender of Canada in 1760.

It was at this point that Amherst's policy of cutting down on cash outlays for gifts angered the Indians. In fact, the Ottawas, Hurons, and Chippewas, who had long been accustomed to French finery for their women, were cut off without any goods. Amherst stubbornly insisted that the Indians must learn to hunt again and to trade for their merchandise at such centers as Fort Pitt, where a trading schedule of prices was posted.[4] Indian hostility was the result of these actions. No less an authority than William Johnson declared that Pontiac's Indian war was caused largely by the lack of presents from both the French and the English.[5] Thus it was that presents

brought about by the Six Nations and Johnson, Teedyuscung laid down the hatchet and entered into an alliance with the English. See *ibid., et seq.* There followed a long series of negotiations and treaties with extensive presents for the Delawares. See accounts of the Easton treaties in the *Pennsylvania Colonial Records*, VII, 207–24, 313–39. For the total presents given Teedyuscung and his allies, see Board of Trade to George III, January 14, 1763, *Sir William Johnson Papers*, IV, 18–20. In memory of this great Indian sachem, a statue has been erected which stands on a cliff overlooking the Wissahickon Creek near Philadelphia. A photograph of this statue can be found in *The National Geographic Magazine*, LXXII (November 1937), No. 5, p. 596.

[4] Jeffery Amherst to William Johnson, December 20, 1761, *Sir William Johnson Papers*, III, 593–95.

[5] William Johnson to the Board of Trade, November 13, 1763 (extract from a letter), Francis Parkman, *The Conspiracy of Pontiac and the Indian War after the Conquest of Canada*, II, Appendix B, pp. 319–20. This letter is not printed in the *Sir William Johnson Papers*. The fact that ". . . . the British governmental policy was parsimonious in the matter of Indian Presents" was listed as an important cause for Indian dissatisfaction in 1760–1761, during the occupation of the Western posts. See *Wisconsin Historical Collections*, XVIII, 228. It is of interest to note that Indians resented the French shortage of goods in Louisiana in 1761. See Kerlerec to Minis-

to the Iroquois and their Ohio brothers became an important issue in controlling the Indians during the last phases of the struggle for empire.

Since this story of Indian diplomacy shifts from the Ohio frontier to the frontier in the North, the role of presents in the Ohio region shall be discussed first. Following Braddock's defeat, the Pennsylvania Assembly rewarded Monacatoocha and the few warriors who had fought at the battle of the Monongahela with gifts of clothing.[6] Croghan, writing to Johnson on December 2, 1755, painted a dismal picture of Indian affairs on the Pennsylvania frontier.[7] In a tone of discouragement, the Pennsylvania trader hinted that he would prefer leaving the Ohio region in order to assist Johnson in conducting the affairs of the Northern Department. By April 5, 1756, Johnson had accepted Croghan's services; and the trader left to assume his new duties in the Mohawk country.[8] Knowing that the Northern superintendent could offer food and security for his small band, Monacatoocha also resolved to leave the Quaker province and to accompany Croghan on his journey north.[9]

Meanwhile, the Delawares and Shawnees, encouraged by French presents and assured of military protection, determined to throw off the yoke of the Six Nations. The alliance of these two tribes with the French forced a crisis in the western parts of Maryland, Pennsylvania, and Virginia. Conrad Weiser declared that no expense should be spared in securing the assistance of the Southern Indians[10] because aid from the Cherokees and Catawbas would be of great help in protecting the frontiers of Pennsylvania against the mighty Delaware leaders—the feared Shingis and the wily Teedyuscung. It was not until July 1756, however, that Governor Robert Hunter Morris could begin treaty-making and present-giving with Teedyuscung.[11]

Before this time, hope to alleviate the miseries of Pennsylvania came from two sources. First, in response to the pressure exerted by Monacatoocha and Sir William Johnson, the Six Nations requested the Delawares and the Shawnees to make the peace. Unfortunately, the prestige of the Six

---

ter, June 18, 1761, A. C., C 13, 42:217 in N. M. Surray (ed.), *Calendar of Manuscripts in the Paris Archives and Libraries Relating to the History of the Mississippi Valley in 1803,* II, 1361.

[6] *Pennsylvania Colonial Records,* VI, 566. Monacatoocha is called Scarroyada here. This sachem was also influential in securing the neutrality of the Wyandots with Pennsylvania gifts. See *ibid.,* VI, 533.

[7] George Croghan to William Johnson, September 10, 1755, *Sir William Johnson Papers,* II, 28–30.

[8] Daniel Claus to William Johnson, April 5, 1756, *ibid.,* II, 438–40.

[9] *Ibid.*

[10] *Ibid.,* II, 401–3.

[11] *Pennsylvania Archives* (1st series), II, 715; Richard Peters to Daniel Claus, August 25, 1756, LO 1580.

Nations did not bring about this peace until July 1756, as has been noted. The second possibility of relief for Pennsylvania hinged upon the actions of the Cherokees and the Catawbas. Governor Morris was worried that even these Southern Indians would turn against his province;[12] but, fortunately, Robert Dinwiddie's long series of negotiations with the Cherokees and Catawbas at last began to pay dividends. For a number of years, Virginia had handed out strouds, halfthicks, duffles, vermilion, guns, powder, lead, and many other presents to these two confederacies.[13] The *Dinwiddie Papers* are filled with correspondence relating to treaties and rewards in goods for these Indians. The colonies of South Carolina and Georgia had also doled out frequent allotments of merchandise to these tribes and to the Creeks, sometimes the enemies of the Cherokees.[14] Of all the Southern tribes, however, the Cherokees and the Catawbas were the

---

[12] Robert Hunter Morris to William Shirley, December 3, 1755, *Sir William Johnson Papers*, II, 368–70. It appears that the Susquehanna Indians were the only tribesmen who remained loyal to Pennsylvania.

[13] As an example, on August 9, 1751, the president of the Virginia council made a gift of £200 to a Cherokee chief. In addition, the Indian expenses for travel were paid. See "Council Meeting," August 9, 1751, *Virginia Council Journals*, typescript copy, pp. 326, 327, 328, Virginia State Library. As examples, also see H. R. McIlwaine (ed.), *Legislative Journals of the Council of Colonial Virginia*, II, 977; H. R. McIlwaine (ed.), *Journals of the House of Burgesses, 1752–1755, 1756–1758*, p. 110; Virginia even had a law which was to prevent the whites from taking guns, blankets, and other articles from the Indians. See William Waller Hening (ed.), *The Statutes at Large; Being a Collection of all the Laws of Virginia from the First Session of the Legislature in the Year 1619*, VI, 286.

[14] *Ibid.* Besides the danger of the Creeks, traders abused Cherokee leaders returning with gifts from Virginia. See John Watts to James Patton, January 20, 1753, Draper MSS 1 QQ 71 (film). Regarding the Cherokee-Creek feud, it appears that the Creeks had a grudge against the Cherokees for joining the English forces in 1715 and attacking them unexpectedly. See Edmond Atkin to the Board of Trade, May 30, 1755, LO 578. Atkin gives a masterly account of each of the Southern tribes in this long detailed report to the Board of Trade. He reported the Upper Creeks as the ". . . . most refined and Political Indians . . . ." while the Lower Creeks were ". . . . not so orderly . . . ." being deteriorated by rum brought by the traders. See *ibid.* Though the French declared that they were better able to supply the Creeks with ammunition than the British, Atkin had a rather complicated plan for carrying presents overland to the Creeks. Moreover, the Southern superintendent said that the Creeks preferred British goods.

Atkin also had a word to say about the Choctaws and Chickasaws. Concerning the former, he asserted that they were beggars from the French, but did revolt in 1746 due to a lack of goods from the French. The Chickasaws, however, were to Atkin the bravest and fiercest of the Southern confederacies. It was only through the aid of arms from South Carolina that these people repelled an assault of the French in 1753. Actually, the Chickasaws were handicapped with their British alliance, being some 750 miles from Charleston. See *ibid.*

most frequent recipients of merchandise from the Southern colonies.[15] As a result, these two "nations" became the main defense of the middle colonies against the French and Indian attacks during the year 1756.

The Cherokees, in particular, were so much in need of goods that, in 1756, they were reported to have been "almost naked."[16] This confederacy, which consisted of upper, middle, and lower towns adjacent to the frontiers of South Carolina, numbered about 3,000 fighting men.[17] The main towns had made an alliance with the English as far back as 1730, at which time some of their chiefs had gone to England, taking with them enemy scalps as a token of their friendship to the king.[18] Despite this alliance, the British could not depend upon these Indians because a historic Cherokee-Catawba enmity made united action with these two allies difficult. Before these natives could be brought into a dependable British alliance, it was necessary to settle this feud. The Catawbas seemed willing to let this matter drop because of their philosophy that ". . . . all Indians who have their supplies from, and are Friends of the English, should be Friends also of each other."[19] Having only 320 warriors, and being destitute of living necessities, this loyal tribe was much dependent upon gifts from Virginia.

At negotiations held during the months of February and March, 1756, William Byrd and Peter Randolph, commissioners for Virginia, used presents to secure a peace treaty with these two tribes.[20] During the course of this conference, Old Hop of the Cherokees and King Hagler[21] of the Catawbas agreed to fight for the English if their warriors were provided with all ". . . . necessary Cloths [sic] Victuals, Arms and Ammunition. . . . ."[22] Shortly after this meeting, these nations promised to furnish Dinwiddie with one thousand warriors in the spring. Indeed,

---

[15] The Cherokees and Catawbas did not receive many presents from Pennsylvania. During the summer of the Forbes campaign in 1758, they were promised gifts if they would go to war. The Cherokees, accompanied by Mohawk friends, then declared, ". . . . wherever they see a Frenchman they will knock his Brains out. . . . ." See *Pennsylvania Colonial Records,* VIII, 124–25; *Pennsylvania Archives* (1st series), III, 405.

[16] See Dinwiddie's treaty with the Cherokees and Catawbas during February and March, 1756, LO 870.

[17] LO 578; Indian Books of South Carolina, Vols. V, VI, *passim.*

[18] LO 578. The "King of England" at this time promised that the Cherokees would "always" have English goods. See LO 870. [19] LO 578.

[20] See "A Treaty Between Virginia and the Catawbas and Cherokees, 1756," *Virginia Magazine of History and Biography,* XII (January 1906), 250–64; LO 870. The Cherokees were so friendly at this time that they accompanied Virginia provincials on an expedition directed at the Ohio Shawnee towns. For an account of this Sandy Creek expedition, see Draper MSS 1 QQ 96–123 (film); Lincoln, *op. cit.,* II, 390–91.

[21] Often spelled King Haigler.

[22] LO 870. The expenses involved in the treaty amounted to £1,319:15:8, sterling. See Palmer, *op. cit.,* I, 251–52.

in anticipation of this treaty, Dinwiddie had already instructed Washington to ". . . . purchase suitable Goods for the Ind's [and] to offer them Presents. . . . ."[23] It was hoped that these presents would nullify the influence of the French priests, who were constantly working with the Southern Indians.[24]

During the years 1756 and 1757, and up to the summer of 1758, at which time the British were again marching against Fort Duquesne, the Cherokees and the Catawbas performed outstanding service in the defense of the Ohio frontier. The Cherokees, in particular, were hard hit during this time, for they lost many warriors and were prevented from caring for their crops.[25] Feeling that they had sacrificed much in order to aid the English, the Cherokees, the Catawbas, and a small number of Tuscaroras, who later joined the Southern tribes, were certainly not backward in their demands for gifts. Washington wrote to Dinwiddie on May 24, 1757, that the Cherokees were ". . . . the most insolent most avaricious, and most dissatisfied wretches I have ever had to deal with . . . ."[26]

The inefficiency of Edmond Atkin was one of the major difficulties in distributing gifts to the Indian allies during the period immediately prior to the Forbes campaign. Though the Southern superintendent's intentions were the best, very few colonials had anything to say in his favor.[27] Perhaps

---

[23] "Instructions to Colonel George Washington," August 14, 1755, *Dinwiddie Papers*, II, 186.

[24] Regarding the activities of the French, see Robert Dinwiddie to Thomas Robinson, November 24, 1755, P.R.O., C.O., 5/17, L.C. 1, C.O. 461 (film).

[25] *New York Colonial Documents*, VII, 284.

[26] *Writings of Washington*, II, 36–37.

[27] George Washington, Robert Dinwiddie, and James Adair are a few of the important colonials who were critical of Edmond Atkin. Despite these criticisms, it is apparent that Atkin was familiar with problems of Indian diplomacy and presents. His detailed plans for periodic visitations, transportation of presents, and classification of subordinates show a true perspective on the duties of his office. See LO 578. Atkin went more into detail in ordering gifts than Sir William Johnson. The conventional items such as strouds, blankets, hatchets, vermilion, brass kettles, looking glasses, flints, together with gold and silver lace, checked linen, calicos, pipes, and gawdy gartering, are found on his memoranda. Besides, Atkin ordered unusual items such as oval copper plates with the picture of the king leaning on a cannon on one side, and a man-of-war under full sail on the other side. The Southern superintendent described in detail the kind of paint boxes that he wished the Indians to have. Some of the tops for the boxes were to have pictures of landscapes, ships, houses, and forts. Others were to show birds, beasts, and fruits. Furthermore, the inside of the top was to contain a mirror, while the box inside was to be divided into two or three compartments for different colored paints. Another interesting gift was an enameled wristband having a picture of an English hand grasping a copper-colored hand, signifying friendship. For a detailed account of these unusual presents see Edmond Atkin, "List of Goods for the Indians," March 1757, LO 3517.

Atkin spent too much time in his very thorough preparations and so was unable to accomplish all that he had planned. Certainly the Southern superintendent made systematic plans for action that find no parallel in the *Sir William Johnson Papers*.[28] Despite these plans, however, Atkin was usually late in delivering presents, or gave too few presents, or even antagonized the Indians.[29] In all fairness to him it must be noted that most of the confusion relating to the distribution of gifts for the defense of the frontier was due to the fact that the Southern tribes were much more populous than the Northern ones. Therefore, Johnson could centralize his contacts with the Iroquois in the North; but Atkin had to carry presents over hundreds of miles of difficult terrain, traveling by horseback in a hot climate.[30]

A controversy between Atkin and George Croghan was another factor which interfered with Atkin's performance of his duties. This controversy arose when the Cherokees appeared on the Ohio frontier.[31] George Croghan, deputy for Johnson, thought that these natives should come under his jurisdiction. Atkin disagreed.

The Southern superintendent's work was too extensive for one man. Although his plans called for an army of interpreters, clerks, Indian surgeons, and provincial soldiers, Atkin actually had few assistants.[32] His most capable deputy was Christopher Gist, who was appointed after Atkin found that he could not personally supervise the handing out of presents and could not conduct Indian affairs in the manner initiated by Dinwiddie.[33] Actually

---

[28] See LO 578; LO 559; LO 3517.

[29] For accounts of Atkin's inefficiency, see *Writings of Washington,* II, 36–37; *Dinwiddie Papers,* II, 669, 707; *New York Colonial Documents,* VII, 282–83; *Adair's History of the American Indians,* p. 268.

[30] Atkin complained of these factors when he compared the office of the Southern superintendent with that of the Northern superintendent. See LO 559.

[31] See *New York Colonial Documents,* VII, 281; Robert Dinwiddie to Edmond Atkin, June 16, 1757, *Dinwiddie Papers,* II, 640.

[32] For Atkin's plan, see LO 578; LO 2502. When Virginia agreed to furnish Christopher Gist as a deputy agent, Atkin also requested a commissary for looking after presents. The Virginia council decided that Gist could look after both duties. See "Council Meeting," October 18, 1757, Virginia Council Journals, typescript copy, p. 62, 2d set, Virginia State Library. By contrast with Atkin, Sir William Johnson had an army of capable assistants. Among these were George Croghan, Andrew Montour, Daniel Claus, the former trader Thomas McKee, and Johnson's nephew, the later superintendent, Guy Johnson. The latter was a careful student of map-making. Some of his drawings and charts are to be found in the *Sir William Johnson Papers.* A complete chronology of Guy Johnson's life is found in *ibid.,* IV, xii–xiii. At one time Croghan, as Johnson's chief deputy, employed ten men as his assistants. One of these was the special assistant of Croghan, who had specified duties in visiting certain tribes at definite times throughout the year.

[33] For Gist's work concerning the handing out of goods, see *Dinwiddie Papers,* II, 669, 713; LO 4640; LO 3990; LO 4723.

it was George Washington who suggested Gist as a deputy agent.[34] By May 30, 1757, Washington's disgust over the confusion in doling out gifts had convinced him that a deputy was the only logical solution. It was particularly painful to the youthful commander to have goods promised to the Indians and then have those promises broken. As a result, he wrote Dinwiddie that ". . . . nothing should be promised but what is performed and only one person empowered to do either."[35]

Another handicap which Atkin could not overcome was the lack of funds. According to orders issued to the superintendent in June 1756, he was to be provided with financial backing by the Earl of Loudoun, at that time commander-in-chief of the British forces in America.[36] Although Loudoun was more than generous in backing Sir William Johnson, he seemed quite reluctant to give the same amount of aid to Atkin.[37] Consequently, the Southern superintendent was dependent upon Virginia to a large degree. Under the continual pressure of Robert Dinwiddie, the Virginia Assembly doled out thousands of pounds for presents to tribesmen defending the frontier. Though some of the cash in Dinwiddie's hands was Crown money, records of £500,[38] £700,[39] and £3,000,[40] for presents to the Southern Indians, punctuate his correspondence during the years 1755–1757. It is not surprising that the people of Virginia complained of the heavy expenses of maintaining the Indians. Because Pennsylvania and Maryland had failed to respond to Atkin's request for their quotas for Indian gifts, Virginia had been forced to bear the entire financial burden.[41]

[34] George Washington to Robert Dinwiddie, June 12, 1757, *Writings of Washington,* II, 57–59.

[35] George Washington to Robert Dinwiddie, May 30, 1757, *Writings of Washington,* II, 39–42.

[36] Atkin's orders read: "That as to the presents for the Indians which he [Atkin] desires, that too must be left to the Commander in Chief who has money impressed to him for that purpose, and who would doubtless upon application furnish him with whatever might be necessary for that service." See *Journals of the Board of Trade,* X, 242–43.

[37] The office of Southern superintendent cost Atkin a personal fortune. See Anne Murray to the Earl of Loudoun, May 24, 1764, LO 6350. Atkin even had difficulty in collecting his salary from Loudoun. See Edmond Atkin to the Earl of Loudoun, May 14, 1756, LO 1148. The royal commission sent to Atkin from George II definitely stated that the Southern superintendent was to receive his yearly £600 salary from the commander-in-chief. See LO 1212.

[38] *Dinwiddie Papers,* II, 283.

[39] *Ibid.,* II, 469.

[40] *Ibid.,* II, 639. See also Indian Books of South Carolina, Vols. V, VI, *passim.*

[41] See Robert Dinwiddie to the Earl of Loudoun, April 8, 1757, *ibid.,* II, 605–6; Robert Dinwiddie to Edmond Atkin, June 20, 1757, *ibid.,* II, 645–46; *Journals of the Board of Trade,* X, 242–43.

The Virginia council examined the "monstrous Acco't of Expences" accumulated by Atkin with a critical eye; if Virginia had to pay, the legislators wanted to know the details of this business of Indian presents.[42]

Despite these problems, gifts did reach the Cherokees, the Catawbas, and their Tuscarora brothers. Guns, flour, cattle, textiles, and even gifts that were so ridiculous that the Indians laughed and refused to accept them —all these reached the fighting front.[43] Regardless of the general Indian dissatisfaction, Dinwiddie was able to report to his superiors in England on May 16, 1757, that approximately four hundred Catawbas, Cherokees, and Tuscaroras were defending the outposts of his colony, being ". . . . extremely expensive in Cloathing, Maintenance and Presents . . . ."[44] He then asked that he be sent home because of poor health. After his departure, no less than six hundred loyal Cherokees, led by William Byrd of Virginia, came to aid General John Forbes in his march toward Fort Duquesne in the early summer of 1758.[45] This campaign was delayed, however, while the Earl of Loudon shifted regiments over thousands of miles. Tired of delay, the Cherokees who ". . . . would have scoured the Woods . . . ." accused the English of being "Trifflers" and dispersed.[46]

The decisive factor in bringing these six hundred warriors to aid in the Fort Duquesne campaign was Atkin, who labored with the Cherokees at Keowee and kept on friendly terms with Attakullakulla,[47] of the Overhill Towns, during March 1758.[48] Governor William Henry Lyttelton, who succeeded James Glen in South Carolina, also collaborated magnificently with Atkin in persuading his assembly to vote the amazing sum of £20,000

---

[42] *Dinwiddie Papers*, II, 707. The Virginia Governor insisted upon good accounts of Indian presents. See *ibid.*, II, 669.

[43] See *Writings of Washington*, II, 169; Draper MSS 1 QQ 85, 1 QQ 142–45, 1 QQ 161 (film) ; "Minutes of the Catawba Conference," May 18–19, 1757, HM 3992.

[44] Robert Dinwiddie to the Earl of Halifax, May 16, 1757, P.R.O., C.O., 5/1329, L.C. 55–58, C.O. 73–76.

[45] Major James Robertson to the Earl of Morton, December 19, 1758, Pargellis, *op. cit.*, pp. 439–42.   [46] *Ibid.*

[47] Attakullakulla was also called Little Carpenter. At this time he was suspected of aiding the French; however, Atkin reported that he was loyal to the English, having recently taken French scalps and prisoners. See Edmond Atkin to the Earl of Loudoun, March 25, 1758, AB 73; Atkin to Lyttelton, August 26, Indian Books of South Carolina, Vol. VI.

[48] AB 73. Edmond Atkin had a rather ingenious method of keeping the Cherokees fighting on the frontier. In 1757, at Winchester, he had a schedule of presents for warriors when they went out to fight. This included guns, ammunition, knives, war paint, and petticoats to interest the women in the project. Upon the return of the warriors, they were handed a different assortment of gifts, such as arm bands, scissors, silver gorgets, pipes, kettles, clasp knives, and needles. See Edmond Atkin, "Rewards and Lists of Goods for the Indians," October, 1757, LO 4753.

for Indian service.[49] Thus it was easier for William Byrd to conduct his Cherokee warriors northward, luring them on by watered spirits and gifts.[50]

When the Forbes army finally did get under way, the Cherokees and the Delawares sent scouting parties to help them. In return for this service they demanded gifts; they even threatened to steal horses if their wishes were not granted.[51] Knives, arm bands, stockings, wampum, strouds, ruffled shirts, gartering, vermilion, and even goods to take home for their wives and children were among the assortment of enticing presents sent to these natives.[52]

Thus the Cherokees, for the time being, proved to be an important ally on the Ohio frontier during the time of French-Indian attacks. Interestingly enough, a few of their important leaders, Attakullakulla, for example, remained loyal to the British throughout the remainder of the war, even through the period of the Cherokee war in 1759–1761.[53] In summary, then, it becomes obvious that presents were a powerful factor in bringing Cherokee help to the frontiers of Virginia, Maryland, and Pennsylvania.

It has been observed already that the Delawares gave some assistance in the Forbes campaign in the summer of 1758. Before this time, however, they had concluded a peace with Pennsylvania, changing their alliance from the French to the British. This treaty brought an end to the Delaware and Shawnee war parties which had been scalping settlers, burning cabins, and stealing domestic animals along the Pennsylvania frontier.[54] The cessation of these hostilities was largely a result of the intervention of the Six Nations in July 1756; but Pennsylvania still had to settle the claims of land fraud as espoused by the Delaware sachem Teedyuscung.[55]

---

[49] AB 73.

[50] Edmond Atkin to William Byrd, March 24, 1758, AB 70; LO 5776.

[51] See *Bouquet Papers*, A 25, 3–6, Canada Archives.

[52] *Colden Papers*, V, 248–49. For the activities of the Delawares and Cherokees in the Forbes campaign, see Sylvester K. Stevens *et al.* (eds.), *The Papers of Col. Henry Bouquet*, Series 21634, *Northwestern Historical Series*, pp. 83, 84, 96, 133, 186, 209–10. Presents were laid out for Catawba, Tuscarora, and Nottaway Indians who were expected to join the expedition. See *Colden Papers*, V, 247.

[53] For a well-documented account of the Cherokee war, see John Richard Alden, *John Stuart and the Southern Colonial Frontier, A Study of Indian Relations, War, Trade, and Land Problems in the Southern Wilderness, 1754–1775.*

[54] Robert Hunter Morris to William Shirley, December 3, 1755, *Sir William Johnson Papers*, II, 368–71; William Shirley to Major General James Abercromby, June 27, 1756, P.R.O., C.O., 5/46, L.C. 521–40; Peter Wraxall to William Johnson, January 9, 1756, *New York Colonial Documents*, VII, 14–31.

[55] The Delawares weakly contended that the reason for their taking up the hatchet against the English was because some of the Six Nations were helping the French. Therefore, since they were allies of the Six Nations, the Delawares joined their brothers. Monacatoocha, acting as spokesman for the Delawares, made this statement be-

The expenses of Indian presents had been such a heavy financial drain upon the Pennsylvania Assembly that they were quite reluctant to turn over still more goods to the Ohio Indians. Pleading that the province of Pennsylvania ". . . . groans under for Indian Affairs . . . . " the assemblymen asserted that such expense should be borne by the proprietaries who acquired the Indian lands.[56] Despite the assembly's complaints about these expenses, it must be remembered that it was actually William Johnson, the Northern superintendent, who financed the gifts which brought about the peace with Delawares.[57] Furthermore, Johnson's work had been hampered by Governor Morris' sudden declaration of war upon the Delawares. This declaration of war was also contrary to the principles of the Quaker element in the assembly. However, the assembly had already acted independently in the matter of Indian presents. Even before the declaration of war against the Delawares, that obstreperous body, under the leadership of Benjamin Franklin, had proceeded to hand out gifts without even consulting Morris, a situation which greatly angered the Governor.[58]

In Teedyuscung, however, the assembly found a most intelligent Indian who demanded his rights in the form of goods, schools, teachers, and houses. To Teedyuscung, these items were "presents."[59] His authority to ". . . . carry the absolute Lead in all their [Indian] Negotiations . . . ."[60] made this "king"[61] of the Delawares a formidable Indian with whom to deal. Assuming authority which William Johnson thought belonged to no Indian in North America, Teedyuscung told the Governor of Pennsylvania that ". . . . All the Indian Nations from the Sun Rise . . . . beyond the Lakes, as far as the Sun setts . . . ." had appointed him as their speaker. This broad

---

fore William Johnson, the Six Nations, and the Shawnees. See "Extracts of Indian Proceedings," July 1, 1755, LO 1269. The Senecas, who always were sympathetic to the French, were suspected of being allies of the French at the time of the Delaware war. See *Sir William Johnson Papers,* II, 427.

[56] *Pennsylvania Colonial Records,* VII, 203.

[57] *Sir William Johnson Papers,* II, 439, 446.

[58] See Robert Hunter Morris to Thomas Penn, November 22, 1755, *Pennsylvania Colonial Records,* VI, 739. Morris declared war on the Delawares on April 14, 1756; see *ibid.,* VII, 88. For Johnson's reaction and the displeasure of the Quakers, see *Sir William Johnson Papers,* II, 447. The Quakers were much pleased when Johnson brought about peace. See *ibid.,* II, 458.

[59] See speech printed in the *Pennsylvania Colonial Records,* VIII, 47, on March 22, 1758, following the conferences at Easton in 1756 and 1757.

[60] William Johnson to James Abercromby, April 28, 1758, *Sir William Johnson Papers,* II, 824–30.

[61] Many of the head Indians were called kings by the English. However, as in the case of Teedyuscung, they were merely chiefs or sachems. Johnson noted this distinction.

definition of authority meant that Teedyuscung was the representative of eighteen nations![62]

Teedyuscung demanded—and received—a clerk to care for his legal records, an action which further evidenced his intelligence and shrewdness.[63] This sachem even refused to assist in fighting the French unless the English who accompanied the warriors were subject to his directions. Furthermore, he pointed out to the whites, "We understand our Way of Fighting better than you."[64]

Although his weakness for rum branded him a drunkard, still this highly intelligent sachem could make a brilliant analysis of the causes of friction between the Indians and the whites. In November 1756, during the second Easton conference,[65] he lambasted the proprietaries for taking lands from the Delawares without giving even so much as ". . . . broken pipes or such Triffles . . . ."[66] in exchange. Teedyuscung shrewdly pointed out that the lands which the proprietaries purchased so cheaply from the Indians were sold to poor settlers at dear prices, and ". . . . the Indians have suffered for it."[67] Although he lacked deeds and other legal papers to back his statements, the Delaware sachem, showing a remarkable memory for details, pointed out exact areas in the Susquehanna and Wyoming valleys which he claimed had been taken by fraud. When asked what he meant by fraud, Teedyuscung replied that the land had been taken by means of forged deeds and by trickery in using the compass, and that no presents had ever been given in return.[68]

From 1756 to 1763, Teedyuscung's charges of fraud enabled him to wangle large numbers of wampum belts, clothes, food, hardware, and lands from the Quaker province.[69] The case was then turned over to William Johnson who brought the matter before the Board of Trade. Now it was the "greedy proprietaries" who were forced to pay the Delawares. A total of £600 was given the Delawares, and they were permitted to live in Pennsylvania's Wyoming and Susquehanna valleys.[70] A temporary lull followed

---

[62] *Sir William Johnson Papers*, II, 826; *Pennsylvania Colonial Records*, VIII, 33. Regarding this claim of Teedyuscung, Johnson said, "Indian manner of speaking [is] indeed somewhat figurative, [but] this is a Rant beyond what I have [ever] met with." See *Sir William Johnson Papers*, II, 826.

[63] Charles Thompson acted as Teedyuscung's clerk. For Thompson's activities on behalf of the sachem, see *Pennsylvania Colonial Records*, VII, 724–25.

[64] *Ibid.*, VII, 714.

[65] The first Easton conference took place in July 1756; see *ibid.*, VII, 207–24.

[66] *Ibid.*, VII, 324.   [67] *Ibid.*, VII, 325.   [68] *Ibid.*, VII, 324–25.

[69] *Pennsylvania Colonial Records*, VII, 324–25; *ibid.*, VII and VIII; *Pennsylvania Archives* (1st series), II.

[70] Board of Trade to George III, January 14, 1763, *Sir William Johnson Papers*, IV, 18–20; *Pennsylvania Colonial Records*, VII, 727–28.

this action. When Connecticut settlers threatened to take over this area in 1762, the Six Nations were aroused because this land belonged to the whole confederacy as well as to the Delawares.[71] Indeed, the Indian land question was far from being settled. Herein is another cause for the Indian rebellion under Pontiac. Insignificant presents doled out in exchange for vast Indian lands might satisfy the tribesmen temporarily; but as civilization made a deeper impression on these primitive people, they realized that they had been cheated out of what had once been a princely patrimony.

Meanwhile, along the British Iroquoian frontier, William Johnson was occupied in obtaining goods to satisfy the wants of the Six Nations. On December 2, 1755, he resigned his commission as major general in order to devote his full time to Indian affairs.[72] Upon Johnson's arrival in New York, the victory at Lake George, won partly through the aid of Six Nations auxiliaries, was celebrated with the firing of ships' guns and the illumination of the city wherever Johnson passed.[73] The bitter rivalry between Shirley and Johnson, each competing with presents for the favor of the Six Nations, came to a head now.[74] The superintendent's influential friends, including the international figure, Thomas Pownall, feared that Shirley would use his influence at the royal court to misrepresent Johnson.[75] Finally, on December 18, 1755, Johnson wrote to the Board of Trade to complain that the constant orders of the Massachusetts Governor had kept him from attending to his Indian affairs for some four months.[76] Apparently Shirley did not take his complaints against Johnson to the Board.

---

[71] *Sir William Johnson Papers*, IV, 18–20.

[72] "William Johnson to Colonial Governors, December 2, 1755," *ibid.*, II, 361–65; William Johnson to William Shirley, November 9, 1755, *ibid.*, II, 282–83; William Shirley to William Johnson, November 15, 1755, *ibid.*, II, 299. The last two letters indicate Shirley's unwillingness to let Johnson resign his military commission.

[73] Daniel Claus, *Narrative of His Relations with Sir William Johnson and Experiences in the Lake George Fight*, p. 18. Herein is the account of the famous meeting in a New York hotel room where Thomas Pownall, Oliver Delancy, Goldsbrow Banyar, Daniel Claus, Peter Wraxall, and John Watts planned the downfall of William Shirley. Claus relates that William Shirley sent a ". . . . Belt of Wampum to the Six Nations clandestinely . . . ." but the Six Nations would not join the Massachusetts Governor's expedition to Niagara. Instead, the Indians preferred to follow Johnson.

[74] For references regarding the hostility aroused between Shirley and Johnson in the campaigns of 1755 regarding presents, see *Sir William Johnson Papers*, I, 737–38, 738–39, 807–9, 826–27, II, 403–4; Lincoln, *op. cit.*, II, 175, 244.

[75] *Supra*, note 73.

[76] William Johnson to the Board of Trade, December 18, 1755, *Documentary History of the State of New York*, II, 1023–24. Shirley was so exasperated with Johnson's reluctance to follow his orders as commander-in-chief that he wrote to the latter on December 24, 1755, declaring, "I must in particular know whether I am to depend upon your following my Instructions now sent you, and those which I shall hereafter send." See *Sir William Johnson Papers*, II, 390–91.

In addition to governing Johnson's military activities, Shirley also controlled Indian affairs. He literally bombarded the superintendent with detailed instructions, directing when and where presents were to be given.[77] He also strenuously objected to Johnson's practice of giving presents in his own name.[78] Naturally Johnson wanted to appear personally responsible for the presents when they were delivered to the Six Nations, but Shirley insisted that they be given in the king's name. Another of Shirley's orders directed the superintendent to furnish the Six Nations with a ". . . . Skillful and Carefull Smith . . . ."[79] This was an order which would gratify many demands on the part of the Indians for such artisans.

While Johnson's friends in the mother country were successfully undermining Shirley's influence, the superintendent held two conferences with the Six Nations and their allies. At Oswego, January 28, 1756, Johnson delivered a long speech to the Six Nations. (Incidentally, this speech had been written out word for word by the Massachusetts Governor.) Johnson supported his oratory with merchandise that would please the Six Nations' sachems. Speaking with all the eloquence of the Iroquois chief, Johnson told of the disloyalty of the Shawnees and the Delawares, who were committing depredations along the Pennsylvania frontier.[80] The Indians countered with the declaration that the French had promised to capture Oswego. Presents and still more presents were necessary to meet Indian discontent of this sort. In fact, the Indians were in such a hostile frame of mind that it was very dangerous even for Johnson to venture into the heart of the

---

[77] Not only did the Earl of Loudoun leave Indian affairs in the North to Johnson, but he made a practice of consulting the superintendent on matters relating to presents. Moreover, Loudoun directed Major General Daniel Webb not to interfere with Indian problems since they were to be the superintendent's concern. Webb was to be commander-in-chief until the arrival of James Abercromby; the latter relinquished the position as commander-in-chief to his superior, Loudoun, who arrived in New York July 23, 1756. See Earl of Loudoun to William Johnson, March 11, 1756, LO 905; "Instructions for Colonel Daniel Webb," February 23, 1756, LO 848; "Instructions for Major General Daniel Webb from George III," March 15, 1756, LO 993. Historians have pictured the Earl of Loudoun as a stern man, devoted to discipline and army regulations. Peter Wraxall, who saw the commander-in-chief on the day of his arrival, left a different impression: "His [Loudoun's] Countenance is full of Candor, his Eyes Sprightly & good Humored, he is short, strong made & seems disposed & fit for Action, he lets himself down with great ease & affability." See Peter Wraxall to William Johnson, July 23, 1756, *Sir William Johnson Papers*, II, 514–16.

[78] *Ibid.*, II, 461.

[79] *Ibid.*, II, 410.

[80] See "Instructions for William Johnson from William Shirley," January 13, 1756, *ibid.*, II, 409–12; William Shirley to the Six Nations, *ibid.*, II, 413–16; "Extract from Records of Sir William Johnson's Indian Proceedings About Oswego," January 28, 1756, LO 1144.

Iroquoian confederacy. Nevertheless, in June 1756 he carried presents to a conference with the Delawares, the Shawnees, and the Six Nations at Onondaga. At this time he found the Indians reluctant to aid the British unless extensive promises of gifts were made. Johnson wrote to Shirley that these Indians would have to be furnished with hats, coats, and ammunition, if any of them could be expected to join the British in a projected Crown Point expedition in 1756.[81] As there was a scarcity of Indian goods during the year 1756, this would be particularly difficult to achieve.[82]

When Johnson returned, he was directed to assist Major General Webb, whose arrogant officers often offended the Indians. Thomas Butler, assistant to the superintendent, so faithfully carried out the Earl of Loudoun's orders to recruit warriors for Webb that the Indians left him without funds.[83] Then it happened. The French offensive, which Indian intelligence had predicted, became a reality. Montcalm's lightning attack at Oswego all but confounded the slow-moving British armies. Appearing before the fortress about August 10, 1756, the French commander laid siege to the fort and wreaked such devastation that the stench from the unburied dead was unbearable for miles around.[84] Thus French Indian allies, "bought" by expensive presents and plunder, had been an important factor in the destruction of the hated Chouaguen, as Oswego was called by the French.[85]

When analyzing the reasons why Montcalm chose Oswego as his objective, it must be remembered that this frontier outpost, in addition to being

---

[81] William Johnson to William Shirley, June 27, 1756, Camp at Onondaga Lake, *Sir William Johnson Papers,* II, 495.

[82] Merchant shipping apparently was almost at a standstill in this year: It will be recalled that Admiral Edward Boscawen was unable to stop all but two French vessels from arriving in Canada in 1755. These vessels contained military supplies, many of which were probably used for presents. Fear was expressed in August 1756, that Boscawen would not be strong enough to meet the Brest fleet. See *ibid.,* II, 532. For a summary of Boscawen's failure to stop the French, see *New York Colonial Documents,* X, 297–99; Gipson, *op. cit.,* VI, 99–126. There was quite a rush for Indian goods when a vessel arrived in New York harbor with arms ". . . . for use of ye Indians. . . ." See Jasper Farmer to William Johnson, June 7, 1756, *Sir William Johnson Papers,* II, 483–83. Johnson himself complained of the scarcity of Indian goods. See William Johnson to the Board of Trade, May 28, 1756, *Documentary History of the State of New York,* II, 422. It appears that Sir Charles Hardy, Governor of New York, was the only one who could secure goods for the superintendent. See *ibid.*

[83] *Sir William Johnson Papers,* II, 553–54; LO 905.

[84] *Ibid.,* II, 552; LO 1603. Apparently British officers were taken as prisoners, while some soldiers and "private persons" were included. See *New York Colonial Documents,* X, 444.

[85] M. de Montcalm to Count d'Argenson, August 28, 1756, *New York Colonial Documents,* X, 464.

a Western fur trade rendezvous, was an important center for giving out presents to the Western Indians and to the Iroquois. Shortly before the post was captured, a road had been built to it, thereby facilitating the shipment of Indian goods to this area.[86] Before that time, goods had been sent by batteaux, which mean that it had to be lugged over the two difficult carrying-places in the Mohawk River.[87] The French looked upon Chouaguen as a place where the English duped the Indians by presents and liquor in order to induce them to murder Canadians.[88] This suspicion was largely true. Johnson had sent as many as four thousand wampum beads at a time for belts to be used at Oswego. Moreover, the superintendent had just completed a conference with the Six Nations, giving presents sufficient to satisfy the appetites of the head sachems.

Other French victories followed. In August 1757 Montcalm was able to capture Fort William Henry in spite of William Johnson's attempts to co-operate with Webb in bringing up Indian allies.[89] In addition, speed and action characterized the French and Indian attack on the palatine settlement at German Flats along the Mohawk River on November 13, 1757.[90]

These brilliant victories of the French greatly affected the British-Indian relations. Once again the Indians were deserting the English in favor of the victors, just as they had done on the Ohio after Braddock's defeat. There were many other reasons which accounted for this wavering allegiance on the part of the Indians. Discontent was evident when Johnson wrote to the Board of Trade in 1757, saying that the tribesmen were ". . . . disgusted and dissatisfied with the extensive purchases of land . . . ." which was usually purchased by presents.[91] In a discouraged tone, the superintendent continued:

By presents & management we may be able to keep some little interest yet alive and perhaps some nations to act a neutral part, yet I am apprehensive, meer expence, Speeches & Promises . . . . Will never be able to effect a favorable Revolution of our Indian interest, and deprive the French of the Great Advantages they have over us by their Indian alliances.[92]

Dissatisfaction among the aborigines was also due to the dishonesty of traders and to quarrels among the tribesmen over the division of gifts.

---

[86] *Sir William Johnson Papers,* II, 553.

[87] Thomas Pownall, "The Carriage of a Ton of Goods from New York to Oswego and Fort Edward," LO 2549.

[88] Vaudreuil to Machault, July 24, 1755, *New York Colonial Documents,* X, 309.

[89] William Johnson to Daniel Webb, August 1, 1757, *Sir William Johnson Papers,* II, 728–29. Loudoun promised Indian presents and urged co-operation between Johnson and Webb. See LO 1587; *New York Colonial Documents,* X, 594, 596, 598–605.

[90] *Sir William Johnson Papers,* II, 757; *New York Colonial Documents,* X, 672–74.

[91] William Johnson to the Board of Trade, September 28, 1757, *New York Colonial Documents,* VII, 276.

[92] *Ibid.*

Losses of chief men among the Mohawks was also a serious problem, and the other loyal tribes of the Six Nations were clamoring for forts to protect their women and children—forts which they did not receive.[93]

Johnson had the assistance of the commander-in-chief, the Earl of Loudoun, to help him meet these problems. Loudoun[94] may have had his shortcomings as a military commander, but he certainly co-operated with Sir William Johnson in the matter of Indian presents. Even before he left England in January 1756 to assume his command in America, Loudoun submitted a memorandum of expenses which included £4,000 for Indian presents and an additional allowance of £600 for the Northern superintendent's salary.[95] The commander-in-chief looked upon the noble Indian from a characteristic European viewpoint. At the same time, with the precision of a military commander, the Earl emphasized the importance of giving presents only to those who had influence. In June 1757 Loudoun declared:

That it was my opinion at present we should treat them [the Indians] like men & talk truth to them; shew them we were sensible of the manner in which they had behaved to us; that now they must declare themselves, for, if they were not friends, we should look on them as enemies & be on our guard accordingly; And in the mean time to be cautious in giving them presents particularly Arms and ammunition. . . . .[96]

It is difficult to explain why Loudoun co-operated so fully with Johnson and neglected Atkin.[97] Perhaps Atkin's geographic isolation may have

---

[93] For references regarding the discontent of the Northern Indians, 1755–1757, see New York Colonial Documents, VII, 276; ibid., VII, 15–31; Sir William Johnson Papers, II, 85–88, 238, 293, 297–98, 385.

[94] John Campell, the fourth Earl of Loudoun, governor of Virginia, and commander-in-chief, arrived in New York on July 23, 1756, to succeed William Shirley. The latter's friends arranged the governorship of Jamaica for Shirley after Thomas Pownall and others of Johnson's party engineered the defeat of Shirley in England. Loudoun served as commander-in-chief until he was replaced by Sir Jeffery Amherst in the spring of 1758. Much of Loudoun's career in America is preserved in the collection of Loudoun Papers in the Henry E. Huntington Library, San Marino, California. These papers, which number thousands of manuscripts, are also descriptive of Loudoun's life in Scotland. Also to be noted is a set of thirteen volumes of "Memorandum Books" kept by Loudoun while in America. These small volumes of almost illegible writing contain some material on Indian affairs. Many of the Loudoun Papers that pertain to William Johnson have been printed in the Sir William Johnson Papers. The cream of Loudoun's military papers have been printed in Pargellis, op. cit.

[95] "Memorandum to the Duke of Newcastle from the Earl of Loudoun," January, 1756, LO 485.

[96] Earl of Loudoun to William Johnson, June, 1757, Sir William Johnson Papers, II, 719–25.

[97] Atkin had even to write to Loudoun for instructions. See Edmond Atkin to the Earl of Loudoun, October 6, 1756, LO 1979.

SIR JEFFERY AMHERST

accounted for this favoritism. Maybe the prestige Johnson achieved as a result of the Crown Point victory of 1755 made Loudoun respect the latter's judgment in native affairs. Possibly the commander-in-chief, who belonged to the nobility, may have felt a kinship with the new superintendent, who was given a baronet and voted £5,000 by Parliament.[98] Whatever the reason, Loudoun constantly supported Johnson's demands for presents through the years 1756–1757;[99] and he gave Johnson complete authority in the handing out of presents. On one occasion, the Earl asserted that he would have no other man in America as the Northern superintendent.[100] He approved Sir William's choice of George Croghan as a deputy agent. Loudoun also chastised William Denny of Pennsylvania, who succeeded Robert Hunter Morris as governor, for treating with the Indians without consulting Johnson.[101] After Montcalm's attack at Oswego, however, the Northern superintendent had to leave Pennsylvania almost completely to her own devices, especially since the Quaker colony was paying for presents to the Ohio Indians.

There was no exaggeration in the French report that Johnson was leaving no stone unturned in his efforts to win the support of the Northern Indians with presents. On June 20, 1757, Johnson severely scolded the chiefs of the Six Nations for their declarations of neutrality following the acceptance of British gifts. He explained that to the English this neutrality meant that no French-Indian war parties were to pass through Iroquoian territory and that the Six Nations were immediately to transmit all intelligence to the English![102] Johnson continued to request gifts for the Indians. The Loudoun Papers contain scores of memoranda for presents such as strouds, gimps, halfthicks, linen, castor hats, gunpowder, needles, flints, clasp knives, verdegris, vermilion, and cutlasses.[103] These presents were Johnson's answer to the Canadians, who were constantly giving out lavish gifts[104] and corrupting the Iroquois by telling them that the English proposed to make slaves of them.

In addition to this competition in presents which he faced, Johnson found that he now had to pay many of his Indian warriors in cash for their

---

[98] The £5,000 voted Johnson by Parliament really was a compensation for the many presents that Johnson had given the Six Nations and their allies from private funds. For a reference on the grant, see *Sir William Johnson Papers*, II, 434–36.

[99] See LO 485; LO 905; LO 5095; *Sir William Johnson Papers*, II, 723–24, 764–67.

[100] Earl of Loudoun to William Johnson, December, 1757, *Sir William Johnson Papers*, II, 764–67.

[101] Earl of Loudoun to William Denny, September 22, 1756, LO 1876; LO 1759.

[102] "Extracts from Indian Records from a Meeting of the Senecas, Cayugas, and Onondagas," June 20, 1757, LO 3823.

[103] See LO 6747; LO 1329; LO 2131.

[104] *New York Colonial Documents*, VII, 234–35.

services. During the period of rivalry between Shirley and Johnson in 1755, the former had initiated the system of paying the Indians in actual money.[105] By 1756, the tribesmen had become aware of the value of their services and were negotiating to fight only as a "nation." It became necessary, therefore, for the superintendent to "buy their assistance." As a matter of fact, on March 15, 1757, Johnson was forced to pay out a total of £ 33,602 : 10 : 0 for the wages of what he termed an Indian regiment, a group consisting of approximately five hundred warriors and their leaders.[106]

Interference from the Quakers was an additional source of trouble for the superintendent. Acting only on their own authority, independently of the colony of Pennsylvania and of the British Government, the Quakers bestowed separate presents upon the Indians; they even went so far as to call the leading sachems aside at conferences to talk independently with them. George Croghan, who was greatly incensed by the pacifistic inclinations of the Quakers, reported that these people sent a speech to the Six Nations in January 1758 in which they declared that the Quakers had nothing to do with the war between the French and the English, and if the Six Nations decided to attack the English, they should attack only the "soldiers." Croghan interpreted this statement as meaning that all who were not Quakers were soldiers! Then he went on to report that the Quakers offered the Indians guns, powder, lead, and hatchets, as well as clothing and provisions![107]

Actually the Quakers, who, for the most part, were prosperous Pennsylvania businessmen, had in reserve a large private fund for treating with the Indians; and they called regular meetings with the natives in order to put into force a "system" of their own creation. Johnson opposed this procedure, stating that the Quaker actions were ". . . . flagrantly illegal. . . . ."[108] No doubt the Quaker policy in dealing with the Indians was designed to bring about an end to hostilities because these people disapproved of the barbaric methods of fighting used among the natives. Croghan's account, as noted above, would indicate that the Quakers were confused. On the one hand, they urged the Indians to cease fighting; on the other, they gave arms and provisions to the natives.

In spite of such competition, Johnson achieved favorable results. A summary of native participation as warriors will serve to reveal how successful

---

[105] *New York Colonial Documents*, VII, 128–29; *Documentary History of the State of New York*, II, 427; *Sir William Johnson Papers*, II, 646. Shirley also made a practice of paying his interpreters high wages. See *ibid.*, II, 400–401.

[106] LO 3063.

[107] See speech sent by the Quakers of Pennsylvania to the Six Nations, January 29, 1758, LO 5491.

[108] William Johnson to James Abercromby, April 28, 1758, *Sir William Johnson Papers*, II, 830–34.

the superintendent was in bringing warriors to aid the British in the period from 1758 to the surrender of Canada in 1760.

During the year 1757, most of Johnson's efforts were devoted to keeping the majority of the Six Nations neutral. He did manage, however, to send out raiding parties, to protect many of the settlements, and to obtain constant intelligence of enemy movements.[109] In 1758, Sir William was able to bring more than four hundred warriors into the field at Ticonderoga— a remarkable feat considering the failure of British arms during the preceding two years.[110] Johnson explained that he was able to obtain this substantial support from the natives because the French had ". . . . neither provisions nor Presents to give them."[111] Finally, in 1759, the long neutrality of the Six Nations was at last broken. At a meeting in their country early in that year, Johnson had ". . . . persuaded the whole Confederacy, to agree to Join, and go with us against Niagara. . . . ."[112] Johnson and five hundred warriors (a number that was later increased to nine hundred) met Brigadier General John Prideaux[113] at Oswego, and the British successfully attacked that stronghold. Prideaux was killed during the battle; but his command devolved on Sir William, and there was a rich harvest in scalps, prisoners, and plunder for the eager warriors.[114]

All the world loves a winner, and the Indians were no exception, espe-

---

[109] William Johnson to William Pitt, October 24, 1760, *ibid.,* III, 269–75. Johnson made it a 'fixt rule" to reward those Indians who would fight the French, but he would not neglect neutral "friends." See *New York Colonial Documents,* VII, 227–29.

[110] *Sir William Johnson Papers,* III, 271. According to General Abercromby, Johnson secured the assistance of 450 Indians. See *ibid.,* II, 870. Montcalm stated that Johnson had 500 warriors. See *New York Colonial Documents,* X, 734. These warriors, however, were merely spectators. See *ibid.,* X, 755.

[111] *Sir William Johnson Papers,* III, 271. Prices were so high for Indian goods during the year 1758 that Johnson urged the purchasing of presents in England. See *ibid.,* II, 832. Despite the high prices, French sources report that the British were furnishing the Indians goods in "profusion." See "Memoire of M. Péar on the Condition of Canada," November 15, 1758, *New York Colonial Documents,* X, 899.

[112] *Sir William Johnson Papers,* III, 27–30, 271.

[113] Brigadier General John Prideaux, apparently a capable officer with European military experience, was killed shortly afterwards. A bay on Lake Ontario bears his name. While Prideaux was to attack Niagara, Amherst moved toward Crown Point and from thence to Montreal. Major General James Wolfe, meantime, was to lead the assault on Quebec.

[114] *Sir William Johnson Papers,* III, 122, 271; William L. Stone, *The Life and Times of Sir William Johnson, Bart.,* II, Appendix, pp. 394–429. Herein is the private manuscript diary of William Johnson covering Indian affairs at Oswego and Niagara in 1759. The Indians flocked to Johnson's headquarters where he handed out pipes, tobacco, and rum. Welcoming the British victory, the natives celebrated by asking for trading agreements and by getting drunk. The Belt, Onondaga sachem, made himself rather troublesome in this respect.

cially when the victor gave large presents. Thus, in June 1760, six hundred warriors heeded Sir William's call for the Montreal campaign. Even the tribesmen living in the vicinity of Montreal, who had hitherto been allied with the French, joined Amherst's victorious army; and Sir William reported sending presents to "Foreign Indians" who were rapidly leaving the sinking French empire.[115] On August 5, 1760, Amherst found that his native auxiliaries numbered 1,330![116] "Thus Sir," related Johnson in a report to William Pitt, "we became Masters of the last place in the Enemys possession in these parts and made those Indians our friends by a peace, who might otherwise have given us much trouble."[117]

On September 28, 1757, when the future looked black, Johnson had written that only by "Presents & management" could the British hope to win the Indians from the French.[118] Certainly it cannot be assumed that the Indians fought for the British from 1758 through 1760 with no thought of reward. The Amherst-Johnson correspondence during this period emphasizes more than once that Indian expenses brought about by "Presents & management" emptied the "War Chest."

Despite these testimonies to the important role of presents in Indian diplomacy, Jeffery Amherst, commander-in-chief, Knight of Bath, insisted that the amount of money expended for native gifts must be cut down.[119] Like his predecessor, the Earl of Loudoun, Amherst at first gave Johnson financial support, turning over to him thousands of pounds at a single warrant. But as the war came to a close, the General's frugal nature gained the

---

[115] *New York Colonial Documents,* VII, 433.

[116] Webster, *op. cit.,* p. 224. Broken down by tribes, the figures were: 329 Sensagos, 114 Senecas, 284 Cayugas, 203 Onondagas, 37 Tuscaroras, 60 Oneidas, 20 Canasaragas, 85 Canjohazys, 51 Mohawks, 22 Scholazys, 12 Mohicans, 35 Chennogas, 18 Oquagos, 3 Mowas, 15 Oswegatchys, 34 Cauadrogas, and 12 warriors with The Belt, Onondaga sachem. The 1,330 included women and children.

[117] William Johnson to William Pitt, October 24, 1760, *Sir William Johnson Papers,* III, 269–75.

[118] William Johnson to the Board of Trade, September 28, 1757, *New York Colonial Documents,* VII, 276.

[119] Jeffery Amherst, 1717–1797, was made Knight of Bath after the conquest of Canada. See *Sir William Johnson Papers,* III, 580–82. Before this time, he had seen service in Europe during the Seven Years' War. After being sent to America, he captured Louisbourg in 1758, and ended his career in the New World with the capture of Montreal in 1760. When he returned to England in 1763, Sir Jeffery was acclaimed a hero and, among other honors, he was made a baron. See Arthur Pound and Richard E. Day, *Johnson of the Mohawks, A Biography of Sir William Johnson, Irish Immigrant, Mohawk War Chief, American Soldier, Empire Builder,* p. 522. According to his signature, Amherst spelled his first name *Jeffery* and not *Jeffrey.* See, for example, Jeffery Amherst to Henry Bouquet, October 3, 1763, Bouquet Papers, A. 4, pp. 421–23, Canadian Archives (photostat).

upper hand, and he began to economize in the giving of presents. Amherst particularly liked to bestow medals upon the Indians. Here was an effective gift that positively identified friendly natives; and, more important, it was inexpensive! After the Montreal campaign the General had 182 silver medals struck off, including one for Silver Heels, who had fought with Braddock.[120] When he sent these articles to Johnson for distribution to the natives, Sir Jeffery thoughtfully enclosed a gold medal for the superintendent himself!

When the Indians were fighting, Amherst willingly approved warrants for gifts.[121] Still, with a wary eye on the king's war chest, he cautioned Sir William Johnson to ". . . . always be as frugal and Oeconomous [sic] of publick money as possible. . . . ."[122] Though the commander-in-chief can be criticized for slicing expenses, it must be remembered that the amount spent for gifts did sometimes seem stupendous. For example, the £3,000 spent for gifts[123] during one campaign represented a large amount of money to the eighteenth-century world.

Amherst's penchant for economy also gave Johnson cause to worry about salary and personnel. For example, it appears that even as late as 1763, Johnson was receiving only the £600 which paid for his duties as superintendent. In Amherst's opinion this compensation was sufficient, and Sir William's constant pleas for reimbursement as colonel of the Six Nations went unanswered. The fact that he also questioned the warrants of George Croghan, Daniel Claus, and Thomas Butler for gifts furnishes another illustration of Amherst's thrift.[124]

Jeffery Amherst did not propose to hand out liberal amounts of goods to the Indians after 1760. He had his own ideas concerning the handling of these natives. He approved of Indian schoolmasters and ministers. Amherst also thought that the Indians should be occupied in bringing in skins; otherwise, they might "hatch mischief." He directed his officers to give the natives powder and arms and a little clothing for hunting purposes, but that was all, and even this small amount must be doled out with caution.[125] In

---

[120] See *Sir William Johnson Papers,* III, 376–78; "Morris Journal," May 19, 1755, Sargent, *op. cit.,* pp. 378–79; G. S. Kimball (ed.), *Correspondence of William Pitt with Colonial Governors and Military and Naval Commissioners in Colonial America,* II, 427.

[121] Jeffery Amherst to William Johnson, October 2, 1759, *Sir William Johnson Papers,* III, 141–42; same to same, February 23, 1760, *ibid.,* III, 192–93.

[122] *Ibid.,* III, 186.

[123] Funds for the Montreal campaign. See *ibid.,* III, 197.

[124] *Ibid.,* III, 330–33, 343–46, 600–601. Croghan alone employed ten men as assistants. See Croghan's return, January 12, 1761, Fort Pitt, *ibid.,* III, 300–301. Also see Jeffery Amherst to George Croghan, May 11, 1763, Bouquet Papers, A. 4, pp. 223–35, Canadian Archives (photostat).

[125] *Sir William Johnson Papers,* III, 345.

addition, a trading schedule was set up at Fort Pitt and at other posts.[126] For example, one of these schedules listed a stroud as being worth two good beaver or three buck skins. The war was over, and the Indians were on their own!

Between July and September, 1761, Sir William, overlooking his poor health, carried Amherst's message of this new policy of frugality to the Western Indians at Niagara and Detroit.[127] In all of these conferences, the flavor of the Indians' conversation indicated rising hostility and disapproval of this policy. Indeed, at times Johnson's very life was in danger. In Illinois belts of wampum were already inviting nations to take up the hatchet against the English.[128] The French Indians, who had been left poverty-stricken after the long war, were particularly in need of goods. For example, on September 6, 1761, at Detroit, the Ottawas "begged" Sir William to consider their needs, especially the lack of powder. According to his instructions, Sir William answered them

That he should in due time consider the Wants which they had represented and hoped they would for the future by their hunting and by an Industrious way of life be enabled to Support their familys without other assistance.[129]

The Ottawas were fortunate if they received any powder, for the total expenditures of the entire journey amounted to only £305, and most of this went to pay for assistants, wampum, and other incidentals.[130]

At Fort Pitt as early as May 1762, George Croghan, deputy agent, was sending in reports of dissatisfaction among the tribesmen, who had begun to miss both the French and the English outlays of free merchandise. With characteristic naïveté the Indians inquired of Croghan ". . . . ye Reason why we allways was Calling them to Council During ye War & giveing them presents & now Take No Notice of them. They say ye French was butt a poor peple [sic] butt they allways Cloathed any Indians that was poor or Naked when they Come to see them."[131]

---

[126] Indian trade regulations at Fort Pitt, *Sir William Johnson Papers*, III, 530–32. Christian Frederick Post reported on September 10, 1757, that the French at Fort Duquesne had a similar system. A store was kept where the Indians might buy goods, but if they would fight the English they could have all they wanted. See *Early Western Travels*, I, 227.

[127] "Minutes of the Proceedings of Sir William Johnson Bart. with the Indians on his Way to, and at the Detroit in 1761 wither he went by his Excellency Sir Jeff. Amhersts Orders to Establish peace & settle all affairs between the English, and the several Nations of Northern and Western Indians," July–September, 1761, *Sir William Johnson Papers*, III, 428–503; Stone, *op. cit.*, II, Appendix, pp. 429–77; *Wisconsin Historical Collections*, XVIII, 229–48.

[128] *Sir William Johnson Papers*, III, 438.   [129] *Ibid.*, III, 472.

[130] "Expenses of Western Indian Meetings," *ibid.*, III, 503.

[131] George Croghan to William Johnson, May 10, 1762, *ibid.*, III, 732–34. It is

Rumors of war were constantly being circulated, and abuses on the part of the whites brought retaliations on the part of the natives throughout the remainder of 1762. As late as March 1763, George Croghan was handing out goods to the downcast tribesmen who had been refused gifts by the commanding officer at Fort Pitt. These goods cost Croghan a year's salary.[132] It was dangerously evident that among other things, such as the encroachment on Indian lands, the lack of presents was bringing on an Indian rebellion. Many of the other abuses suffered by the natives are clearly pointed out in a contemporary drama which is attributed to Robert Rogers.[133] This work is entitled *Ponteach: Or the Savages of America, A Tragedy*.[134]

Indeed, it is clearly established in Johnson's writings that an outstanding cause of the rebellion was the failure to supply the Western Indians with goods. Francis Parkman recognized this factor in a brief paragraph in his great work on Pontiac's rebellion, and Howard H. Peckham in his recent study on Pontiac mentions the importance of presents in relation to the Indian uprising of 1763.[135] According to Johnson, the contemporary authority,

---

of interest to note that Croghan made a preliminary treaty of peace in 1764 with Pontiac after the conspiracy was crushed. See *Wisconsin Historical Collections*, XVIII, 275.

[132] George Croghan to William Johnson, March 12, 1763, *Sir William Johnson Papers*, IV, 62–63. Of all the Six Nations, the Senecas were the only "nation" (the Senecas were really composed of many tribes) who joined the Indian rebellion of 1763. Actually, according to a contemporary account, the Senecas numbered more than all of the remainder of the Iroquoian confederacy together. See *ibid.*, IV, 240–41. Showing loyalty to Sir William, other members of the Six Nations assisted British forces in putting down the conspiracy. The loyal warriors, characteristically enough, were, in appreciation of their efforts, given supplies and presents.

[133] Robert Rogers (1731–1795), the famous frontiersman, was the author of several other works. See his "Journals" and *A Concise Account of North America*, published in London, 1765. While Allan Nevins supports the claim that Rogers wrote the above drama, Francis Parkman is in doubt as to its authorship. See Parkman, *op. cit.*, Vol. I, note 1, p. 175.

[134] In this play, two traders talk of a colleague named Old Ogden. Their conversation goes like this:

> By this old *Ogden* built his stately House,
> Purchas'd Estates, and grew to a little King.
> He, like an honest Man, bought all by Weight,
> And made the ign'rant Savages believe
> That his Right Foot exactly weigh'd a Pound:
> By this for many Years he bought their furs,
> And died in Quiet like an honest Dealer.

See Robert Rogers, *Ponteach: Or the Savages of America, A Tragedy*, edited by Allan Nevins.

[135] Parkman, *op. cit.*, I, 175. Parkman cites a letter from Sir William Johnson to Cadwallader Colden, January 24, 1763; it has been printed in the *Sir William Johnson Papers*, IV, 273–77. Also see Howard H. Peckham, *Pontiac and the Indian Uprising,*

the French had found it a great deal cheaper to control the Indians by bestowing lavish gifts upon them than to maintain a standing army which would hold them in check by force.[136] In 1765, in a letter to the Board of Trade, the superintendent repeated his conviction that "kindness" on the part of the French and loads of presents made the Indians overlook injustices.[137] Moreover, the Western tribes expected to partake of British gifts after the "reduction" of Canada. But the British were especially cautious about giving ammunition to the French Indians. This refusal of the English to grant goods—even those items which were absolutely essential for hunting—led the Indians to believe the rumors that the British meant to make slaves of them.[138] Here was an opportunity for Pontiac to make the most of Indian discontent. It was an opportunity he did not overlook.[139]

Thus, in 1759, following the fall of Fort Duquesne, the Indians had been eager to receive large amounts of British merchandise in the form of gifts.[140] Strouds, cattle, guns, jews'-harps, and a hundred other favors helped to bring vast numbers of Western Indians under the British flag. The very name of the kind Warraghiyagey, as Sir William was called by the tribes-

---

pp. 97–98, 101–2. Peckham disagrees with Parkman on the origin of the Indian war of 1763 and maintains there was no "grand conspiracy." For an evaluation of this disagreement, see Wilbur R. Jacobs, "Was the Pontiac Uprising a Conspiracy?" *The Ohio State Archaeological and Historical Quarterly*, LI (January 1950), 26–37.

[136] *Ibid.* Croghan advocated this policy for the British in 1764. See George Croghan to the Board of Trade, June 8, 1764, Clarence Walworth Alvord *et al.* (eds.), *Collections* of the Illinois Historical Library, British Series, Vol. I, *The Critical Period, 1763–1765*, pp. 256–63. Hereafter cited as *The Critical Period, 1763–1765*.

[137] William Johnson to the Board of Trade, May 24, 1765 (extract from a letter), Parkman, *op. cit.*, Vol. II, Appendix A, pp. 316–18. Not printed in the *Sir William Johnson Papers*. See *The Critical Period, 1763–1765*, pp. 500–511 for the complete letter.

[138] William Johnson to the Board of Trade, November 13, 1763 (extract from a letter), Parkman, *op. cit.*, Vol. II, Appendix B, pp. 319–20. Not printed in the *Sir William Johnson Papers*. See also William Johnson to the Board of Trade, August 30, 1764, *The Critical Period, 1763–1765*, p. 263.

[139] As an example, the Chippewas and other tribes plundered Mackinac in the summer of 1763, sharing the spoils of goods and prisoners with the Ottawas. See Daniel Claus to William Johnson, August 6, 1763, *Wisconsin Historical Collections*, XVIII, 256–58; "Indian Hostilities, 1763, Summary of Pontiac's Conspiracy at the Upper Posts," *ibid.*, XVIII, 250–52. Pontiac, previous to this attack, urged the Ottawas, Hurons, and Foxes to attack the English who refused supplies to the sick, made no condolence for the dead, and gave no credit for trade. This conference took place near Detroit on May 3, 1763. See "The Pontiac Manuscript, Journal or a History of a Conspiracy by the Indians Against the English, and of the Seige of Detroit Beginning the 7th of May, 1763," *Collections* of the Pioneer Society of the State of Michigan together with the County Pioneer Societies, VIII, 273–74; "Accounts of the Conspiracy of Pontiac and the Siege of Detroit," *ibid.*, VIII, 340–64.

[140] Memorial of James Abercromby, Agent for Virginia, to William Pitt, January 20, 1759, P.R.O., C.O., 5/1329, L.C. 161–62, C.O. 221–24.

men, served to rally the Indian hosts. It was this "kindness" in satisfying even the most insignificant needs of the natives that made Johnson so beloved by the Indians. A bit of clothing or food to an old woman, a ruffled shirt and a brilliant waistcoat for a chief, a gun for a warrior, a toy for a child—all of these appear in the detailed and illuminating accounts of the superintendent.[141] Knowing the Indians' childlike desire for a constant flow of presents, Johnson's numerous assistants continued to carry out the well-tested policy of bestowing gifts. In 1760, when Sir Jeffery's policy of economy took effect, Johnson pleaded to allow officers at the frontier posts to give the Indians a few articles of clothing whenever they visited the British. The pleas were in vain. The commander-in-chief made stern reply to the effect that the Indians would now have to shift for themselves.

The situation was not promising. After the long wars the natives faced especially grave economic problems. Crops had not been cared for; tools were needed; women demanded the old French finery; and, worst of all, there was no ammunition. Fierce young warriors would "tear the heart out of a trader" to get these prizes.[142] The result was the Indian war of 1763. The proclamation of the same year[143]—supposed to be a solution to all Indian problems—was only a palliative. The old conflict went on.

---

[141] See *Sir William Johnson Papers*, II, 566–646, III, 149–82.

[142] *Vide* note 139.

[143] The Proclamation of October 7, 1763, announcing the famous Indian boundary line, separating Indian territory from white settlement, was preceded by Colonel Henry Bouquet's earlier proclamation of October 13, 1761, at Fort Pitt. This action on Bouquet's part was contested by the lieutenant-governor of Virginia, Francis Fauquier. See Francis Fauquier to Henry Bouquet, January 17, 1762, Bouquet Papers, ff. 5–500, British Museum (photostat). Colonel Henry Bouquet (1719–1765), a naturalized officer in the British army who had been born in Switzerland, clearly saw the defects in Amherst's Indian policy. See, for example, Henry Bouquet to Jeffery Amherst, May 19, 1763, Bouquet Papers, A. 4, pp. 249–51 (Canada Archives, photostat). During Pontiac's uprising (which should be considered a war for Indian independence rather than a "conspiracy"), Sir Jeffery actually urged Bouquet to spread the scourge of smallpox among the attacking tribes! See Bouquet's answer to Amherst dated July 13, 1763, Stevens, *op. cit.*, Series 21634, pp. 214–15. Captain Simeon Ecuyer, commander at Fort Pitt during the siege, did give the Indians some blankets from the smallpox hospital. See A. T. Volwiler, ed., "William Trent's Journal at Fort Pitt, 1763," *Mississippi Valley Historical Review*, XI (1924), 400.

Regarding the Indian boundary line, it is of interest to note that John Stuart was able to secure Indian agreement to a boundary line on the frontier of Georgia at the Augusta conference with the Southern Indians in the fall of 1763. The exact delineation of this line can be seen on a map later drawn by Joseph Purcell (probably completed in 1776—the map has no date) under Stuart's direction for the Board of Trade. An original copy of this map is located at the Newberry Library, Chicago.

BIBLIOGRAPHY

I. GUIDES AND CALENDARS

ANDREWS, CHARLES M. *Guide to the Materials for American History to 1783 in the Public Record Office of Great Britain.* Carnegie Institution of Washington, Publication No. 90A I and II, Washington, D.C., 1912–1914. 2 vols.

Andrews' work should be used in connection with the Library of Congress transcripts, although this guide is not complete for the vast collection at this library.

ANDREWS, CHARLES M., AND DAVENPORT, FRANCES G. *Guide to the Manuscript Materials for the History of the United States to 1783, in the British Museum, in Minor London Archives, and in the Libraries of Oxford and Cambridge.* Carnegie Institution of Washington, Publication No. 90, Washington, D.C., 1908.

Both guides of Andrews are now supplemented by Grace Gardner Griffin's *A Guide to Manuscripts Relating to American History in British Depositories*, Washington, 1946.

DAY, RICHARD E. (ed.). *Calendar of the Sir William Johnson Manuscripts in the New York State Library.* Albany, New York, 1909.

Many of the Sir William Johnson manuscripts were destroyed by fire in 1911. This calendar is invaluable for checking the content of these lost documents.

DEPUY, HENRY F. *A Bibliography of English Colonial Treaties with the American Indians Including a Synopsis of Each Treaty.* Printed for the Lenox Club, New York, N.Y., 1917.

Although this bibliography is by no means complete, it is valuable because of the facsimile title page of each treaty. DePuy also gives the location of the original manuscripts.

PALMER, WILLIAM P. *et al.* (eds.). *Calendar of Virginia State Papers and Other Manuscripts Preserved in the Capitol at Richmond.* Richmond, Virginia, 1875–1893. 11 vols.

Volume I (1652–1781) covers much material relating to Indian affairs and presents.

PARKER, DAVID W. *Guide to the Documents in the Manuscript Room at the Public Archives of Canada.* Ottawa, Canada, 1911.

This guide gives a brief description of the contents of the Bouquet and Haldimand papers. It has an excellent index.

————. *Guide to the Materials for United States History in the Canada Archives.* Carnegie Institution of Washington, Publication No. 172, Baltimore, Maryland, 1913.

This guide also has a general description of Series B, the Haldimand Collection, and Series A, the Bouquet Collection.

Report of the Canada Archives. Ottawa, Canada, 1882–

These reports were originally begun by Douglas Brymer, archivist, and have a calendar for French documents in the report of 1887. The Bouquet and Haldimand papers are covered in the report of 1889.

Roy, J. Edmond (ed.). *Rapport Sur Les Archives de France Relative à L'Histoire du Canada.* Ottawa, 1911.

This calendar of French manuscripts is a useful guide for French transcripts in the Canada archives. The annotations are particularly valuable.

Swem, E. G. (comp.). *Virginia Historical Index.* Roanoke, Virginia, 1934–1936. 2 vols.

Swem's index is in reality a guide to various sources, historical works, and periodicals relating to Virginia and her neighbors. It has proved extremely useful in selecting materials regarding presents.

Stevens, Benjamin Franklin (comp.). *Catalogue Index of Manuscripts in the Archives of England, Holland, and Spain Relating to America, 1763–1783.* London, 1870–1902.

A manuscript of this calendar is preserved in the Library of Congress. It covers many of the Library of Congress transcripts relating to presents given the Indians after 1763.

Surrey, N. M. Miller (ed.). *Calendar of Manuscripts in the Paris Archives and Libraries Relating to the History of the Mississippi Valley to 1803,* privately printed, 1926–1928. 2 vols.

This calendar covers the correspondence of French officials during the period of the French and Indian War with a note on the content of each letter.

II. PRIMARY MATERIAL

A. Manuscript Sources

Canada Archives (Ottawa, Canada).

Manuscripts from the Bouquet Papers have been examined. These have proved especially useful in the study of Indian presents used in the frontier campaigns.

Clements, William L., Library (Ann Arbor, Michigan).

The William Knox Papers, Volume X, have been used for the study of records of Indian presents both in the Northern and in the Southern Department of Indian Affairs in the period immediately following 1763. The accounts of Guy Johnson, John Stuart, and General Frederick Haldimand have been examined.

Historical Commission of South Carolina (Columbia, South Carolina).

The Indian Books of South Carolina, Vols. II–VI (film), are extremely valuable for Southern Indian politics.

Historical Society of Pennsylvania (Philadelphia, Pennsylvania).

The Etting Collection of Ohio Company Papers includes considerable material on Indian affairs as they relate to the Ohio Company. See Volume I.

Huntington, Henry E., Library (San Marino, California).

Abercromby Papers. This collection, which supplements the Loudoun Papers, contains letters relating to the use of Indian warriors.

Blathwayt Papers. These papers are concentrated upon the Colonial period before 1700. Herein are preserved lists of presents with their cost.

Huntington Manuscripts. Like the Loudoun Papers, the Huntington Manuscripts contain a wide assortment of materials concerning the use of presents in the

Northern as well as in the Southern Department of Indian Affairs. Such items as lists of presents, Indian treaties, and the correspondence of agents who distributed goods have been used. The Loudoun Memorandum Books have been examined. These thirteen small volumes, in Loudoun's almost indecipherable handwriting, contain much material upon Indian affairs.

Loudoun Papers. This large, carefully preserved collection includes a large portion of the material used for the study of presents to the Indians along the Ohio and Northwest frontiers. These papers, which are heavy in detail for the years 1756–1760, also contain much material relating to French-Indian politics and the use of gifts. In addition, there are to be found numerous accounts of treaties, correspondence between Loudoun and the Northern as well as the Southern Department of Indian Affairs, and lists of presents. Many of the documents that strictly pertain to the Northern superintendency have been printed in the *Sir William Johnson Papers.*

LIBRARY OF CONGRESS (Washington, D.C.). See also the University of California at Los Angeles.

Collections of British transcripts. The Additional Manuscripts from the British Museum have put much light upon presents to the Indians as they concerned the Board of Trade. Here is to be found the materials relating to the trial of Governor John Reynolds revolving chiefly around the alleged misappropriation of expensive presents.

The Colonial Office papers in class 5 contain a large amount of data covering the use of presents during the entire period, 1748–1763. This includes Indian treaties, lists of presents, prices as they varied in different years, insurance and freight charges, correspondence of governors and British officials in England, and documents relating to the military campaigns and the use of Indian warriors as auxiliaries during the French and Indian War.

Society for the Propagation of the Gospel in Foreign Parts. See University of California at Los Angeles.

The Treasury Board Papers include long lists of presents. These lists contain charges for treating fabrics used for gifts such as pressing, dyeing, and tilloting.

Collections of French transcripts. The Archives Nationales, Ministre des Colonies have, in series F, a large portion of the material relating to the use of Indian warriors in the campaigns throughout the French and Indian War. These materials are especially valuable for the study of the campaigns of 1755.

The Archives de Ministre des Affairs Étrangères, Memoires et Documents Angleterre, contain many accounts of Indian problems as they affected the state of the French colonies in America. For example, some documents are concentrated upon the status of the Iroquois confederacy.

UNIVERSITY OF CALIFORNIA AT BERKELEY.

This collection of photographic enlargements of the records of British-American customs from the Public Record Office has proved valuable. Dr. Lawrence A. Harper, custodian, was good enough to make this material available. Customs 3/73 contains references on the prices of materials used for Indian presents.

UNIVERSITY OF CALIFORNIA AT LOS ANGELES.

The collection of Library of Congress transcripts of Professor Louis Knott Koontz includes film and typescript copies of the Colonial Office papers in class 5, Additional Manuscripts from the British Museum, documents from the Archives de Ministre des Affairs Étrangères and the Archives Nationales, Ministre des Colonies.

This collection has proved invaluable in the study of Indian presents during the years 1748–1763.

Professor Frank J. Klingberg's film collection of the records of the Society for the Propagation of the Gospel in Foreign Parts (S.P.G. MSS), Library of Congress transcripts has much material relating to Indian missionary work. S.P.G. MSS, Letters 1759–1782 Series B, Vol. 2, Parts 1 and 2 (Library of Congress film). This film contains letters from Sir William Johnson indicating his interest in helping the Society extend its work among the Indians. In addition, letters from the Mohawk missionary, John Ogilvie, are included.

VIRGINIA STATE LIBRARY (Richmond, Virginia).

The Virginia Council Journals have proved invaluable in the study of presents to the Ohio and Southern Indians. Included here are accounts of the transportation, appropriations, and matters of policy as they concerned Indian presents.

WISCONSIN STATE HISTORICAL SOCIETY (Madison, Wisconsin).

Draper Manuscripts. The Preston Papers (QQ) are valuable for materials relating to Indian affairs throughout the period of the French and Indian War. Together with the newspaper extracts (JJ), much of which has been taken from the *Maryland Gazette*, the famous collection made by Draper covers frontier Indian diplomacy, the use of presents, Indian traders, the Southern Indians, the Ohio Indians, and the Northern confederacies.

B. GENERAL PRINTED SOURCES

BLAIR, EMMA HELEN (ed. and trans.). *Indian Tribes of the Upper Mississippi Valley and Region of the Great Lakes as Described by Nicolas Perrot, French Commandant in the Northwest; Bacqueveille de la Potherie, French Royal Commissioner to Canada; Morrell Marston, American army officer; and Thomas Forsyth, United States Agent at Fort Armstrong.* Cleveland, Ohio, 1911. 2 vols.

The description of the Algonquian and Iroquois Indians in the old Northwest by Nicolas Perrot relates in detail native customs as they concerned the exchange of presents. Perrot describes the use of presents in almost every phase in the customs of the aborigines.

BOUQUET, HENRY. Sylvester K. Stevens, *et al.* (eds.). *The Papers of Col. Henry Bouquet* (Series 21643 *Northwestern Pennsylvania Historical Series*). Prepared by the Pennsylvania Historical Survey, Work Projects Administration, Harrisburg, Pennsylvania, 1941.

This mimeographed edition of Bouquet's papers has been useful in the study of presents to the Indians on the Forbes campaign of 1758.

BOYD, JULIAN P. (ed.). *The Susquehanna Company Papers, 1750–1772.* Wilkes-Barre, Pennsylvania, 1930–1933. 4 vols.

The Susquehanna Company Papers contain scattered accounts of the merchants who supplied the province of Pennsylvania with goods for presents in volumes I and II.

CLAUS, DANIEL. *Narrative of His Relations with Sir William Johnson and Experiences in the Lake George Fight.* Printed by the Society of Colonial Wars for the State of New York, June 1904.

Daniel Claus' *Narrative* includes an account of the Lake George campaign in 1755 and, more important, the only record of the famous meeting between William Johnson and his friends when the downfall of William Shirley was planned.

COLDEN, CADWALLADER. *The Letters and Papers of Cadwallader Colden* in the *Collections* of the New York Historical Society. Printed for the Society, New York, 1917–1923, 1934–1935. 9 vols.

Colden's correspondence with William Johnson and other Colonial leaders throws much light upon the use of presents by the British to secure Indian warriors.

DARLINGTON, WILLIAM M. (ed.). *Christopher Gist's Journals with Historical, Geographical, and Ethnological Notes and Biographies of His Contemporaries.* Pittsburgh, Pennsylvania, 1893.

Gist's journals are of particular importance in connection with the large present given the Ohio Indians at the Logstown Treaty in 1752.

DINWIDDIE, ROBERT. R[obert] A[lonzo] Brock (ed.). *The Official Records of Robert Dinwiddie, Lieutenant Governor of Virginia, 1751–1758.* (Vols. III and IV of the Virginia Historical Society *Collections,* n.s.) Commonly known as the *Dinwiddie Papers.* Published by the Society, Richmond, Virginia, 1883–1884.

These papers comprise all of the letters of Dinwiddie known to Brock; however, the forthcoming edition of Dinwiddie letters, to be known as the Dinwiddie Correspondence, edited by Professor Louis Knott Koontz, make available all known Dinwiddie materials. The *Dinwiddie Papers,* as edited by Brock, have been valuable in the study of Indian presents in the Ohio Valley during the years 1751–1758. Because Dinwiddie's correspondence reach almost all of the important Colonial officials of the British colonies, his letters almost form a basis for any study of the early history of the French and Indian War.

ILLINOIS. *Collections* of the Illinois Historical Library, X, British Series Volume I, *The Critical Period, 1763–1765,* edited by Clarence Walworth Alvord and Clarence Edwin Carter. Published by the Trustees of the Illinois Historical Library, Springfield, Illinois, 1915.

This volume carries the correspondence of William Johnson and George Croghan relating to the scarcity of presents after the conquest of Canada in 1760. Some of these letters concern the Indian rebellion under Pontiac showing the connection of this uprising with the lack of presents for the Western Indians.

————. *Collections* of the Illinois Historical Library, XXVII, XXIX, French Series, Volumes II and III, *Anglo French Boundary Disputes in the West, 1749–1763,* and *Illinois on the Eve of the Seven Years' War, 1747–1755,* edited by Theodore Calvin Pease. Published by the Trustees of the Illinois Historical Library, Springfield, Illinois, 1936, 1940 (respectively).

In both of these volumes Pease has written a stimulating introduction. Since Volume II is concerned with political affairs more than an account of events, it contains less material on Indian presents. Volume III, however, covers the conspiracy of the insubordinate branch of the Miamis under Old Briton and the use of French presents in order to quell the rebellion.

JOHNSON, WILLIAM. James Sullivan *et al.* (eds.). *The Papers of Sir William Johnson.* Albany, New York, 1921– . 9 vols to date.

The *Sir William Johnson Papers* have proved to be for this study the most valuable source on presents to the Indians. Volumes I, II, III, and IV contain lists of presents, accounts of treaties, the correspondence of Johnson with almost all the important Colonial officials in the Northern colonies, and numerous reports of assistants to the Northern superintendent relating to the use of presents to the Six Nations and their allies.

Journal of the Commissioners for Trade and Plantations From April 1704 to May 1782. London, 1920–1938. 14 vols. Usually known as the *Journals of the Board of Trade.*

Volumes IX, X, and XI are indispensable for the study of the imperial machinery regarding the British distribution of presents.

KENNEDY, ARCHIBALD. *The Importance of Gaining and Preserving the Friendship of the Indians to the British Interest Considered.* New York, 1751.

This contemporary publication emphasizes the importance of presents and gunsmiths in securing the favor of the Six Nations and their allies.

KIMBALL, GERTRUDE S. (ed.). *Correspondence of William Pitt with Colonial Governors and Military and Naval Commissioners in Colonial America.* New York, 1906. 2 vols.

Amherst's correspondence with Pitt contains references to Indian presents.

MARYLAND, ARCHIVES OF, XXI. *Correspondence of Governor Horatio Sharpe 1753–1771,* edited by William Hand Brown. Baltimore, Maryland, 1888–1911. 4 vols.

Horatio Sharpe's correspondence contains references to Indian affairs.

————, L. *Proceedings and Acts of the General Assembly of Maryland 1752–1754,* edited by J. Hall Pleasants. Baltimore, Maryland, 1933.

This volume contains some material on Thomas Cresap.

MICHIGAN. *Collections* of the Pioneer Society of the State of Michigan Together with Reports of the County Pioneer Societies. Lansing, Michigan, 1874–1929. 40 vols.

Volume VIII is of particular value, including the "Pontiac Manuscript" and "Accounts of a Conspiracy of Pontiac and the Siege of Detroit."

MISSISSIPPI. Dunbar Rowland (ed.). *Mississippi Provincial Archives, 1763–1766, English Dominion Letters and Enclosures to the Secretary of State from Major Robert Farmar and Governor George Johnstone.* Nashville, Tennessee, 1911. 1 vol.

Volume I has material on French presents that were annually given the Indians before the English took control. Only one volume has been published.

————. Dunbar Rowland *et al.* (eds.). *Mississippi Provincial Archives, 1704–1743, French Dominion.* Jackson, Mississippi, 1927. 3 vols.

Volume III includes lists of French presents.

MUNRO, JAMES, *et al.* (eds.). *Acts of the Privy Council, Colonial Series . . . .* Hereford, England, 1908–1912. 6 vols.

Volume IV touches on correspondence relating to the Virginia condolence present for the Twightwees.

NEVINS, ALLAN (ed.). *Ponteach: Or the Savages of America, A Tragedy by Robert Rogers.* Chicago, Illinois, 1914.

This contemporary drama attributed to Rogers reviews many of the abuses along the frontier, besides the scarcity of presents, that led to Pontiac's rebellion in 1763.

NEW YORK. E. B. O'Callaghan (ed.). *Documentary History of the State of New York.* Albany, New York, 1850–1851. 4 vols.

In this work is included much of Johnson's correspondence relating to the distribution of presents.

————. E. B. O'Callaghan *et al.* (eds.). *Documents Relative to the Colonial History of the State of New York Procured in Holland, England and France.* Albany, New York, 1853–1887. 15 vols.

Volumes VI and IX were of particular value in the study of Johnson's distribution of presents as Northern superintendent and the use of presents by Montcalm in the later campaigns of the French and Indian War.

PARGELLIS, STANLEY McCRORY (ed.). *Military Affairs in North America 1748–1765, Selected Documents From the Cumberland Papers in the Windsor Castle.* New York, 1936.

This volume of documents includes the cream of the Loudoun military correspondence. Concerning this study, it reveals the problems in connection with securing Indians for the Forbes campaign in 1758.

PENNSYLVANIA. *Minutes of the Provincial Council of Pennsylvania, from the Organization to the Termination of the Proprietary Government.* Philadelphia, Pennsylvania, 1851–1853. 10 vols.

Volumes IV, V, VI, VII, and VIII illuminate the policy of the Quaker colony in detail regarding Indian presents. Lists of goods, Indian treaties, correspondence, and other data relating to Indian affairs have been preserved. These volumes are to be used in connection with *Pennsylvania Archives* (1st series) which supplement the *Pennsylvania Colonial Records.*

————. Samuel Hazard (ed.). *Pennsylvania Archives* (1st series). Philadelphia, Pennsylvania, 1852–1856. 12 vols.

Volumes I and II have proved invaluable in the study of Pennsylvania Indian politics. In addition, scattered references are to be found in the 4th and 8th series of events relating to the frontier during the period 1748–1763.

REICHEL, WILLIAM C. (ed.). *Memorials of the Moravian Church.* Philadelphia, Pennsylvania, 1870.

Volume I (the only volume published) contains the journal of Count Zinzendorf recording his travels with Conrad Weiser among the Ohio and Iroquois Indians.

RHODE ISLAND. *Collections* of the Rhode Island Historical Society, 1827–1941. Providence, Rhode Island. 34 vols.

Volume I contains Roger Williams' *Key to the Indian Language* which was originally published in 1643. Williams has noted details concerning the making of wampum beads and mentions the value of these grains.

SARGENT, WINTHROP (ed.). *The History of an Expedition Against Fort Du Quesne in 1755; Under Major General Edward Braddock, Generalissimo of H.B.M. Forces in America* (Volume V of the *Memoirs of the Historical Society of Pennsylvania*). Philadelphia, Pennsylvania, 1856.

Herein is the journal of Robert Orme and the "Morris" journal covering the activities of Croghan and Braddock's eight Indian guides.

SHEA, JEAN MARIE (ed.). *Relations Diverses sur La Bataille du Malnagueulé Gagné le 9 Juillet, 1755, par les François sous m. de Beaujeau, Commandant du Fort du Quesne sur les Anglois m. Braddock, Général en Chef des Troupes Angloises.* New York, 1760.
Beaujeau's account of the participation of the French Indians in Braddock's defeat has been useful.

SHIRLEY, WILLIAM. Charles Henry Lincoln (ed.). *Correspondence of William Shirley, Governor of Massachusetts and Military Commander in America, 1731–1760.* New York, 1912. 2 vols.
Shirley's letters to and from William Johnson reveal much information regarding the use of presents during the campaigns of 1755 and the dispute between these men.

THWAITES, REUBEN GOLD (ed.). *Early Western Travels, 1748–1849, A Series of Annotated Reprints of Some of the Best and Rarest Contemporary Volumes of Travel, Descriptive of the Aborigines, Social, and Economic Conditions of the Middle and Far West During the Period of Early American Settlement.* Cleveland, Ohio, 1904–1907. 32 vols.
Volume I contains the journals of George Croghan, Conrad Weiser, and Christian Frederck Post which, although printed elsewhere, were found valuable because of the accompanying explanatory notes. However, these notes must be used with caution.

————. (ed.). *The Jesuit Relations and Allied Documents, Travels, and Explorations of the Jesuit Missionaries in New France 1610–1791, The Original French, Latin and Italian Texts, with English Translations and Notes; Illustrated by Portraits, Maps, and Facsimiles.* Cleveland, Ohio, 1896–1901. 72 vols.
Throughout the *Jesuit Relations* there are scattered references to the custom of using presents among the Indians.

TYLER, LYON GARDINER (ed.). *Narratives of Early Virginia, 1606–1625.* New York, 1907.
Mention is made of the presents given by John Smith to the Indians living in the vicinity of Jamestown.

VAN DOREN, CARL, BOYD, JULIAN P. (eds.). *Indian Treaties Printed by Benjamin Franklin, 1736–1762: Their Literary, Historical and Bibliographical Significance.* Philadelphia, Pennsylvania, 1938.
This beautifully printed work covers many of the treaties included in the *Pennsylvania Colonial Records.* The editors have written an excellent introduction.

VIRGINIA. William Waller Hening (ed.). *The Statutes at Large; Being a Collection of all the Laws of Virginia from the First Session of the Legislature in the Year 1619.* Richmond, Virginia, 1819–1823. 13 vols. Universally referred to as *Hening's Statutes.*
This collection, despite the limited title, contains some material relative to Indian affairs.

————. H. R. McIlwaine (ed.). *Legislative Journals of the Council of Colonial Virginia.* Richmond, Virginia, 1918–1919. 3 vols.
These journals include material relating to Indian problems.

VIRGINIA. H. R. McIlwaine *et al.* (eds.). *Journals of the House of Burgesses of Virginia.* Richmond, Virginia, 1905–1915. 13 vols.

Herein is much material relating to the French advances in the Ohio region with some reference to Indian presents.

———. *The Virginia Gazette, 1736–1780.* Reproduced in photostat by the Massachusetts Historical Society, Boston, Massachusetts, 1925.

Herein are contained scattered accounts of Indian affairs on the frontier. Also to be noted are the descriptions of runaway servants which describe clothing in detail. Much of this type of clothing was given to the Indians as presents.

———. *Virginia Magazine of History and Biography.* William G. Stanard *et al.* (eds.). Richmond, Virginia, 1893–.

Manuscripts relating to the Treaty of Logstown in 1752 have been printed in Volume XIII (October 1905).

WASHINGTON, GEORGE. John C. Fitzpatrick (ed.). *The Diaries of George Washington, 1748–1799.* New York, 1925. 4 vols.

Washington's diaries include the famous trip made by the young officer in 1754 to Venango and Le Boeuf. This account illustrates the fierce competition between the French and English for Indian friendship by the use of presents.

———. John C. Fitzpatrick (ed.). *The Writings of George Washington from the Original Manuscript Sources, 1745–1799.* Washington, D.C., 1931–1944. 39 vols.

This collection of Washington's writings is the most complete available. Volumes I and II have proved most valuable for the study of Washington and Indian affairs.

———. Worthington C. Ford (ed.). *The Writings of George Washington.* New York, 1889–1893. 14 vols.

Ford's annotations in Washington's diary of 1754 have proved useful.

———. Stanislaus Murray Hamilton (ed.). *Letters to Washington and Accompanying Papers.* Boston, Massachusetts, 1898–1902. 5 vols.

Hamilton's footnotes have been used to advantage.

WEBSTER, J. CLARENCE (ed.). *The Journal of Jeffery Amherst Recording the Military Career of General Amherst in America from 1758–1763.* Chicago, Illinois, 1931.

The journal of Amherst includes much material relating to the use of Indian auxiliaries and the presents that were given to warriors.

WILLIAMS, SAMUEL COLE (ed.). *Adair's History of the American Indians.* Johnson City, Tennessee, 1930.

Adair's work is filled with references to presents as they were given to the Indians both by the French and by the English.

WISCONSIN. *Collections* of the State Historical Society of Wisconsin, edited by Reuben Gold Thwaites. Madison, Wisconsin, 1854–1911. 21 vols.

Volumes XII, XVII, and XVIII have been found to cover materials relating to the distribution of gifts. Volume XVIII is of particular value, since it includes the journal of Céloron de Blainville and documents relating to presents and to the Indian war of 1763.

WRAXALL, PETER. Charles Howard McIlwain (ed.). *An Abridgement of the Indian Affairs Contained in Four Folio Volumes Transacted in the Colony of New York, From the Year 1678 to the Year 1751 by Peter Wraxall (Harvard Historical Studies, XXI).* Cambridge, Massachusetts, 1915. Commonly referred to as *Wraxall's Abridgement.*
McIlwain's introduction is quite valuable. The abridgement, however, is rather limited considering the fact that it does not go beyond the year 1751.

III. SECONDARY MATERIALS

ALDEN, JOHN RICHARD. *John Stuart and the Southern Colonial Frontier, A Study of Indian Relations, War, and Land Problems in the Southern Wilderness, 1754–1775.* Ann Arbor, Michigan, 1944.

ALVORD, CLARENCE WALWORTH. *The Mississippi Valley in British Politics, A Study of the Trade, Land Speculation, and Experiments in Imperialism Culminating in the American Revolution.* Cleveland, Ohio, 1917. 2 vols.

BAILEY, KENNETH P. *The Ohio Company of Virginia and the Westward Movement, 1748–1792, A Chapter in the History of the Colonial Frontier.* Glendale, California, 1939. See also his *Ohio Company Papers,* 1947.

———. *Thomas Cresap, Maryland Frontiersman.* Boston, Massachusetts, 1944.

BEER, GEORGE LOUIS. *British Colonial Policy, 1754–1765.* New York, 1922.

CRANE, VERNER W. *The Southern Frontier, 1670–1732.* Philadelphia, Pennsylvania, 1929.

FREEMAN, DOUGLAS SOUTHALL. *George Washington, A Biography.* New York, 1948. 2 vols.

GAYARRÉ, CHARLES. *History of Louisiana.* New Orleans, Louisiana, 2d edition, 1879. 4 vols.

GIPSON, LAWRENCE HENRY. *The British Empire Before the American Revolution,* 1936– 7 vols. to date. Volume IV, *Zones of International Friction, North America South of the Great Lakes Region, 1748–1754,* and Volume VI, *The Great War for Empire, the Years of Defeat, 1754–1757.* These volumes have proved invaluable in the study of Indian affairs.

HODGE, FREDERICK WEBB. *Handbook of the American Indians North of Mexico.* Smithsonian Institution, Bureau of American Ethnology, Bulletin No. 30, Washington, D.C., 1907. 2 vols.

JACOBS, WILBUR R. "Wampum, the Protocol of Indian Diplomacy," *Wiliam and Mary Quarterly, A Magazine of Early American History,* Third Series, IV (October 1949), 596–604.

———. "Was the Pontiac Uprising a Conspiracy?" *Ohio State Archaeological and Historical Quarterly,* LI (January 1950), 26–37.

KLINGBERG, FRANK J. *Anglican Humanitarianism in Colonial New York.* Philadelphia, Pennsylvania, 1940.

KOONTZ, LOUIS KNOTT. *Robert Dinwiddie, His Career in American Colonial Government and Westward Expansion.* Glendale, California, 1941.

————. *The Virginia Frontier, 1754–1763.* Baltimore, Maryland, 1925.

LYDEKKER, JOHN W. *The Faithful Mohawks.* New York, 1938.

MACLEOD, WILLIAM CHRISTIE. *The American Indian Frontier.* New York, 1928.

MORGAN, LEWIS H., *League of the HO-DÉ-NO-SAU-NEE or Iroquois* (edited by Herbert M. Lloyd). New York, 1901. 2 vols.

OSGOOD, HERBERT L. *The American Colonies in the Eighteenth Century.* New York, 1924. 4 vols. Complemented by C. M. Andrews' recent volumes.

PARGELLIS, STANLEY MCCRORY. *Lord Loudoun in North America.* New Haven, Connecticut, 1933.

PARKMAN, FRANCIS. *The Conspiracy of Pontiac and the Indian War After the Conquest of Canada.* Boston, Massachusetts, 1912. 2 vols.

PECKHAM, HOWARD H. *Pontiac and the Indian Uprising.* Princeton, New Jersey, 1947.

The Penn Wampum Belts, Leaflets of the Museum of the American Indian. Heye Foundation, New York, No. 4 (March 22, 1925).

POUND, ARTHUR, AND DAY, RICHARD E. *Johnson of the Mohawks, A Biography of Sir William Johnson, Irish Immigrant, Mohawk War Chief, American Soldier, Empire Builder.* New York, 1930.

SHAW, HELEN LOUISE. *British Administration of the Southern Indians, 1756–1783.* Lancaster, Pennsylvania, 1931.

STEPHENSON, NATHANIEL WRIGHT, AND DUNN, WALDO HILARY. *George Washington.* New York, 1940. 2 vols.

STONE, WILLIAM L. *The Life and Times of Sir William Johnson, Bart.* Albany, New York, 1865. 2 vols.

VOLWILER, ALBERT T. *George Croghan and the Development of Central New York, 1763–1800.* Reprint from the *Quarterly Journal* of the New York State Historical Association for January 1923.

————. *George Croghan and the Westward Movement, 1741–1782.* Cleveland, Ohio, 1926.

WALLACE, PAUL H. W. *Conrad Weiser, 1696–1760, Friend of Colonist and Mohawk.* Philadelphia, Pennsylvania, 1945.

WINSOR, JUSTIN. *The Mississippi Basin: The Struggle in America Between England and France, 1697–1763.* New York, 1895.

WOODWARD, ASHBEL M. D. *Wampum: A Paper Presented to the Numismatic and Antiquarian Society of Philadelphia.* Albany, New York, 1880.

INDEX